Microsoft®

Windows® 2000

Professional Edition

Illustrated Introductory

Microsoft®

Windows® 2000

Professional Edition

Illustrated Introductory

Steven M. Johnson
Neil J. Salkind

ONE MAIN STREET, CAMBRIDGE, MA 02142

Australia • Canada • Denmark • Japan • Mexico • New Zealand • Philippines
Puerto Rico • Singapore • South Africa • Spain • United Kingdom • United States

Microsoft Windows 2000—Illustrated Introductory is published by Course Technology

Managing Editor:	**Nicole Pinard**
Senior Product Manager:	**Kathryn Schooling**
Product Manager:	**M.T. Cozzola**
Developmental Editor:	**M.T. Cozzola**
Associate Product Manager:	**Emily Heberlein**
Production Editor:	**Elena Montillo**
Marketing Manager:	**Andrea Loeb**
Editorial Assistant:	**Stacie Parillo**
Composition House:	**GEX, Inc.**
QA Manuscript Reviewer:	**Nicole Ashton, John Freitas**
Text Designer:	**Joseph Lee, Joseph Lee Designs**
Cover Designer:	**Doug Goodman, Doug Goodman Designs**

For more information contact:

Course Technology
One Main Street
Cambridge, MA 02142

or find us on the World Wide Web at: www.course.com

Disclaimer

Course Technology reserves the right to revise this publication and make changes from time to time in its content without notice.

ISBN 0-7600-5473-8

Printed in the United States of America

4 5 6 7 8 9 BM 04

Exciting New Products

Master Microsoft Office 2000

Master Microsoft Office 2000 applications with the Illustrated series. With *Microsoft Office 2000—Illustrated Introductory* students will learn the basics of Microsoft Office 2000 Professional. For deeper coverage, *Microsoft Office 2000—Illustrated Second Course* focuses on the more advanced skills of Office 2000 applications.

Illustrated also offers individual application books on Access, Excel, Word, and PowerPoint 2000. Each book covers basic to advanced skills for the application and meets Microsoft Office User Specialist (MOUS) Expert certification.
Other titles include:

▶ Microsoft Access 2000—Illustrated Introductory and Complete

▶ Microsoft Publisher 2000—Illustrated Essentials
▶ Microsoft Publisher 2000—Illustrated Introductory
▶ Microsoft Outlook 2000—Illustrated Essentials
▶ Microsoft FrontPage 2000—Illustrated Introductory
▶ Microsoft FrontPage 2000—Illustrated Essentials
▶ Microsoft Office 2000—Illustrated Introductory and Second Course
▶ Microsoft Office 2000—Illustrated Brief
▶ Microsoft PowerPoint 2000—Illustrated Brief and Introductory
▶ Microsoft Word 2000—Illustrated Introductory and Complete
▶ Microsoft PhotoDraw (Version 2) —Illustrated Essentials

Check Out Computer Concepts

Computer Concepts—Illustrated Essentials and Introductory, Third Edition is the quick and visual way to learn cutting-edge computer concepts. The third edition has been updated to include advances to the Internet and multimedia, changes to the industry, and an introduction to e-commerce and security.

Create Your Ideal Course Package with CourseKits™

If one book doesn't offer all the coverage you need, create a course package that does. With Course Technology's CourseKits—our mix-and-match approach to selecting texts—you have the freedom to combine products from more than one series. When you choose any two or more Course Technology products for one course, we'll discount the price and package them together so your students can pick up one convenient bundle at the bookstore.

Try out Illustrated's New Product Line: Multimedia Tools

What are Multimedia Tools?

Multimedia tools teach students how to create text, graphics, video, animations, and sound; all of which can be incorporated for use in printed materials, Web pages, CD-ROMs, and multimedia presentations.

New Titles
▶ Adobe Photoshop 5.5—Illustrated Introductory (0-7600-6337-0)
▶ Abobe Illustrator 8.0—Illustrated Introductory (0-619-01750-3)
▶ Adobe InDesign 1.0—Illustrated Introductory (0-619-01751-1)

▶ Macromedia Director 7—Illustrated Introductory (0-619-01772-4)
▶ Macromedia Director 7—Illustrated Complete (0-619-01779-1)

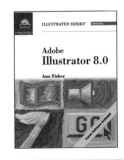

Preface

Welcome to *Microsoft Windows 2000—Illustrated Introductory*. This highly visual book offers users a hands-on introduction to Microsoft Windows 2000, Professional Edition, and also serves as an excellent reference for future use. If you would like additional coverage of Microsoft Windows 2000, we also offer *Microsoft Windows 2000—Illustrated Complete*, an expanded version of the Introductory edition.

► Organization and Coverage

This text contains eight units that cover basic through intermediate Microsoft Windows 2000 skills. In these units, students learn how to manage files using both My Computer and Windows Explorer. They also learn how to access the Internet, send e-mail with Outlook Express, and manage shared files using a network.

► About this Approach

What makes the Illustrated approach so effective at teaching software skills? It's quite simple. Each skill is presented on two facing pages, with the step-by-step instructions on the left page, and large screen illustrations on the right. Students can focus on a single skill without having to turn the page. This unique design makes information extremely accessible and easy to absorb, and provides a great reference for after the course is over. This hands-on approach also makes it ideal for both self-paced or instructor-led classes.

Each lesson, or "information display," contains the following elements:

Each 2-page spread focuses on a single skill.

Clear step-by-step directions explain how to complete the specific task, with what students are to type in green. When students follow the numbered steps, they quickly learn how each procedure is performed and what the results will be.

Concise text that introduces the basic principles discussed in the lesson. Procedures are easier to learn when concepts fit into a framework.

Windows 2000

Disconnecting a Network Drive

Usually, you map a network drive to automatically reconnect every time you log on. However, sometimes you may find it necessary to manually disconnect a mapped drive. Your system administrator may have added new hard drives to the server, or he or she may have reorganized the directory structure, in which case the network path for the mapped drive may now be incorrect. Windows makes the process of disconnecting a mapped drive very easy in the case of such an event. John was informed by the system administrator of a network reorganization that will take place over the weekend. He disconnects the drive mapped to (F:) until he finds out what changes have been made. Before disconnecting the mapped drive, John cleans up his hard drive and the mapped drive.

Steps

1. Double-click the **My Computer** icon, then double-click the **mapped drive**
   The contents of the mapped drive appears.

2. Right-click the **Suppliers** file, click **Delete**, then click **Yes** to confirm the deletion

3. Click the **Back** button `⇦ Back ▾` on the toolbar

4. Click the **Address list arrow**, then click **My Documents**
   John wants to delete the Sales folder.

5. Right-click the **Sales shared folder**, then click **Delete**
   The Confirm Folder Delete dialog box opens.

6. Click **Yes**, click **Yes** again, then click the **Close** button in the My Documents window

7. Right-click the **My Network Places** icon on the desktop
   A pop-up menu appears for My Network Places, as shown in Figure H-14. This menu provides several commands for working in a network environment. See Table H-2 for a description of the commands available through this menu.

8. Click **Disconnect Network Drive** on the pop-up menu
   The Disconnect Network Drive dialog box opens, as shown in Figure H-15. The dialog box displays a list of all the network drives that you have mapped from your computer. You should check with your system administrator or instructor before actually disconnecting a drive. To quit without actually disconnecting a drive, click Cancel.

9. Click the **mapped drive** with the Wired Coffee folder (or the one you previously mapped), click **OK**, then click **Yes** if necessary to the warning message
   Windows disconnects the drive you have selected and closes the Disconnect Network Drive dialog box.

QuickTip

To disconnect a network drive in Windows Explorer, right-click a mapped network drive in the left pane, then click Disconnect.

Network paths

The path to a shared network directory is like the path to a file on a hard or floppy disk. For example, the path to the Suppliers file on your Project Disk is A:\Wired Coffee\Sales\Suppliers. Network paths replace the drive designation with the host computer name, as in \\Server\Wired Coffee. In either example, the path tells the computer where to look for the files you need.

► WINDOWS H-16 **MANAGING SHARED FILES USING MY NETWORK PLACES**

Hints as well as trouble-shooting advice, right where you need it – next to the step itself.

Clues to Use boxes provide concise information that either expands on one component of the major lesson skill or describes an independent task that is in some way related to the major lesson skill.

Every lesson features large-size, full-color representations of what the students' screen should look like after completing the numbered steps.

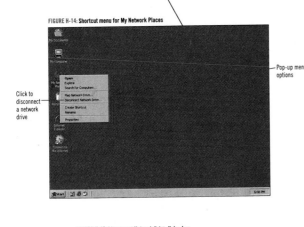

FIGURE H-14: Shortcut menu for My Network Places

Click to disconnect a network drive

Pop-up menu options

FIGURE H-15: Disconnect Network Drive dialog box

Disconnect Network Drive

Select the drive(s) you want to disconnect:

F: \\Server\Wired Coffee

Your list of drives might be different

OK   Cancel

TABLE H-2: Pop-up menu commands for My Network Places

command	function
Open	Opens My Network Places
Explore	Opens Windows Explorer in order to copy and move files from one folder to another, whether on your local computer or the network
Search for Computers	Finds a computer whose name you know but not its location
Map Network Drive	Maps a drive from your computer to a shared directory on another computer
Disconnect Network Drive	Disconnects a drive on your computer from a shared directory on another computer
Create Shortcut	Creates a shortcut to My Network Places
Rename	Renames the My Network Places icon
Properties	Displays the properties of your network

MANAGING SHARED FILES USING MY NETWORK PLACES   WINDOWS H-17 ◀

Quickly accessible summaries of key terms, toolbar buttons, or keyboard alternatives connected with the lesson material. Students can refer easily to this information when working on their own projects at a later time.

The page numbers are designed like a road map. Windows indicates the Windows section, H indicates the eigth unit, and 17 indicates the page within the unit.

Other Features

The two-page lesson format featured in this book provides the new user with a powerful learning experience. Additionally, this book contains the following features:

▶ Real-World Case

The case study used throughout the textbook, a fictitious coffee company called Wired Coffee Company, is designed to be "real-world" in nature and introduces the kinds of activities that students will encounter when working with Microsoft Windows 2000. With a real-world case, the process of solving problems will be more meaningful to students.

▶ End of Unit Material

Each unit concludes with a Concepts Review that tests students' understanding of what they learned in the unit. The Concepts Review is followed by a Skills Review, which provides students with additional hands-on practice of the skills. The Skills Review is followed by Independent Challenges, which pose case problems for students to solve. The Visual Workshops that follow the Independent Challenges help students develop critical thinking skills. Students are shown completed screens and are asked to re-create them.

Instructor's Resource Kit

The Instructor's Resource Kit is Course Technology's way of putting the resources and information needed to teach and learn effectively into your hands. With an integrated array of teaching and learning tools that offers you and your students a broad range of technology-based instructional options, we believe this kit represents the highest quality and most cutting edge resources available to instructors today. Many of these resources are available at www.course.com. The resources available with this book are:

Instructor's Manual   Available as an electronic file, the Instructor's Manual is quality-assurance tested and includes unit overviews, detailed lecture topics for each unit with teaching tips, an Upgrader's Guide, solutions to all lessons and end-of-unit material, and extra Independent Challenges. The Instructor's Manual is available on the Instructor's Resource Kit CD-ROM, or you can download it from **www.course.com**.

Course Test Manager   Designed by Course Technology, this Windows-based testing software helps instructors design, administer, and print tests and pre-tests. A full-featured program, Course Test Manager also has an online testing component that allows students to take tests at the computer and have their exams automatically graded.

Course Faculty Online Companion   You can browse this textbook's password-protected site to obtain the Instructor's Manual, Solution Files, Project Files, and any updates to the text. Contact your Customer Service Representative for the site address and password.

Project Files   Project Files contain all of the data that students will use to complete the lessons and end-of-unit material. A Readme file includes instructions for using the files. Adopters of this text are granted the right to install the Project Files on any standalone computer or network. The Project Files are available on the Instructor's Resource Kit CD-ROM, the Review Pack, and can also be downloaded from www.course.com.

Solution Files   Solution Files contain every file students are asked to create or modify in the lessons and end-of-unit material. A Help file on the Instructor's Resource Kit includes information for using the Solution Files.

Figure Files   Figure files contain all the figures from the book in bitmap format. Use the figure files to create transparency masters or in a PowerPoint presentation.

WebCT   WebCT is a tool used to create Web-based educational environments and also uses WWW browsers as the interface for the course-building environment. The site is hosted on your school campus, allowing complete control over the information. WebCT has its own internal communication system, offering internal e-mail, a Bulletin Board, and a Chat room.

Course Technology offers pre-existing supplemental information to help in your WebCT class creation, such as a suggested Syllabus, Lecture Notes, Figures in the Book / Course Presenter, Student Downloads, and Test Banks in which you can schedule an exam, create reports, and more.

Brief Contents

Contents

Windows 2000

Contents

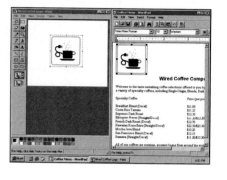

Managing Files Using My Computer   WINDOWS C-1

Managing Folders and Files Using Windows Explorer

Contents

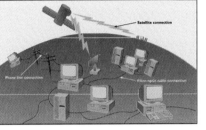

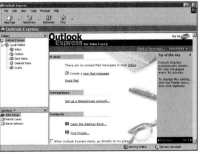

Contents

Managing Shared Files Using My Network Places

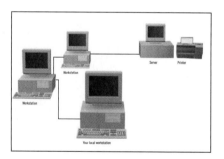

Getting
Started with Windows 2000

Microsoft Windows 2000 is an **operating system**, a computer program that controls the basic operation of your computer and the programs you run on it. **Programs**, also known as **applications**, are task-oriented software you use to accomplish specific tasks, such as word processing, managing files on your computer, and performing calculations. When you work with Windows 2000, you will notice many **icons**: small pictures on your screen intended to be meaningful symbols of the items they represent. You will also notice **windows**: rectangular frames that can contain icons, the contents of a file, or other usable data. This use of icons and windows is called a **graphical user interface** (**GUI**), meaning that you interact ("interface") with the computer through the use of graphics. This unit introduces you to basic Windows skills.

Windows 2000

Starting Windows and Viewing the Windows Desktop

Microsoft Windows 2000 is an operating system that provides a secure file management system in which you can work on your computer and share information with others on a network. When you first start Windows, you will see the logon screen. In the logon procedure, you identify yourself to Windows using a user name and password. After completing the logon procedure, you see the Windows Active Desktop. The **Active Desktop** is an on-screen version of a regular desk, containing all the information and tools you need to accomplish your tasks. From the desktop, you can access, store, share, and explore information in a seamless manner, whether it resides on your computer, a network, or the Internet. (The **Internet** is a worldwide collection of over 40 million computers linked together to share information.) The desktop is called "active" because (unlike other Windows desktops) it allows you to access the Internet and view content from the desktop. Figure A-1 shows what the desktop looks like when you start Windows 2000 for the first time. The bar at the bottom of your screen is called the **taskbar**, which allows you to start programs and switch among currently running programs. (At the moment, none are running.) At the left end of the taskbar is the **Start button**, which you use to start programs, find and open files, access Windows Help and so on. Next to the Start button on the taskbar is the **Quick Launch toolbar**, which contains buttons you use to quickly start Internet-related programs and show the desktop. Use Table A-1 to identify the icons and other elements you see on your desktop. ➤➤➤ Windows 2000 automatically starts when you turn on your computer. If Windows is not currently running, follow the steps below to start it now.

1. Turn on your computer

Windows automatically starts, and the desktop appears, as shown in Figure A-1. If you are working on a network at school or at an office, you might see a Welcome to Windows dialog box or a Network Password dialog box. If so, continue to Step 2 for the Windows dialog box or continue to Step 3 for the Network Password dialog box; if not, continue to Step 5. When you start Windows 2000, the Getting Started with Windows 2000 dialog box might appear. You can click Register Now to register your Windows 2000 software, Discover Windows to learn about Windows 2000, or Connect to the Internet to set up your computer to access the Internet.

Trouble?

To perform this step, you press all three keys at the same time. Hold down [Ctrl] and [Alt] with one hand, then press [Del] with the other.

▶ 2. Press **[Ctrl][Alt][Del]** to begin the logon process

After you press the three keys, the Log On to Windows dialog box opens, with spaces for you to enter your user name and password. Your instructor or technical support person (the person in charge of your network) assigns your user name. If you are using your own computer, you selected your user name when you installed Windows 2000. A user name might automatically appear. If your user name appears on the screen, proceed to Step 4.

Trouble?

If you don't know your password, see your instructor or technical support person.

▶ 3. In the User name box, type your user name, then press **[Tab]**

4. Type your password, then click **OK**

When you type the password, only asterisks will appear as you type. This helps to prevent other people from learning your password. When you enter a valid password, you are given privileges to use the network.

QuickTip

To open this dialog box, click the Start button, point to Programs, point to Accessories, point to System Tools, then click Getting Started.

▶ 5. In the Getting Started with Windows 2000 dialog box, click to clear the **Show this screen at startup** check box, then click **Exit**

The Windows desktop appears on your screen, as shown in Figure A-1.

FIGURE A-1: Windows Active desktop

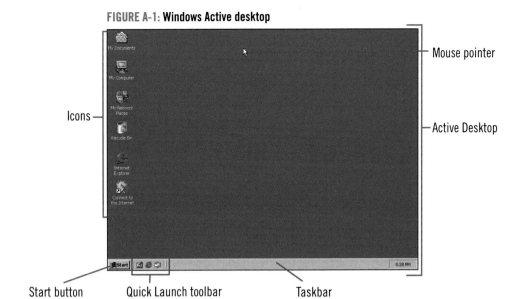

Icons

Mouse pointer

Active Desktop

Start button   Quick Launch toolbar   Taskbar

TABLE A-1: Elements of the Windows desktop

desktop element	allows you to
My Documents folder	Store programs, documents, graphics, or other files
My Computer	Work with different disk drives and printers on your computer system
My Network Places	Work with different disk drives and printers on a network
Recycle Bin	Delete and restore files
Internet Explorer	Start Internet Explorer, a program you use to access the Internet
Internet Connection Wizard	Set up your computer to access the Internet; changes to Connect to the Internet icon after you create a connection
Taskbar	Start programs and switch among open programs
Start button	Start programs, open documents, find a file, and more
Quick Launch Toolbar	Show the desktop, start Internet Explorer, and start Outlook Express

CLUES TO USE

Using and changing a password

Passwords are used to maintain security on a local or network computer. When choosing a password, remember that the Windows 2000 password program is case-sensitive. Your password should be at least six to eight characters long. It should include, if possible, combinations of capital letters, lowercase letters, and non-alphabetic characters. Using a word from the dictionary as a password is not a good idea, as someone trying to gain unauthorized access to your account could guess it more easily than a non-dictionary password that you can remember easily. Never write down your password on paper or let someone look over your shoulder as you log on to the system. Always be sure to log out when you walk away from your desk. To change your password, press [Ctrl][Alt][Del], click Change Password in the Windows Security dialog box, type the old password in the Old Password text box, type the new password in the New Password and Confirm New Password text boxes, then click OK.

Windows 2000

Using the Mouse

A **mouse** is a handheld input device you roll across a flat surface (such as a desk or a mousepad) to position the **mouse pointer**, the small symbol that indicates the pointer's relative position on the desktop. When you move the mouse, the mouse pointer on the screen moves in the same direction. The shape of the mouse pointer changes to indicate different activities. Table A-2 shows some common mouse pointer shapes. Once you move the mouse pointer to a desired point on the screen, you use the **mouse buttons**, shown in Figure A-2, to "tell" your computer what you want it to do. Table A-3 describes the basic mouse techniques you'll use frequently when working in Windows. ✎ Try using the mouse now to become familiar with these navigational skills.

Steps

1. Place your hand on the mouse, locate the mouse pointer ⬉ on the Windows desktop, then move the mouse back and forth across your desk
As you move the mouse, the mouse pointer moves correspondingly.

Trouble?

If pointing to the icon high-lights it, you are not using default Windows 2000 set-tings. Consult your instructor or technical support person. This book assumes you are using the Windows 2000 default double-click mouse setting.

2. Move the mouse to position the mouse pointer over the **My Computer icon** 🖳 in the upper-left corner of the desktop
Positioning the mouse pointer over an icon or over any specific item on the screen is called **pointing**. When you position the mouse pointer over an icon or button, a **ScreenTip** appears, which describes the icon or gives the name of the button.

3. Press and release the **left mouse button**
The act of pressing a mouse button once and releasing it is called **clicking**. The icon is now highlighted, or shaded differently than the other icons on the desktop. The act of clicking and highlighting an item, such as an icon, indicates that you have **selected** it to perform some future operation on it. To perform any type of operation on an icon (such as moving it), you must first select it.

4. Point to the **My Computer icon** 🖳, press and hold down the **left mouse button**, move the mouse down and to the right, then release the mouse button
The icon becomes dimmed and moves with the mouse pointer. When you release the mouse button, the icon relocates on the desktop. This skill is called dragging and allows you to move icons and other Windows elements. Next you will use the mouse to display a pop-up menu.

5. Point to the **My Computer icon** 🖳, then press and release the **right mouse button**
Clicking the right mouse button is known as **right-clicking**. Right-clicking an item on the desktop displays a **pop-up menu**, shown in Figure A-3. This menu lists the commands most commonly used for the item you have clicked; the available commands are not therefore the same for every item.

QuickTip

When a step tells you to "click," it means, by default, to left-click. The directions will say "right-click" if you are to click with the right mouse button.

6. Click anywhere outside the menu to close the pop-up menu

7. Move the **My Computer icon** 🖳 back to its original position in the upper-left corner of the desktop using the pointing and dragging skills you have just learned

8. Point to the **My Computer icon** 🖳, then click the **left mouse button** twice quickly
The My Computer window opens, containing several icons. Clicking the mouse button twice is known as **double-clicking**, and it allows you to open a window, program, or file that an icon represents. Leave the desktop as it is and move on to the next lesson.

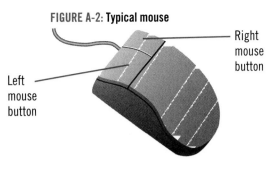

FIGURE A-2: **Typical mouse**

Right mouse button

Left mouse button

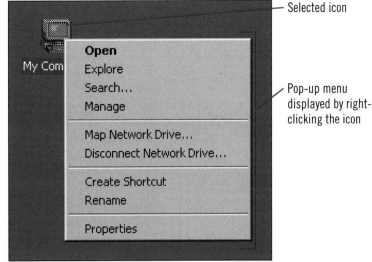

FIGURE A-3: **A pop-up menu**

Selected icon

Pop-up menu displayed by right-clicking the icon

TABLE A-2: **Common mouse pointer shapes**

shape	used to
⬈	Select items, choose commands, start programs, and work in programs
I	Position mouse pointer for editing or inserting text; called the insertion point or cursor
⬈⧗	Indicate Windows is busy processing a command
↔	Position mouse pointer on the border of a window for changing the size of a window
🖑	Position mouse pointer for selecting and opening Web-based content

TABLE A-3: **Basic mouse techniques**

task	what to do
Pointing	Move the mouse to position it over an item on the desktop
Clicking	Press and release the left mouse button once
Double-clicking	Press and release the left mouse button twice quickly
Dragging	Point to an item, press and hold the left mouse button, move the mouse to a new location, then release the mouse button
Right-clicking	Point to an item, then press and release the right mouse button

CLUES TO USE

Using the mouse with the Internet

When you use the Internet, you point to an item to select it and single-click an item to open it, which is different from the standard Windows operating system. Because Windows 2000 integrates use of the Internet with its other functions, it allows you to choose whether you want to extend the way you click on the Internet to the rest of your computer work. Windows 2000 gives you two choices for selecting and opening icons using the mouse buttons: single-click mode (known as the Internet or Web style) or double-click mode (known as the Classic style). To change the way Windows 2000 uses the mouse button to select and open icons, click the Start button on the taskbar, point to Settings, click Control Panel, double-click Folder Options, and click the Single-click to open an item or Double-click to open an item option. Windows 2000 is set by default in double-click mode.

Windows 2000

Getting Started with the Windows Desktop

The key to getting started with the Windows desktop is learning how to use the Start button on the taskbar. Clicking the Start button on the taskbar displays the **Start menu**, which is a list of commands that allows you to start a program, open a document, change a Windows setting, find a file, or display help information. Table A-4 describes the available categories on this menu that are installed with Windows 2000. As you become more familiar with Windows, you might want to customize the Start menu to include additional items that you use most often and change Windows settings in the Control Panel to customize your Windows desktop. **Personalized Menus** is a Windows setting that reduces the size of the Programs menu to reflect how you use your computer. When Personalized Menus is turned on, Windows keeps track of which programs you use and hides the programs you have not used recently, while still keeping all of your programs easily accessible. To view hidden programs, click the down arrow at the bottom of the Programs submenu. ◤ Begin by viewing the Start menu and opening the **Control Panel**, a window containing various programs that allow you to specify how your computer looks and performs. The My Computer window should still be open on your screen.

1. Click the **Start button** on the taskbar

The Start menu opens.

2. Point to **Settings** on the Start menu

An arrow next to a menu indicates a **cascading menu**, or a **submenu**—a list of commands for the menu item with the arrow next to it. Pointing at the arrow displays a submenu from which you can choose additional commands. The Settings submenu opens, as shown in Figure A-4, listing commands to open the Control Panel, Network and Dial-up Connections, and Printers; and to change settings for the Taskbar & Start Menu.

QuickTip

To turn on Personalized Menus, click Taskbar & Start Menu on the Settings submenu, then click the Use Personalized Menus check box on the General tab.

3. Click **Control Panel** on the submenu

The Control Panel window opens, as shown in Figure A-5, containing icons for various programs that allow you to specify how your computer looks and performs. Leave the Control Panel window open for now, and continue to the next lesson.

Accessing the Internet from the desktop

One of the important differences between Windows 2000 and other versions of Windows is that Windows 2000 allows you to access the Internet right from the desktop. This is possible because a program called Internet Explorer is integrated into the Windows 2000 operating system. **Internet Explorer** is an example of a **browser**, a computer program designed to access the Internet. Windows 2000 adds Web enhancements to the Start menu and the taskbar.

The Favorites command on the Start menu makes it easy to access places on the Internet you visit frequently. New commands on the Search submenu (On the Internet and For People) make it easy to find and access places on the Internet you want to visit. To provide additional Internet access, the Quick Launch toolbar is available on the taskbar to help you launch Internet-related programs and show the desktop. Windows 2000 makes it easier than ever to access the Internet.

FIGURE A- 4: Cascading menus

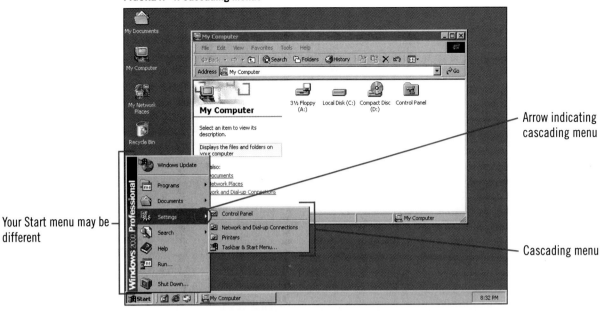

Arrow indicating cascading menu

Your Start menu may be different

Cascading menu

FIGURE A- 5: Control Panel

Icons for various programs to change Windows settings

TABLE A-4: Start menu categories

category	description
Windows Update	Connects to a Microsoft Web site and updates your Windows 2000 files as necessary
Programs	Opens programs included on the Start menu
Favorites	Connects to favorite Web sites, or opens folders or documents that you previously selected; available when the Display Favorites feature is turned on in the Taskbar & Start Menu dialog box
Documents	Opens documents most recently opened and saved
Settings	Allows you to set user preferences for system settings, including the Control Panel, Network and Dial-Up Connections, Printers, and Taskbar & Start Menu
Search	Locates programs, files, folders, or computers on your computer network, or finds information or people on the Internet
Help	Lists Windows help information by topic, alphabetical index, or search criteria
Run	Opens a program or file based on a location and filename that you type or select
Log Off	Allows you to log off the system and log on as a different user; available when the Display Logoff feature is turned on in the Taskbar & Start Menu dialog box
Shut Down	Provides options to shut down the computer, restart the computer, or log off a user and restart the computer

Moving and Resizing Windows

One of the powerful things about working in Windows is that you can open more than one window or program at once. This means, however, that the desktop can get cluttered with many open windows for the various windows and programs you are using. To organize your desktop, sometimes it is necessary to change the size of a window or move it to a different location. Each window, no matter what it contains, is surrounded by a standard border that you can drag to change the size of the window. Each window also has three standard buttons in the upper-right corner that allow you to change the size of windows. Table A-5 shows the different mouse pointer shapes that appear when resizing windows. ▰▰▰ Try moving and resizing the Control Panel window now.

Steps 1 2 3 4

1. **Click anywhere in the My Computer window or click the My Computer button on the taskbar**
   The My Computer window moves in front of the Control Panel window. The My Computer window is now **active** (title bar color changes from gray to blue); this means that any actions you perform will take place in this window.

QuickTip

You can click the Show the Desktop button 🗗 on the Quick Launch toolbar to minimize all open windows and programs in order to show the desktop.

2. **Click the Minimize button ▬ in the My Computer window**
   The window no longer appears on the desktop, but you can still see a button named My Computer on the taskbar. When you **minimize** a window, you do not close it but merely reduce it to a button on the taskbar so that you can work more easily in other windows. The button on the taskbar reminds you that the program is still running.

3. **Point to the title bar on the Control Panel window**
   The **title bar** is the area along the top of the window that contains the name of the file and the program used to create it. When a window is active, the title bar color changes from gray to blue. You can move any window to a new location on the desktop by dragging the window's title bar.

4. **With the mouse pointer over any spot on the title bar, click and drag the title bar to center the window on the desktop**
   This action is similar to dragging an icon to a new location. The window is relocated.

QuickTip

You can double-click the title bar of a window to switch between maximizing and restoring the size of a window.

5. **Click the Maximize button ▢ in the Control Panel**
   When you **maximize** a window, it takes up the entire screen.

6. **Click the Restore button 🗗 in the Control Panel**
   The **Restore button** returns a window to its previous size, as shown in Figure A-6. The Restore button only appears when a window is maximized. Now try making the window smaller.

QuickTip

You can resize windows by dragging any corner, not just the lower-left. You can also drag any border to make the window taller, shorter, wider, or narrower.

7. **Position the mouse pointer on the lower-right corner of the Control Panel window until the pointer changes to ↘, as indicated in Figure A-6, then drag the corner up and to the left**
   The window is now resized. In the next lesson you will work with the menus and toolbars in the Control Panel, so you can leave this window open.

8. **Click the My Computer button on the taskbar**
   The My Computer window returns to the size it was before it was minimized and is now active.

9. **Click the Close button ☒, located in the upper-right corner of the My Computer window**
   The My Computer window closes. You will learn more about My Computer in later lessons.

FIGURE A-6: Restored Control Panel window

Title bar

Active window

Sizing buttons

Drag here to size both height and width

TABLE A-5: Mouse pointer shapes that appear when resizing windows

mouse pointer shape	use to
↔	Drag the right or left edge of a window to change its width
↕	Drag the top or bottom edge of a window to change its height
↖ or ↗	Drag any corner of a window to change its size proportionally

Moving and resizing the taskbar

In addition to windows, you can also resize and move other elements on the desktop, such as the taskbar, using the methods in this lesson. You can move the taskbar by dragging it to any edge (right, left, top, or bottom) of the desktop. You can also change the size of the taskbar by dragging its edge.

Using Menus and Toolbars

A **menu** is a list of commands that you use to accomplish certain tasks. You've already used the Start menu to open the Control Panel. A **command** is a directive that provides access to a program's features. Each Windows program also has its own set of menus, which are located on the menu bar along the top of the program window. The **menu bar** organizes commands into groups of related operations. Each group is listed under the name of the menu, such as "File" or "Help." To access the commands in a menu, you click the name of the menu. See Table A-6 for examples of items on a typical menu. Some of the most frequently used commands on a menu can also be carried out by clicking a button on a toolbar. A **toolbar** contains buttons that are convenient shortcuts for menu commands. ◀━━━ Use a menu and toolbar button to change how the contents of the Control Panel window appear.

Steps

You can add or remove buttons to or from a toolbar to customize it. To customize the toolbar, click View on the menu bar, click Toolbars, then click Customize.

If you do not see the views button, click the More Buttons button ≫ to display it.

1. Click **View** on the menu bar

The View menu for the Control Panel appears, listing the View commands available in the Control Panel, as shown in Figure A-7. When you click a menu name, a general description of the commands available on that menu appears in the status bar. On a menu, a **check mark** identifies a feature that is currently selected (that is, the feature is enabled or "on"). To disable ("turn off") the feature, you click the command again to remove the check mark. A menu can contain more than one enabled check mark. A **bullet mark** also indicates that an option is enabled, but a menu can contain only one enabled bullet mark. To disable a command with a bullet mark next to it, you must select a different bullet option on the menu. On the View menu, the Large Icons bullet option is enabled, so the Control Panel window displays large icons.

2. On the View menu, click **Small Icons**

The window now displays smaller icons, so they take up less room. The Control Panel toolbar includes buttons for the commands that you use most frequently while you are in the Control Panel window. When you position the mouse pointer over a button, a ScreenTip appears. Use the ScreenTip feature to view the name of a button on the toolbar.

3. On the Control Panel toolbar, position the pointer over the **Views button** 📰▾ to view the ScreenTip

Some toolbar buttons appear with an arrow, which indicates that the button contains several choices. You can click the button arrow to display a menu of choices.

4. On the Control Panel toolbar, click the **Views button** 📰▾, as shown in Figure A-8, then click **Details**

The Details view includes a description of each Control Panel program. The ellipsis (. . .) at the end of a column line of text indicates more text to the right. You can adjust the column width to see the additional text. To adjust the column width, position the pointer (which changes to ↔), then drag to the right.

FIGURE A-7: **View menu in the Control Panel**

Check mark

Bullet mark

Menu bar

Commands in menu

Description of menu in status bar

FIGURE A-8: **Control Panel toolbars**

Toolbars

Click to display button menu

Views button menu

Click this view in Step 4

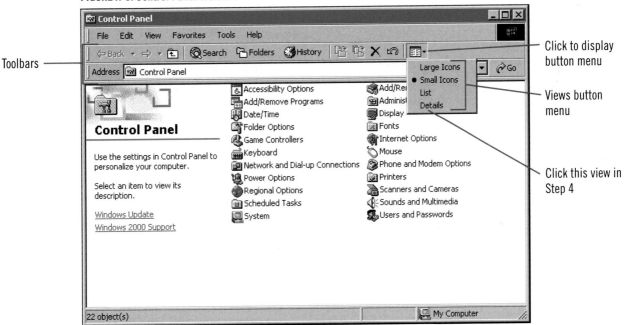

TABLE A-6: **Typical items on a menu**

item	description	example
Dimmed command	A menu command that is not currently available	Undo Ctrl+Z
Ellipsis	Choosing this menu command opens a dialog box that allows you to select from several options	Save As...
Triangle	Choosing this menu command opens a cascading menu containing an additional list of menu commands	Zoom ▶
Keyboard shortcut	An alternative to using the mouse for executing a menu command	Paste Ctrl+V
Underlined letter	Pressing the underlined letter while the [Alt] key is also pressed executes the menu command	Print Preview

Using Scroll Bars

When you cannot see all of the items available in a window, scroll bars appear on the right and/or bottom edges of the window. **Scroll bars** allow you to move around in a window to display the additional contents of the window. See Figure A-9 for the components of scroll bars. The vertical scroll bar moves your view up and down through a window; the horizontal scroll bar moves your view from left to right. There are several ways you can use scroll bars. When you need to scroll only a short distance, you can use the scroll arrows. When you need to scroll more quickly, you can click in the scroll bar above or below the scroll box, which moves the view up or down one window's height (the line that was at the bottom of the screen is moved to the top, and vice versa). Dragging the scroll box moves you even more quickly to a new part of the window. See Table A-7 for a summary of the different ways to use scroll bars. ➤ Use the scroll bars to view and read the description of each Control Panel program.

Steps

QuickTip

When scroll bars don't appear in a window, it means that all the information fits completely in the window.

1. **In the Control Panel window, click the down scroll arrow once in the vertical scroll bar, as shown in Figure A-9**
   Clicking this arrow once moves the view down one line. Clicking the up arrow once moves the view up one line at a time.

2. **Click the up scroll arrow in the vertical scroll bar**
   The view moves up one line.

3. **Click anywhere in the area below the scroll box in the vertical scroll bar**
   The contents in the window scroll down in a larger increment.

4. **Click the area above the scroll box in the vertical scroll bar**
   The contents in the window scroll back up. To move in even greater increments, you can drag the scroll box to a new position.

QuickTip

If you have a mouse with a wheel button in between the left and right buttons, you can roll the wheel button to quickly scroll up and down or click the wheel button and move the mouse in any direction.

5. **Drag the scroll box to the middle of the scroll bar**
   The scroll box indicates your relative position within the file, in this case, the halfway point.

6. **On the Control Panel toolbar, click the Views button ⊞▾, then click Large Icons**
   This restores the Control Panel to its original display.

FIGURE A-9: Scroll bars in Control Panel

Drag to adjust column width

Details view

Up scroll arrow

Vertical scroll bar

Scroll box

Down scroll arrow

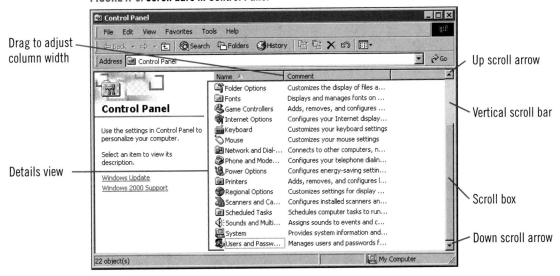

TABLE A-7: Using scroll bars in a window

to	do this
Move down one line	Click the down arrow at the bottom of the vertical scroll bar
Move up one line	Click the up arrow at the top of the vertical scroll bar
Move down one window's height	Click in the area below the scroll box in the vertical scroll bar
Move up one window's height	Click in the area above the scroll box in the vertical scroll bar
Move up or down a greater distance in the window	Drag the scroll box in the vertical scroll bar
Move a short distance side to side in a window	Click the left or right arrows in the horizontal scroll bar
Move to the right one window's width	Click in the area to the right of the scroll box in the horizontal scroll bar
Move to the left one window's width	Click in the area to the left of the scroll box in the horizontal scroll bar
Move left or right a greater distance in the window	Drag the scroll box in the horizontal scroll bar

CLUES TO USE

Accessibility for special needs

If you have difficulty typing or using a mouse, have slightly impaired vision, or are deaf or hard of hearing, you can adjust the appearance and behavior of Windows 2000, making your computer easier to use. The **Accessibility Wizard** helps you configure Windows for your vision, hearing, and mobility needs. The Accessibility Wizard also enables you to save your settings to a file that can be used on another computer. To open the Accessibility Wizard, click Start, point to Programs, point to Accessories, point to Accessibility, then click Accessibility Wizard. You can also use the Control Panel to adjust the way your keyboard, display, and mouse function to suit varying vision and motor abilities. Some of the accessibility tools available include StickyKeys, which enables simultaneous keystrokes while pressing one key at a time; FilterKeys, which adjusts the response of your keyboard; ToggleKeys, which emits sounds when certain locking keys are pressed; SoundSentry, which provides visual warnings for system sounds; ShowSounds, which instructs programs to provide captions; High Contrast, which improves screen contrast; MouseKeys, which enables the keyboard to perform mouse functions; and SerialKeys, which allows the use of alternative input devices.

Using Dialog Boxes

A **dialog box** is a window that opens when you choose a command from a menu that is followed by an ellipsis (...). The ellipsis indicates that more information is required before the program can carry out the command you selected. Dialog boxes open in other situations as well, such as when you open a program in the Control Panel. In a dialog box, you specify the options you want using a variety of elements. See Figure A-10 and Table A-8 for some of the typical elements of a dialog box. ➤ Practice using a dialog box to control your mouse settings.

Steps 123 4

1. **In the Control Panel window, double-click the Mouse icon 👆 (you might need to scroll down the Control Panel window to find this icon)**
   The Mouse Properties dialog box opens, shown in Figure A-11. The options in this dialog box allow you to control the way the mouse buttons are configured, select the types of pointers that appear, choose the speed of the mouse movement on the screen, and specify what type of mouse you are using. Tabs at the top of the dialog box separate these options into related categories.

2. **Click the Motion tab**
   This tab has three boxes. The first, labeled Speed, has a slider for you to set how fast the mouse pointer moves on the screen in relation to how you move the mouse in your hand. The slider lets you specify the degree to which the option is in effect—the speed of the mouse pointer.

3. **In the Speed box, drag the slider to the left**
   As you move the mouse, notice the slower speed.

4. **Click the other tabs in the Mouse Properties dialog box and examine the options that are available in each category**
   Now, you need to select a command button to carry out the options you've selected. The two most common command buttons are OK and Cancel. Clicking OK accepts your changes and closes the dialog box; clicking Cancel leaves the settings intact and closes the dialog box. The third command button in this dialog box is Apply. Clicking the Apply button accepts the changes you've made and keeps the dialog box open so that you can select additional options. Because you might share this computer with others, it's important to return the dialog box options back to the original settings.

5. **Click Cancel**
   The original settings stay intact and the dialog box closes.

6. **Click the Close button in the upper-right corner of the Control Panel window**

FIGURE A-10: Dialog box elements

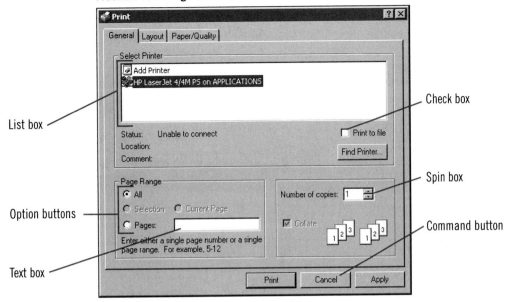

List box

Check box

Option buttons

Spin box

Text box

Command button

FIGURE A-11: Mouse Properties dialog box

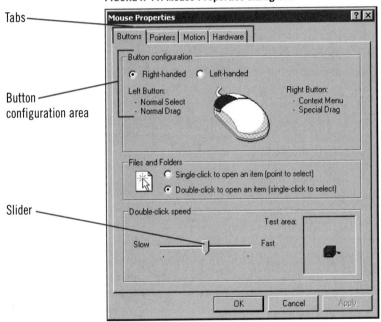

Tabs

Button
configuration area

Slider

TABLE A-8: Typical items in a dialog box

item	description
Check box	A square box that turns an option on (when the box is checked) and off (when the box is blank)
Command button	A rectangular button with the name of the command on it; it carries out a command in a dialog box
List box	A box containing a list of items; to choose an item, click the list arrow, then click the desired item
Option button	A small circle that selects a single dialog box option (you cannot check more than one option button in a list)
Spin box	A box with two arrows and a text box; allows you to scroll numerical increments or type a number
Slider	An icon you slide to set the degree to which an option is in effect
Tab	A place to organize related options
Text box	A box in which you type text

Windows 2000

Using Windows Help

When you have a question about how to do something in Windows 2000, you can usually find the answer with a few clicks of your mouse. There are a variety of different ways to access **Windows Help**, which is like a book stored on your computer, complete with an index and a table of contents to make finding information easier. You can click Help on the Start menu to open the main Windows Help dialog box. To get help on a specific program, you can click Help on the program's menu bar. You can also access **context-sensitive help**, help specifically related to what you are doing, using a variety of methods that you will practice (such as pointing to or right-clicking an object). Use Help to find out about the Windows desktop.

Steps

1. **Click the Start button on the taskbar, click Help, then click the Contents tab if necessary**
   The Windows Help dialog box opens, as shown in Figure A-12, with the Contents tab in front. The Contents tab provides you with a list of help categories. Each book icon has several "chapters" (subcategories) that you can see by clicking the book icon or the name of the help category next to the book.

2. **Point to the Introducing Windows 2000 Professional category, then click to view the subcategories underneath**
   When you point to a help category, the mouse changes to the hand pointer and the help category text is selected. The text changes to blue and underlined. This is similar to the way selecting on the Internet works. You continue to click categories to find the help topic you want.

> **QuickTip**
> You can hide the left pane of the Help window to make reading the help information easier. Click the Hide button on the Help toolbar to hide the left pane; click the Show button to re-open it.

3. **Click the What's new? topic**
   The What's New topic appears in the right pane, as shown in Figure A-13. **Panes** divide a window into two or more sections. Read the information on the new features in Windows 2000 Professional. Within a help topic, you can click ⊞ to expand a topic heading or click ⊟ to collapse a topic heading. You can move back and forth between help topics you have already visited by clicking the Back button and the Forward button on the Help toolbar.

4. **Click the Favorites tab**
   The Favorites tab allows you to add a frequently used help topic to the Topics list. If you want to add the selected topic to the Topics list, known as a **bookmark**, click Add. Later, you can return to this list and double-click the bookmark to quickly display the topic.

5. **Click the Index tab**
   The Index tab provides you with an alphabetical list of all the help topics that are available, much like an index at the end of a book. You can find out about any Windows feature by either entering the topic in the text box, or by scrolling down to the topic for which you want help, selecting a topic, and then clicking Display.

> **QuickTip**
> To print all or part of the help information, click the Options button on the Help toolbar, then click Print.

6. **Click the Search tab**
   The Search tab helps you locate the topic you need using keywords. You can find a topic by entering a keyword in the text box, clicking List Topics, selecting a topic, and then clicking Display.

7. **Click the Web Help button on the Help toolbar**
   Windows online support and information appears in the right pane. You can access the Windows Web site by clicking any one of the topics. The Web site topics provide technical support, answers to frequently asked questions, upgrade information, and late-breaking tips about working with Windows 2000.

8. **Click the Close button in the Windows Help window**
   The Help window closes.

FIGURE A-12: Windows 2000 dialog box

Help tabs

Help toolbar

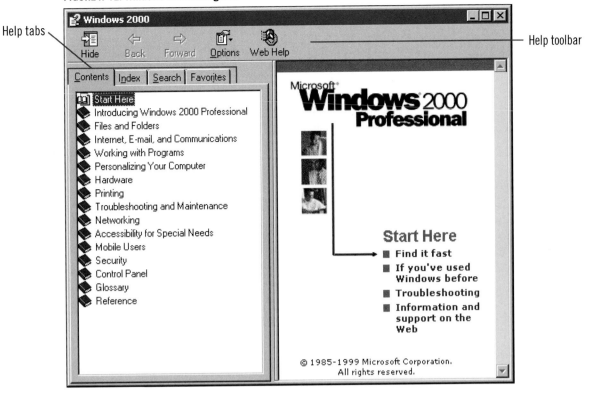

FIGURE A-13: Getting help on a particular topic

Left pane lists Help categories

Right pane displays help on the topic you select

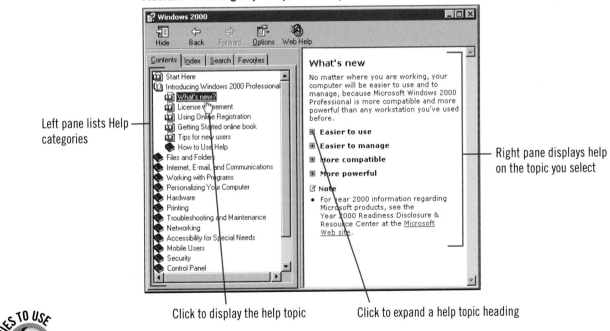

Click to display the help topic

Click to expand a help topic heading

CLUES TO USE

Context-sensitive Help

To receive help in a dialog box, click the Help button [?] in the upper-right corner of the dialog box; the mouse pointer changes to ⬚?. Click on the item in the dialog box for which you need additional information. A pop-up window opens, providing a brief explanation of the selected feature. You can also click the right mouse button on an item in a dialog box, then click the What's This? button to view the explanation. In addition, when you click the right mouse button in a help topic window, you can choose commands to annotate, copy, and print the contents of the topic. Help windows always appear on top of the currently active window, so you can see help topics while you work.

Shutting Down Windows

When you are finished working at your computer, you need to make sure to **shut down**, or turn off, your computer properly. This involves several steps: saving and closing all open files, closing all open windows, exiting all running programs, shutting down Windows itself, and, finally, turning off the computer. If you turn off the computer while Windows or other programs are running, you could lose important data. Once all files, windows, and programs are closed, you choose the Shut Down command from the Start menu. The Shut Down Windows dialog box opens with several options, as shown in Figure A-14. See Table A-9 for a description of each option. Depending on your Windows settings, your shut down options might be different. ▶ Close all your open files, windows, and programs, and then exit Windows.

Steps 1 2 3 4

1. If you have any open windows or programs, click the **Close button** ☒ in the upper-right corner of the window
   Complete the remaining steps to shut down Windows and your computer only if you have been told to do so by your instructor or technical support person.

2. Click the **Start button** on the taskbar, then click **Shut Down**
   The Shut Down Windows dialog box opens, as shown in Figure A-14. In this dialog box, you have the option to shut down the computer, restart the computer, log off a user, stand by for a while, or hibernate.

3. Click the **What do you want the computer to do? list arrow**, then click **Shut down**, if it isn't already selected, or click outside the list to close it.

4. If you are working in a lab, click **Cancel** to return to the Windows desktop; if you are working on your own machine or if your instructor or technical support person told you to shut down Windows, click **OK** to exit Windows

5. If you see the message "It's now safe to turn off your computer", turn off your computer and monitor
   Some computers power off automatically, so you may not see this message.

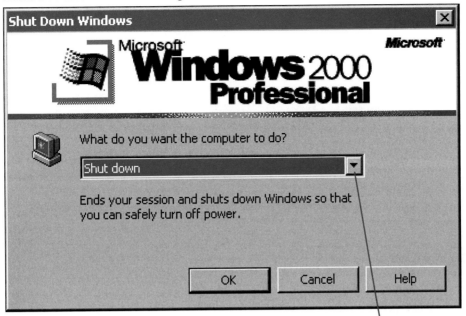

FIGURE A-14: Shut Down Windows dialog box

Windows 2000

Click to select a Windows shut down option

TABLE A-9: Shut down options

option	function	when to use it
Shut down	Prepares the computer to be powered off	When you are finished working with Windows and you want to shut off your computer
Restart	Restarts the computer and reloads Windows	When you want to restart the computer and begin working with Windows again (your programs might have frozen or stopped working)
Log off	Ends your session and restarts the computer for a new user	When you want to change to another user on the same computer
Stand by	Maintains your session, keeping the computer running on low power	When you want to stop working with Windows for a few moments and conserve power (for a laptop or portable computer)
Hibernate	Saves your session to disk so that you can safely turn off power; your session is restored the next time you start Windows	When you want to stop working with Windows for a while and start working again later; available when the Power Management setting (in the Control Panel) is turned on

CLUES TO USE

Logging off Windows

Many users may use the same computer, so each user has his or her own identity in Windows. This allows many users to use the same machine with complete privacy over their files, and with the ability to customize the operating system for their own preferences. Windows manages these separate identities by giving each user a unique user name and password. For a quick change between users of the same computer, you can choose the Log Off command on the Start menu or in the Shut Down Windows dialog box. This command identifies the name of the user who is currently logged on. When you choose this command, Windows 2000 shuts down and automatically restarts to the Enter Network Password dialog box. When the new user enters a user name and password, Windows starts with their configuration settings and network permissions.

Practice

▶ Concepts Review

Label each of the elements of the screen shown in Figure A-15.

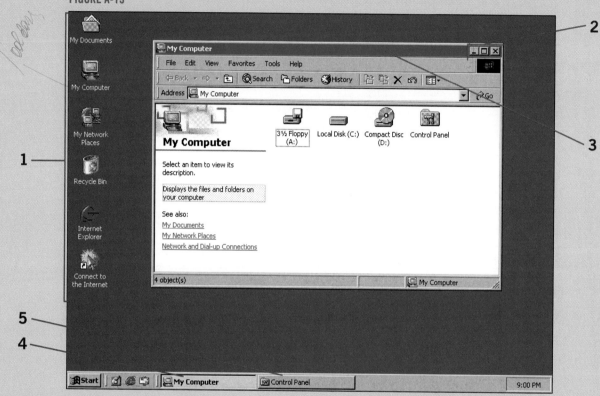

Match each of the terms with the statement that describes its function.

6. Recycle Bin
7. Sizing buttons
8. Start buttons
9. Taskbar
10. Title bar
11. Mouse

a. Allows you to minimize, maximize, and restore windows
b. The item you first click to start a program using the Start menu
c. Used to point to screen elements and make selections
d. Area where the name of an open program and file appear
d. Area where deleted files are placed
e. Displays the Start button and buttons for currently open programs and windows

Select the best answer from the list of choices.

12. **The term for moving an item to a new location on the desktop is**
    a. pointing.
    b. clicking.
    c. dragging.
    d. restoring.

13. **The Maximize button is used to**
    a. return a window to its original size.
    b. expand a window to fill the entire screen.
    c. scroll slowly through a window.
    d. reduce a window to a button on the taskbar.

14. **The Minimize button is used to**
    a. return a window to its original size.
    b. expand a window to fill the entire screen.
    c. scroll slowly through a window.
    d. reduce a window to a button on the taskbar.

15. **The Menu bar provides access to a program's functions through**
    a. toolbar buttons.
    b. scroll buttons.
    c. commands.
    d. dialog box elements.

16. **To move the contents of the window up one screen,**
    a. click the up scroll arrow.
    b. click the down scroll arrow.
    c. click in the scroll bar above the scroll box.
    d. click in the scroll bar below the scroll box.

▶ Skills Review

1. **Start Windows and view the Windows desktop.**
   a. Identify and write down as many items on the desktop as you can, without referring to the lesson material. Write them down as a list.
   b. Compare your results to Figure A-1.

2. **Use the mouse.**
   a. Move the mouse on your desk and watch how the mouse pointer moves across the screen.
   b. Point to the My Documents icon on the desktop.
   c. Click the My Documents icon once. Notice that the icon's title is highlighted.
   d. Press and hold down the mouse button, then drag the My Documents icon to the opposite side of the desktop. Release the mouse button when you are finished.
   e. Drag the My Documents icon back to the original location.
   f. Practice clicking and dragging other icons on the desktop.
   g. Double-click the My Documents icon.

3. **Get started with Windows desktop.**
   a. Click the Start button on the taskbar.
   b. Point to Settings.
   c. Click Control Panel.

4. Move and resize windows.

a. Click the My Documents button on the taskbar.

b. Click the Minimize button.

c. Point to the title bar on the Control Panel window, then drag the window to the center of the desktop.

d. Click the Maximize button.

e. Click the Restore button.

f. Position the mouse pointer on any corner of the Control Panel window and drag to resize the Control Panel window smaller, so that the vertical and horizontal scroll bars appear.

g. Click the My Documents window button on the taskbar.

h. Click the Close button on the My Documents window.

5. Use menus and toolbars.

a. Click View on the menu bar, then click Small Icons.

b. Click View on the menu bar, then click List.

c. Click the Views button on the toolbar, then click Details.

6. Use scroll bars.

a. Click below the vertical scroll box.

b. Click the vertical up scroll arrow.

c. Drag the horizontal scroll box to the middle of the scroll bar.

d. Click the View button arrow on the toolbar, then click Large Icons.

7. Use dialog boxes.

a. Double-click the Display icon.

b. Click the Appearance tab.

c. Click the Scheme list arrow.

d. Select a color scheme.

e. Click Apply (do not click OK).

f. Click the Scheme list arrow, then click Windows Standard to return the color scheme back to the way it was.

g. Click OK, then close the Control Panel window.

8. Use Windows Help.

a. Click the Start button, then click Help.

b. Click the Index tab.

c. In the Type in the keyword to find text box, type **accessibility**.

d. Click Accessibility Wizard in the list of topics, then click Display twice.

e. Read the help topic in the right pane. Use the buttons on the vertical scroll bar if necessary to read all of the information.

f. Click the Close button.

9. Shut down Windows.

a. Click the Start button, then click Shut Down.

b. Click the What do you want the computer to do? list arrow, then click Restart.

c. Click OK if you are not working in a lab or if your lab manager approves of shutting down the computer. Otherwise, click Cancel.

► Independent Challenges

1. Windows 2000 provides extensive online Help. At anytime, you can select Help from the Start menu and get the assistance you need. Use the Help options to learn about the topics listed below.

To complete this independent challenge:

a. Locate and read the help information on the following topics: My Computer, adjusting the double-click speed of the mouse, changing the color of the desktop, changing the appearance of scroll bars, and exiting programs.

b. If you have a printer connected to your computer, print one or more of the help topics you located.

c. Close the Windows Help window.

2. You can customize many Windows features to suit your needs and preferences. One way you do this is to change the appearance of the taskbar on the desktop.

To complete this independent challenge:

a. Position the mouse pointer over a blank area of the taskbar, then drag to the top of the screen to move the taskbar.

b. Position the mouse pointer over the bottom border of the taskbar. When the pointer changes shape, drag upwards to increase the size of the taskbar.

c. Click the Start button, point to Settings, and click Taskbar & Start Menu. On the General tab, click the Show Clock check box to deselect the option and observe the effect on the taskbar in the Preview window.

d. Print the Screen using the Windows Paint accessory (Press the Print Screen key to make a copy of the screen. Start the Paint program by clicking the Start button, pointing to Programs, pointing to Accessories, then clicking Paint. Click Edit on the menu bar, click Paste to paste the screen into Paint, then click Yes to paste the large image if necessary. Click File on the menu bar, click Print, then click Print in the dialog box.)

e. Restore the taskbar to its original setting, size, and location on the screen.

3. You have accepted a new job in New York City. After moving into your new home and unpacking your stuff, you decide to set up your computer. Once you set up and turn on the computer, you decide to change the date and time settings to reflect the time zone in New York.

To complete this independent challenge:

a. Open the Control Panel window, then double-click the Date/Time icon.

b. Click the Time Zone tab.

c. Select Eastern Time (US & Canada) from the list.

d. Click the Date & Time tab, change the month and year to September 2001, then click Apply.

e. Print the screen. (See Independent Challenge 2, Step d for screen printing instructions.)

f. Return the date and time zone back to their original settings, then click OK.

g. Close the Control Panel window.

4. You are a student in a Windows 2000 course. After learning basic Windows 2000 desktop skills, you want to learn how to customize the desktop. Use the online version of the Getting Started Book in Windows Help to find information on customizing your desktop and then print the related help topics.

To complete this independent challenge:

a. Open the Windows Help window.

b. In the Contents tab, go to the Introducing Windows 2000 Professional category.

c. Go to the Getting Started online book topic.

d. In the right pane, click Windows 2000 Professional Getting Started, then open Ch 1 – Welcome.

e. View the Windows 2000 Professional at a Glance topic, then print the topic.

f. Close the Windows Help windows.

► Visual Workshop

Re-create the screen shown in Figure A-16, which shows the Windows desktop with My Documents and My Computer open. Print the screen. (See Independent Challenge 2, Step d for screen printing instructions.)

FIGURE A-16

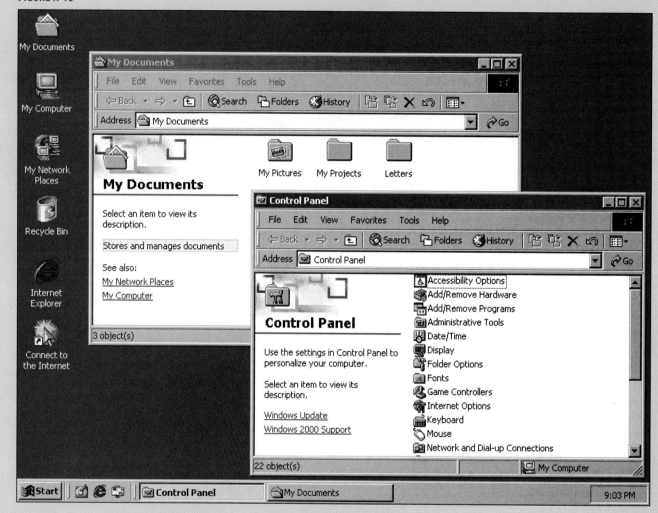

Working
with Windows Programs

Objectives

- ▶ **Start a program**
- ▶ **Open and save a WordPad document**
- ▶ **Edit text in a WordPad document**
- ▶ **Format text in a WordPad document**
- ▶ **Use Paint**
- ▶ **Copy data between programs**
- ▶ **Print a document**
- ▶ **Play a video clip**
- ▶ **Play a sound**

Now that you know how to work with common Windows graphical elements, you're ready to work with programs. Windows comes with several **accessories,** built-in programs that, while not as feature-rich as many programs sold separately, are extremely useful for completing basic tasks. In this unit, you will work with some of these accessories. John Casey is the owner of Wired Coffee Company, a growing company that uses Windows 2000. John needs to prepare a new coffee menu, so he will use two Windows accessories, WordPad and Paint, to create it. He will use another accessory, Windows Media Player, to play video and sound clips on his computer.

Windows 2000

Starting a Program

A **Windows program** (also called an application), is software designed to run on the Windows operating system. All Windows accessories are located on the Accessories submenu of the Programs submenu. John wants to use **WordPad**, a word-processing accessory that comes with Windows, to prepare the text of his new coffee menu, so he needs to start this program.

1. Click the **Start button** on the taskbar
The Start menu opens.

QuickTip

If a single arrow appears at the top or bottom of the Programs submenu, point to the arrow to scroll up or down the menu to view more elements.

2. Point to **Programs** on the Start menu
The Programs submenu opens, listing the programs and categories for programs installed on your computer. WordPad is on the Accessories submenu.

3. Point to **Accessories** on the Programs submenu
The Accessories submenu opens, as shown in Figure B-1. The Accessories submenu lists a personalized menu of the programs you have used most recently. To reduce the number of elements on the Programs submenus and customize your Windows environment, Windows keeps track of which programs you use and hides the programs you have not used recently.

4. Click the **More menu items indicator** ☽ at the bottom of the Accessories submenu, if necessary
The full Accessories submenu appears. Locate the WordPad item on this submenu.

Trouble?

If the Toolbar, Format Bar, ruler, or status bar does not appear, click View on the menu bar, then click the element (without a check mark) you want to view.

5. Click **WordPad** on the Accessories submenu
The mouse pointer briefly changes to an hourglass, indicating that you are to wait while Windows starts the WordPad program. The WordPad window then appears on your desktop, as shown in Figure B-2. The WordPad window includes two toolbars, the **Toolbar** and the **Format Bar**, as well as a ruler, a work area, and a status bar. A blinking cursor, known as the **insertion point**, appears in the work area of the WordPad window, indicating where new text will be inserted. The WordPad program button appears in the taskbar, indicating that the WordPad program is now running.

6. Click the **Maximize button** ▢ in the WordPad window
WordPad expands to fill the screen.

FIGURE B-1: Starting WordPad using the Start menu

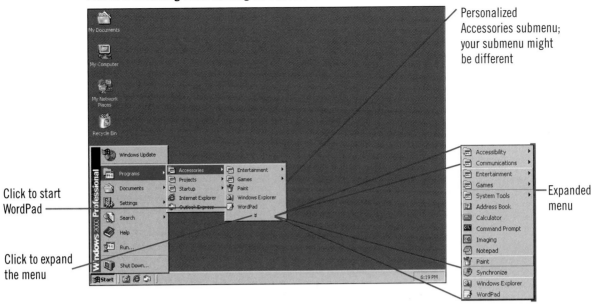

Personalized
Accessories submenu;
your submenu might
be different

Click to start
WordPad

Click to expand
the menu

Expanded
menu

FIGURE B-2: Windows desktop with the WordPad window open

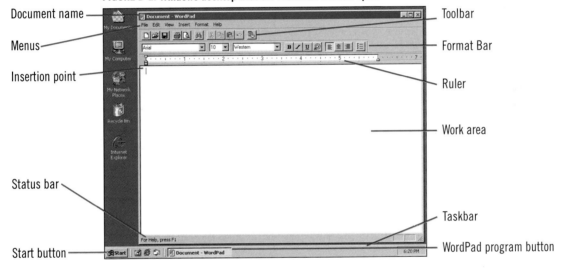

Document name
Menus
Insertion point

Status bar

Start button

Toolbar
Format Bar
Ruler

Work area

Taskbar
WordPad program button

Creating documents in other languages

You can install multiple languages on your computer, such as Hebrew, Arabic, Japanese, Korean, French, Spanish, German, and many others. You can choose which language you want to use when you create a document. Then Windows 2000 makes the characters for that language available, so you can start writing. You can create documents in other languages using WordPad and NotePad, word-processing accessories that come with Windows 2000. To install additional languages, click the Start button, point to Settings, click Control Panel, double-click Regional Options, click the General tab, and then click the check box next to the language group you want to install. To complete the installation, you must insert the Windows 2000 CD-ROM. To add an input locale and keyboard layout, click the Input Locales tab in the Regional Options dialog box, click Add, and then click the locale and layout you want. Once you have added one or more input locale(s), an input locale indicator appears in the status area of the taskbar. The indicator displays the first two letters of the current input language (such as EN for English). You can compose documents that contain more than one language. Any recipients of multilanguage documents must also have the same languages installed on their computer to read and edit the documents. To compose a document using multiple languages, click the input locale indicator on the taskbar, click the language you want to use in the list that opens, and then type your message.

Opening and Saving a WordPad Document

A **document** is the piece of work you create using a word-processing program. You can use WordPad to create documents such as letters, memos, and resumes. When you start WordPad, a blank document appears in the work area of the WordPad window, known as the **document window**. You can enter new information to create a new document and save the result as a file, or you can open an existing file and save the document with any changes you made. To prevent any accidental changes to the original document, you can save the document with a new name. This makes a copy of the document, so you can make changes to the new document and leave the original file unaltered. John wants to open an existing WordPad document that contains the text of the coffee menu rather than typing the menu from scratch. He needs to open the document and save it with a new name before making any changes to it, so that the original file remains intact.

QuickTip

Make sure you have made a copy of your Project Disk, to protect the original. If you need assistance, contact your instructor or technical support person.

1. Insert a copy of your Project Disk into the appropriate floppy drive, click the **Open button** 📂 on the WordPad toolbar

The Open dialog box opens, as shown in Figure B-3. In this dialog box, you locate and choose the file you wish to open. You can click icons in the **Places bar** on the left side of the dialog box to navigate to common locations or recently used files and folders on your computer or network. The file John created is stored on your Project Disk.

Trouble?

If a list of files doesn't appear in the file list, click the Files of Type list arrow, then click Text Document or Word for Windows 6.0.

2. Click the **Look in list arrow**, click the **drive that contains your Project Disk**, then click the **Unit B Folder**

A list of the files in this folder on the Project Disk appears in the file list. You can select a file in the file list or type the name of the file you want in the File name text box. When you type a name, **AutoComplete** suggests possible matches with previous filename entries. You can continue to type or click the File name list arrow, then click a matching filename from the list. The list is constrained by the Files of Type list, which means you will see different lists depending on the file type you select.

3. In the file list click **Win B-1**, then click **Open**

The file named Win B-1 opens. This is a menu for the coffee company.

4. Click **File** on the menu bar, then click **Save As**

The Save As dialog box opens, as shown in Figure B-4. The Save As command allows you to save an existing document under a new name and also in a different folder or drive location.

QuickTip

To provide a consistent place to store all your files, Windows 2000 saves and opens all your documents to and from the My Documents folder on your desktop unless you choose a different location.

5. If **Win B-1** is not already selected, click in the **File name text box**, then select the entire filename by dragging the mouse pointer over it

In WordPad, as in most other Windows programs, you must select text in order to modify it. When you select text, the selection appears **highlighted** (white text on a black background) to indicate that it has been selected. Any action you now take will be performed on the selected text.

6. Type **Coffee Menu** to replace the selected text

As soon as you start typing, the selected text is replaced by the text you are typing. It's a good idea to use descriptive names for your files so you can identify their contents more easily.

QuickTip

When an existing document is open, you can click the New button 🗋 on the toolbar to create a blank new document.

7. Click **Save**

The file is saved under the new name, Coffee Menu, in the same folder and drive location as the Win B-1 file. The original file, called Win B-1, is automatically closed, and the new filename appears in the title bar of the WordPad window.

FIGURE B-3: **Open dialog box**

Click an icon in the Places bar to open a common location on your computer or network

Type filename here; AutoComplete suggests possible matches with previous filenames

Click to specify the location of file to open

List of files and folders stored in the selected location (such as the My Documents folder); your list may be different

Click to open selected file

Select type of file here

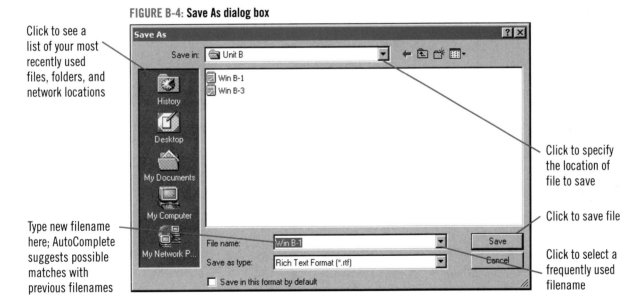

FIGURE B-4: **Save As dialog box**

Click to see a list of your most recently used files, folders, and network locations

Type new filename here; AutoComplete suggests possible matches with previous filenames

Click to specify the location of file to save

Click to save file

Click to select a frequently used filename

About saving files

Until you save them, the documents you create are stored in the computer's **Random Access Memory** (**RAM**). RAM is a temporary storage space that is erased when the computer is turned off. To store a document permanently, you must save it as a file to a disk. A **file** is a collection of information that has a unique name, distinguishing it from other files. You can save files to a **floppy disk** that you insert into the disk drive

of your computer (usually the A: or B: drive) or a **hard disk**, which is built into the computer (usually the C: drive). This book assumes that you will save all of your files to your Project Disk, which your instructor or technical support person has provided to you. Windows 2000 lets you save files using names that have up to 255 characters, including spaces.

Editing Text in a WordPad Document

One of the major advantages of using a word processor is that you can **edit**, or change the contents of a document, without having to retype it. You can also move whole sections of a document from one place to another using the Cut and Paste commands. ▬▬▬ John wants to add a greeting and change the price for a pound of coffee in the Coffee Menu document. He also wants to change the order of the menu items, so that the coffees are listed in alphabetical order.

Steps

1. Press ↓ three times or click in the line just above "Specialty Coffees"
Figure B-5 shows the insertion point where you want to insert new text. Repositioning the insertion point in a document (called **navigating**) is an important skill to learn. In addition to the arrow keys, WordPad offers another set of keys and key combinations, as shown in Table B-1, that enable you to navigate a document quickly.

Trouble?

If you make a mistake while typing, press [Backspace] (which deletes the character to the left of the insertion point) until you have deleted your mistake, then retype the text.

2. Type Welcome to the taste tantalizing coffee selections offered to you by Wired Coffee Company. You will find a variety of specialty coffees, including Single-Origin, Blends, Dark Roasts, and Decaffeinated., then press [Enter]
WordPad automatically puts the text that won't fit on the current line onto the next line, using a feature called **wordwrap**.

3. In the price of the Breakfast Blend coffee, click to the right of the last digit, 0
This number needs to be changed from "11.90" to "11.00".

4. Press [Backspace] twice, then type 00
Now John wants to rearrange the list so that the coffees are listed in alphabetical order. The fourth coffee in the list (Espresso Dark Roast) needs to be moved so it comes before the third (Ethiopian Harrar). To do this, John first has to select the entire line so that he can move the text up the list. You can select text three different ways. You can drag the mouse to highlight the text you want to select. If you need to select just a word, you can double-click it. If you need to select a line or paragraph, you can position the pointer to the left of the first character in the line or paragraph, then click once to select a line or twice to select an entire paragraph.

5. Position the pointer to the left of the first character in the line "Espresso Dark Roast"
The pointer changes from I to ↖.

6. Click once
The entire line is selected. Now, John can move the line.

QuickTip

To select the entire paragraph, you can triple-click anywhere in the paragraph.

7. Click the Cut button ✂ on the toolbar
When selected text is **cut** from a document, Windows removes it from the document and places it on the **Clipboard**, a temporary storage place where it remains available to be pasted somewhere else. When text is **copied**, a copy of it is placed on the Clipboard to be pasted in another location, but the text also remains in its original place in the document.

8. Press ↑ once to move up one line in the list
This is where John wants to paste the line he cut. Selections you paste are inserted at the location of the insertion point.

9. Click the Paste button 📋 on the toolbar, then click the Save button 💾 on the toolbar
Figure B-6 shows the line pasted into the list. The coffees are now in alphabetical order and the changes you made to the file are saved.

FIGURE B-5: Positioning the insertion point

Insertion point —

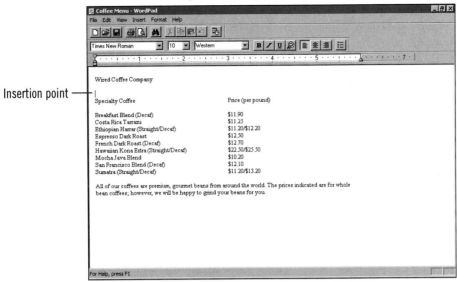

FIGURE B-6: Editing a WordPad file by cutting and pasting

List is now in
alphabetical order

Your lines
might wrap
differently

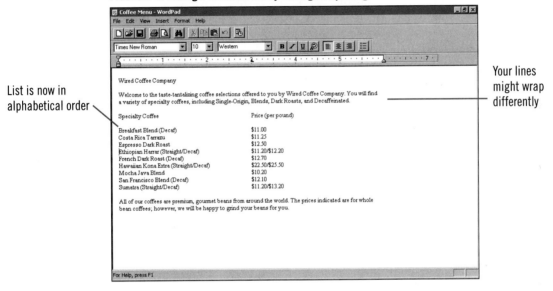

TABLE B-1: Moving around a WordPad document

key(s)	navigation
↑	Move up one line
↓	Move down one line
←	Move left one character
→	Move right one character
[PgUp]	Move to the previous page
[PdDn]	Move to the next page
[Ctrl][End]	Move to the end of the document
[Ctrl][Home]	Move to the beginning of the document
[Ctrl]→	Move to the beginning of the next word to the right
[Ctrl]←	Move to the beginning of the previous word to the left

Windows 2000

Formatting Text in a WordPad Document

You can change the **format**, or the appearance of the text and graphics in a document, so that the document is easier to read or more attractive. Almost all formatting changes in WordPad can be achieved using the Format Bar, which appears below the Toolbar in the WordPad window. Table B-2 describes the function of each button on the Format Bar. John wants to make the Coffee Menu document more attractive. He does this by centering the title, bolding it, and increasing its size.

QuickTip

To insert a special character, such as a trademark or symbol, click the Start button on the taskbar, point to Accessories, point to System Tools, and then click Character Map. Click a character, click Select, click Copy, place the insertion point in your document at the desired location, and then click the Paste button on the Toolbar.

1. Select the text **Wired Coffee Company**

Remember that the first step in making any editing or formatting change is to select the text you want to change. Then, you can carry out the desired command.

2. Click the **Center button** 🗒 on the Format Bar

Notice that the title is centered and the button appears indented.

3. Click the **Bold button** 🅱 on the Format Bar

The selected material appears in bold. If you wanted to turn bold off, you would click the button again. Buttons act as **toggle** switches—click once to turn the format feature on, click again to turn it off.

4. Click the **Italic button** 🇮 on the Format Bar

Italicizing does not provide the effect that John wanted.

5. Click the **Undo button** 🔄 on the Toolbar

This command reverses the last change that was made, such as typing new text, deleting text, and formatting existing text. Undo cannot reverse all commands (such as scrolling or saving a document), but it is a quick way to reverse most editing and formatting changes.

6. Click the **Font list arrow** `Times New Roman ▾` on the Format Bar, then click **Arial**

The **font**, or typeface, of the text changes from Times New Roman to Arial.

7. Click the **Font Size list arrow** `10 ▾` on the Format Bar, then click **14**

The selected text increases in size from 10-point to 14-point. One **point** is 1/72 of an inch in height. Whenever you want to know the type and size of a font on your screen, place the insertion point anywhere in the text and look at the size that appears in the Font list box and Font Size list box.

8. Click anywhere in the document to deselect the text

As Figure B-7 shows, the title is centered and changed in typeface to Arial and size to 14-point.

9. Click the **Save button** 💾 on the toolbar

The changes made to the Coffee Menu are saved.

FIGURE B-7: Formatted text

Click to change the font type

Click to change the size of text

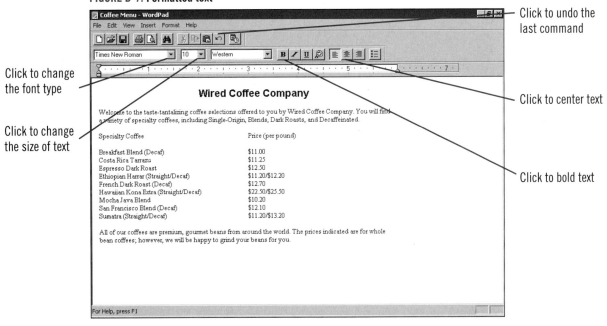

Click to undo the last command

Click to center text

Click to bold text

TABLE B-2: Format Bar buttons and list arrows

button	function	button	function
Times New Roman	Select a font	(color icon)	Add or change color
10	Select a font size	(left align icon)	Left align
B	Bold	(center align icon)	Center align
I	Italic	(right align icon)	Right align
U	Underline	(bulleted list icon)	Create bulleted list

Formatting text as you type

As you've learned, one way to format text is to select it, then apply a formatting change. Another way is to first apply the formatting you want, then enter text. This approach is helpful when you are starting a new document and are familiar with the effect that different formatting options create. For example, if you were creating a new list of items and knew that you wanted the title to be 24-point underlined text, you could click the Underline button U on the Format Bar, then click 24 in the Font Size list box. Anything that you type from that point will have those format characteristics. When you finish typing the title, you can change the font back to a smaller point size and click the Underline button to toggle the option off, then continue typing.

Using Paint

Windows 2000

When it comes to creating and working with images, Paint is a useful Windows accessory. You can draw images and manipulate them with commands such as rotate, stretch, and invert colors. You can open more than one Windows program at a time, so while WordPad is still running, you can open Paint and work on drawings and images. This is called multitasking. John already created a logo for his coffee company. Now he wants to review the logo and revise it as necessary before using it on his promotional materials.

Steps 1234

1. **Click the Start button on the taskbar, point to Programs, point to Accessories, click Paint, then click the Maximize button on the Paint title bar**
   The Paint window opens and is maximized in front of the WordPad window. You can find buttons for frequently used commands in the Paint Tool Box, located along the left edge of the window. Table B-3 describes these tools.

QuickTip

To provide a consistent place to store all your images, Windows 2000 saves and opens all your image files to and from the My Pictures folder located in the My Documents folder.

2. **Click File on the menu bar, click Open**
   The Open dialog box opens.

3. **Click the Look in list arrow, click the drive that contains your Project Disk, then double-click the Unit B folder**
   A list of the files stored in this folder on the Project Disk appears.

4. **In the file list, click Win B-2, then click Open**
   The file named Win B-2 opens, shown in Figure B-8. If you cannot see the logo on your screen, use the scroll buttons to adjust your view. John decides the logo could use some final modifications.

5. **Click File on the menu bar, click Save As, then save the document as Wired Coffee Logo to your Project Disk**
   A copy of the file is saved under the new name, and the original file remains intact. John wants to add a rounded border around the logo. To use any tool in Paint, you first click it in the Tool Box, and then "paint" or "draw" with it using the mouse.

QuickTip

You can press and hold down [Shift] while you drag a drawing tool to create a proportional drawing, such as a square or circle.

6. **Click the Rounded Rectangle tool 🔲 in the Tool Box, then move the cursor into the Paint work area**
   When you move the mouse pointer back into the work space, it changes to $+$, indicating that the Rounded Rectangle tool is active.

Trouble?

If your rounded rectangle doesn't match Figure B-9, click Edit on the menu bar, then click Undo to reverse the last command. If Undo is not available, click the Erase tool 🖊, drag to erase the rounded rectangle, then repeat Step 6.

7. **Beginning above and to the left of the logo, drag $+$ so that a rounded rectangle surrounds the image, then release the mouse button below and to the right of the image, as shown in Figure B-9**
   John likes this new look.

8. **Click File on the menu bar, then click Save**
   Now John can use the logo in his other documents.

FIGURE B-8: Company logo in Paint

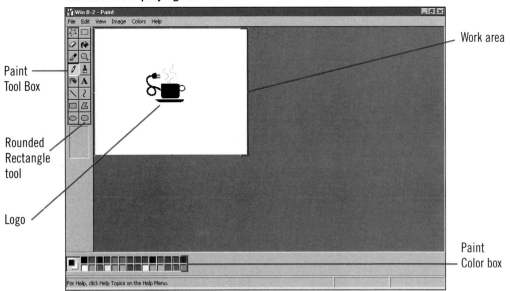

Paint Tool Box

Rounded Rectangle tool

Logo

Work area

Paint Color box

FIGURE B-9: Company logo with rounded rectangle

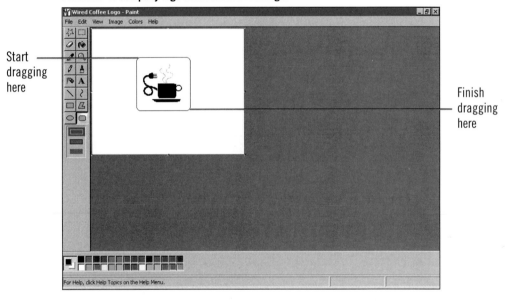

Start dragging here

Finish dragging here

TABLE B-3: Buttons in the Paint Tool Box

tool	description	tool	description
	Selects a shape that is not regular		Creates dispersed lines and patterns
	Selects a shape that is regular		Enters text in drawings
	Erases part of a drawing		Draws a straight line
	Fills a shape with a color or texture		Draws a free-form line
	Picks up a color from the picture for drawing		Draws a regular shape
	Magnifies part of an image		Draws an irregular shape
	Draws freehand		Draws an oval or circle
	Designates the size and shape brush to draw with		Draws a rectangle or square with rounded corners

Copying Data Between Programs

One of the most useful features that Windows offers is the ability to use data created in one document in another document, even if the two documents were created in different Windows programs. To work with more than one program or document at a time, you simply open each of them on your desktop. Any window that is open on the desktop is represented by a **program button** on the taskbar. When you want to switch from one open window to another, click the correct program button on the taskbar. If you **tile** or arrange open windows on the desktop so that all are visible, you can switch among them simply by clicking in the window you want to work in. Just as you used the Clipboard to rearrange text in WordPad, you can use it to move and copy data between two different documents. Table B-4 reviews the Cut, Copy, and Paste commands and their associated keyboard shortcuts, which can be used in Paint, WordPad, and many other Windows programs. ➤ John wants to add the company logo, which he created with Paint, to the Coffee Menu document, which he created with WordPad. He'll first switch to WordPad, which is still running, to decide exactly where he wants to place the logo. Then he'll switch to Paint, copy the logo, and finally switch back to WordPad and paste it in the menu.

Steps

Trouble?

If your windows don't appear tiled, click the program button on the taskbar for each program (Paint and WordPad) to ensure that both windows are maximized, then repeat Step 1.

1. **Make sure both WordPad and Paint are open, place the mouse pointer on an empty area of the taskbar, right-click, then click Tile Windows Vertically from the shortcut menu**
   The windows (Paint and WordPad) are arranged next to one another vertically, as shown in Figure B-10, so that John can maneuver quickly between them while working.

2. **Click the Paint program button on the taskbar or click anywhere in the Paint window**
   The Paint program becomes the **active program** (the title bar changes from gray to blue).

3. **Click the Select tool [icon] in the toolbox, then drag a rectangle around the coffee logo to select it**
   Dragging with the Select Tool selects an object in Paint for cutting, copying, or performing other modifications.

QuickTip

When Windows are tiled, you can drag a selected item from one program to another to copy the item between programs.

4. **Click Edit on the Paint menu bar, then click Copy**
   The logo is copied to the Windows Clipboard. The Copy command is similar to the Cut command you used when working with the coffee list, but when you copy a selection, the original remains intact and a copy is placed on the Clipboard.

5. **Click the first blank line of the WordPad document, above the title**
   The WordPad program becomes active and the insertion point is placed on the WordPad page, where John wants the logo to appear. If you cannot see enough of the page, use the scroll buttons to adjust your view.

6. **Click the Paste button [icon] on the WordPad Toolbar**
   The logo is pasted into the document, as shown in Figure B-11.

7. **Click the Maximize button in the WordPad window, click the Center button [icon] on the Format Bar, then click below the logo to deselect it**
   The logo is centered in the document.

8. **Click the Save button [icon] on the WordPad Toolbar**
   The document is complete and ready for John to print.

9. **Click the Paint program button on the taskbar, then click Close button [icon] in the Paint window**

FIGURE B-10: **Tiled windows**

Click to
activate the
Paint program

Right-click to
open the pop-up
menu and tile
windows vertically

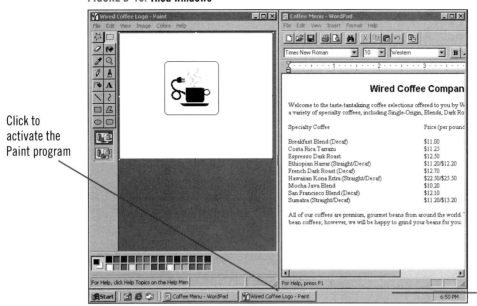

FIGURE B-11: **Copying a selection between programs**

Copy
selected logo
from Paint
document

Paste logo in
WordPad
document

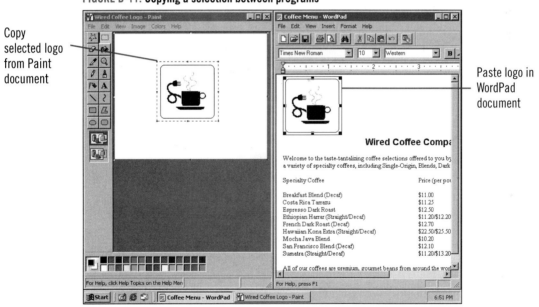

TABLE B-4: **Overview of cutting, copying, and pasting**

function	toolbar button	keyboard shortcut
Cut: Removes selected information from a file and places it on the Clipboard	✂	[Ctrl][X]
Copy: Places a copy of selected information on the Clipboard, leaving the file intact	▤	[Ctrl][C]
Paste: Inserts whatever is currently on the Clipboard into another location (within the same file or in a different file)	▥	[Ctrl][V]

Windows 2000

Printing a Document

Printing a document creates a **printout** or **hard copy**, a document on paper that you can share with others or review as a work in progress. Most Windows programs have a print option that you access through the Print Dialog box and a Print button on the Toolbar. Although your printing options vary from program to program, the process works similarly in all of them. It is a good idea to use the **Print Preview** feature to look at the layout and formatting of a document before you print it. You may catch a mistake, find that the document fits on more pages than you wanted, or notice formatting that you want to do differently. Making changes before you print saves paper. John decides to preview the coffee menu before printing the document.

Steps

1. **In the WordPad window, click the Print Preview button 🖺 on the Toolbar**
   A reduced but proportionate image of the page appears in the Preview window, as shown in Figure B-12.

QuickTip

To zoom out from the zoom in position, click the print preview area or click the Zoom Out in Print Preview.

2. **Move the mouse pointer (which changes to 🔍) over the logo and click, or click Zoom In in Print Preview**
   The preview image of the page appears larger, easier to see. John notices extra space around the dotted rectangle, the area determined by the **margin** setting, so he is not yet ready to print.

3. **Click Close in Print Preview**
   The Preview window closes and you return to the Coffee Menu document.

4. **Click File on the menu bar, then click Page Setup**
   The Page Setup dialog box opens. In this dialog box, you can change the margin setting to decrease or increase the area outside the dotted rectangle. You can change other printing options here, such as paper size, page orientation, and printer source. Table B-5 describes the Page Setup dialog box options.

5. **Select the number in the Top text box, then type 1.25, select the number in the Bottom text box, type 1.25, then click OK**
   You return to the WordPad document. You should verify that you like the new margins before printing.

6. **Click 🖺**
   The menu contains smaller margins.

QuickTip

To quickly print a document, click the Print button 🖨 on the Toolbar. To open the Print dialog box, click File on the menu bar, then click Print.

7. **Click Print in the Print Preview window**
   The Print dialog box opens, as shown in Figure B-13, showing various options available for printing. Check to make sure you are printing to the correct printer. If you need to change printers, select a printer. If you want to add a printer, double-click the Add Printer icon, then follow the Add Printer Wizard instructions. When you are done, accept all of the settings.

QuickTip

To see the number of documents waiting to print, right-click the printer in the Print dialog box, then click Open.

8. **Click Print**
   The WordPad document prints. While a document prints, a printer icon 🖨 appears in the status area on the taskbar. You can point to the printer icon to get status information. To **close**, or quit, a program and any of its currently open files, you select the Exit command from the File menu. You can also click the Close button in the upper right-corner of the program window.

9. **Click the Close button ✕ in the WordPad window**

FIGURE B-12: **Coffee Menu in Print Preview**

Click to print document —

Click to magnify the view in Print Preview —

Click to close Print Preview

Dotted lines indicate margins

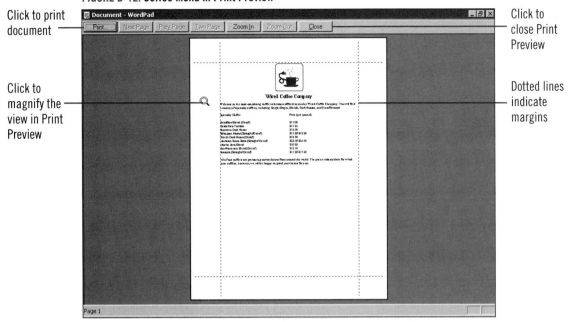

FIGURE B-13: **Print dialog box**

Double-click to add a printer —

Printer information —

In a multiple-page document, set which pages to print here —

Your print options might differ

Click to select a printer; your printer name and location might be different

Click to find a network printer

Set number of copies here

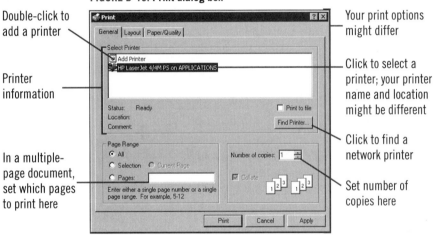

TABLE B-5: **Page Setup dialog box options**

page setup option	function
Size	Defines the size of the paper on which you want to print
Source	Defines the location of the paper, such as another paper bin or an envelope feeder
Orientation	Allows you to select between Portrait (the page being taller than it is wide) and Landscape (the page being wider than it is tall)
Margins	Allows you to define top, bottom, left, and right page margins

Printer properties

You can select Layout or Paper/Quality tabs from the Print dialog box and adjust several facets of the printing operation. For example, to control the intensity with which graphics images are printed, you would click the Paper/Quality tab, then adjust the intensity slider. You can also adjust fonts, paper sizes, and other printing dimensions in the Print dialog box.

Playing a Video Clip

Windows 2000 comes with a built-in accessory, called **Windows Media Player**, that you can use to play video, sound, and mixed-media files. You can use it to play movies, sounds, and other multimedia files from your computer, a local network, or the Internet. The Windows Media Player delivers high-quality continuous video and sound playback, known as **streaming media**. With the Windows Media Player, you can modify the media and control settings. ▄▄▄ John wants to play a video, so he needs to use the Windows Media Player.

Steps

QuickTip

To make sure you are using the most recent version of Windows Media Player, click Help on the menu bar, then click Check for Player Upgrade. (You must have an open connection to the Internet to perform this check.)

1. Click the **Start button** on the taskbar, point to **Programs**, point to **Accessories**, point to **Entertainment**, then click **Windows Media Player**
   Windows Media Player opens, as shown in Figure B-14.

2. Click **File** on the menu bar, click **Open**, then click **Browse**
   The Open dialog box opens.

3. Click the **Look in list arrow**, click the **drive that contains your Project Disk**, then double-click the **Unit B folder**
   A list of the files in this folder on the Project Disk appears in the file list.

QuickTip

You can change the size of the Windows Media Player window by clicking View on the menu bar, then clicking Standard, Compact, or Minimal.

4. In the file list, click **Coffee Cup**, click **Open**, then click **OK** in the Open dialog box
   The video opens in the Media Player window and starts to play. A **Seek bar** in the Windows Media Player window moves indicating the progress of the video, as shown in Figure B-15. You can drag the Seek bar backward or forward to play different parts of the video. Below the Seek bar is the Control bar. The **Control bar** allows you to play all or part of a video. Table B-6 describes the function of each button on the Control bar. Above the Seek bar is the Navigation bar. With the **Navigation bar** buttons, you can move backward and forward between open files and start your Web browser and open media Web sites on the Internet. (You must have an open connection to the Internet to perform this check.)

QuickTip

To customize playback settings, click View on the menu bar, click Options, click the Playback tab, select the settings you want, then click OK.

5. Click the **Play button** ▶ on the toolbar

6. Click **File** on the menu bar, then click **Close**
   The video closes. Leave the Windows Media Player window open for the next lesson.

FIGURE B-14: Windows Media Player window

Click to move between open media files

Navigation bar

Seek bar

Control bar

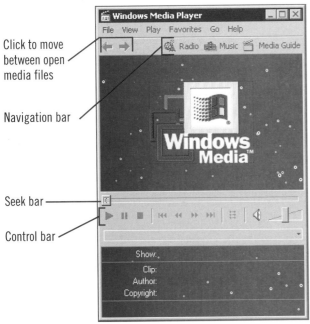

FIGURE B-15: Windows Media Player window playing a video

Slider indicating current play time

Click to play video

Information about video

Current status of video

Length of video in seconds

TABLE B-6: Control bar buttons on the Windows Media Player

button	description
▶	Play a video or sound
‖	Pause a video or sound
■	Stop a video or sound
◄◄	Return to the beginning of the current video or sound
◄◄	Rewind the video or sound
►►	Advance forward through the video or sound
►►|	Begin to play the beginning of the next video or sound
▦	Play a short section of each video or sound in a show
◁	Silence the audio content of the file
◢	Control the volume level of the content you are viewing

CLUES TO USE

Changing Windows Media Player Options

You can change the way Windows Media Player plays video and audio, the way the player opens, the size of the player window, and the types of files you can play. To change Windows Media Player options, click View on the menu bar, then click Options. In the Options dialog box, click the Playback tab to change audio volume, balance, playback options such as whether files should repeat and rewind; click the Player tab to specify how Windows Media Player opens and the window appears; click the Custom Views tab to specify what controls appear in Compact and Minimal view; click the Advanced tab to change streaming settings; and click the Formats tab to specify the file formats you want to use with Windows Media Player.

Playing a Sound

You can play sounds using the Windows Media Player. In order to listen to sounds, your computer must have a sound card and self-powered speakers. Windows Media Player can play a variety of sounds. To play a sound, you click the Play button. If you want to pause while playing the sound, you click the Pause button. If you want to change the starting position of the sound, you drag the slider. John enjoyed playing a video, so he decides to play a sound.

1. **Make sure the Windows Media Player is open, click File on the menu bar, then click Open**
   The Open dialog box opens. John decides to play a sound located on your Project Disk.

2. **Click Browse, click the Look in list arrow, then click the drive that contains your Project Disk**
   A list of the files and folders stored on the Project Disk appears in the file list.

> **QuickTip**
> To adjust the volume, use [↑] and [↓] on the keyboard to raise and lower the volume.

3. **In the file list, click Better Coffee, click Open, then click OK**
   The sound plays, as shown in Figure B-16. The Seek bar in the Windows Media Player window moves, indicating the current play time of the sound. John decides to pause the sound, change the starting position of the sound, and then resume playing.

4. **Click the Play button ▶ on the toolbar, then before the sound finishes, click the Pause button ▐▌ on the toolbar**
   You can drag the Seek bar backward or forward to play different parts of the sound.

> **QuickTip**
> To display the volume control icon on the taskbar, double-click the Sound and Multimedia icon in the Control Panel, click the Sound tab, click the Show volume control on the taskbar check box, then click OK.

5. **Drag the Seek bar back to the beginning, then click the Play button ▶ to restart the sound**

6. **When you are finished playing the sound, click the Close button ✖ on the Windows Media Player window**

FIGURE B-16: Windows Media Player window playing a sound

Drag to a new position to hear a different part of the sound

Click to open audio and media Web sites on the Internet

Drag to change volume

Click to pause sound

Playing a music CD

To accommodate the many people who like to play audio CDs in their CD-ROM drives while working, Windows 2000 includes the CD Player program in its accessories. The controls on the player, shown in Figure B-17, look just like those on a regular CD player. The Windows 2000 CD Player supports many of the same features found in CD players, such as random play, programmable playback order, and the ability to save programs so that users don't have to re-create their playlists each time they play a CD. To play an audio CD, insert the CD in your CD-ROM drive; the CD Player will automatically start playing the audio CD. You can click the CD Player button on the taskbar to open the CD Player window

FIGURE B-17: CD Player window

Practice

► Concepts Review

Label each of the elements of the screen shown in Figure B-18.

FIGURE B-18

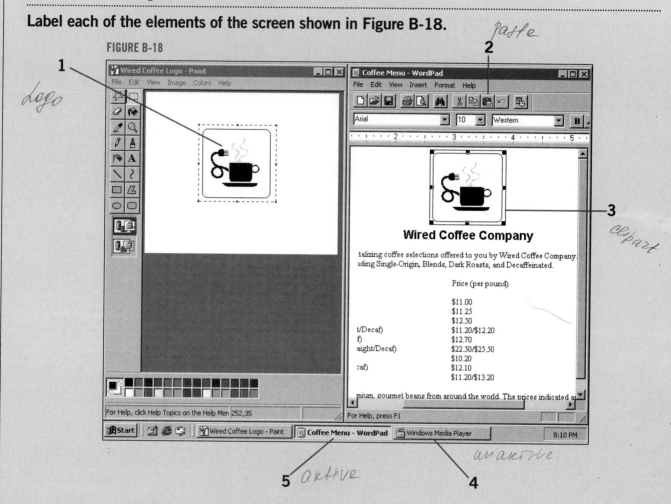

(handwritten labels: 2 — paste; 1 — Logo; 3 — clipart; 5 — active; 4 — unactive)

Match each of the terms with the statement that describes its function.

6. **Copy**   a. Removes selected text or an image from its current location

7. **Accessories**   b. Copies selected text or an image from its current location

8. **Cut**   c. A set of characters you assign to a collection of information

9. **Select**   d. A collection of programs that come built-in with Windows and enable you to perform certain tasks

10. **filename**   e. What you must first do to existing text before you can format, move, or copy it

Select the best answer from the list of choices.

11. The first step in starting any Windows accessory is to click

    a. the Start button.

    b. the taskbar.

    c. the Open icon.

    d. anywhere on the desktop.

12. **What program command makes a copy of a file?**
    a. Save
    b. Save As
    c. Copy
    d. Duplicate
13. **The WordPad feature that automatically moves words to the next line when there is not room for them on the previous line is called**
    a. Wordwrap.
    b. Format insert.
    c. Margin.
    d. Tab.
14. **Which of the following is NOT a way to select text?**
    a. Double-click a word
    b. Drag over the text
    c. Click File on the menu bar, then click Select
    d. Click to the left of the first character in a line of text
15. **What is the name of the Windows location where information is placed after it is cut or copied?**
    a. Clipboard
    b. Paint
    c. Start Up menu
    d. Hard drive
16. **Which of the following is an option to change the outside edge size of a document?**
    a. Paper Size
    b. Paper Source
    c. Orientation
    d. Margins

▶ Skills Review

1. **Start a program.**
    a. Start WordPad.
    b. Review the elements of the WordPad program window.
2. **Open and save a WordPad document.**
    a. Open the WordPad file named Win B-3 on your Project Disk.
    b. Save the file as *Choose Coffee* to your Project Disk.
3. **Edit text in a WordPad document.**
    a. Change the spelling of the word *neuances* to *nuances* in the first paragraph.
    b. Insert a space between the characters *r* and *a* in *ora* in the second paragraph.
    c. Delete the word *heavy* in the last line of text and replace it with *medium*.
4. **Format text in a WordPad document.**
    a. Select all the text in the file named Choose Coffee.
    b. Change it from the present font to Garamond, and change the size to 12-point.
    c. Center the title (*Wired Coffee*) and change it to bold, 16-point.
    d. Underline each title (*How to Choose a Coffee* and *How to Taste the Difference*) and change them to 14-point.
    e. Click anywhere in the WordPad window outside of the selected text.
    f. Save the document.

5. **Use Paint.**
   a. Start Paint.
   b. Open the Paint file named Win B-2 on your Project Disk, then save it as *Wired Coffee Logo 2* to your Project Disk.
   c. Draw a circle around the logo.
   d. Use the Undo command or Eraser tool as necessary if the circle doesn't fit around the logo.
   e. Save the file.
6. **Copy data between programs.**
   a. Tile the WordPad and Paint windows vertically. (*Hint:* Maximize both windows first.)
   b. Select the logo in the Paint window, then copy it to the Clipboard.
   c. In WordPad, insert the cursor at the beginning of the document.
   d. Maximize WordPad, then paste the logo in the blank line.
   e. Center the logo.
   f. Save the Choose Coffee file.
   g. Close the Wired Coffee Logo 2 file and Paint.
7. **Print a document.**
   a. Print two copies of the file named Choose Coffee.
   b. Close all open documents.
   c. Close WordPad.
8. **Play a video clip.**
   a. Start Windows Media Player.
   b. Open the video file named Coffee Cup on your Project Disk.
   c. Play the video, then close it.
9. **Play a sound.**
   a. Open the sound file named AM Coffee on your Project Disk.
   b. Play the sound, and then pause it.
   c. Drag the Seek bar to the beginning of the sound, then replay it.
   d. Close the Windows Media Player window.

▶ Independent Challenges

1. You just opened a small, independent bookstore and are working on your inventory. You need to create a list of books that can be consulted when customers come in and want to know what kind of books you carry. Start WordPad and create a new document that lists the first 10 books in your stock. Above the list, include your name, the name of your book store; a street address, city, zip code, and phone number for the store. For each book in the list, include the author's name (last name first), the title, and the date of publication.

To complete this independent challenge:

   a. Start WordPad.
   b. Type the heading (the name of the bookstore, address, city, state, zip code, and phone number).
   c. Center the heading information.
   d. Enter the information for at least 10 books, using [Tab] to create columns for the author's name, the title, and the date of publication. Be sure that the columns line up with one another.
   e. Proofread your list and correct any errors you may have made.
   f. Italicize the last and first name of each author, and bold the name of each book.
   g. Save the list as *Book Inventory* to your Project Disk.
   h. Print two copies of the list.
   i. Exit WordPad.

2. You parents are celebrating their 25th wedding anniversary. You want to create an invitation to a party for them. Using WordPad, create an invitation, including the invitation title, your parents' names, date and time of the party, location of the party (use *35 Crow Canyon Road* for the address), written directions to the party, your name, and the date to respond by and phone number to reach you. Using Paint, then paste a map of the party location into the invitation. Remember that you can open more than program at a time, and you can easily switch between programs using the taskbar.

To complete this independent challenge:

a. Start WordPad and type the information needed for the invitation.

b. Select the title text and click the Center button on the toolbar.

c. Change the title text to 18-point, bold.

d. Change the rest of the text to 14-point Arial.

e. Save the WordPad document as *Invitation* to your Project Disk.

f. Start Paint, then open the *Invitation Map* file on your Project Disk.

g. Copy the map to the Clipboard.

h. Place the insertion point above the written instructions in the Invitation document.

i. Click the Paste button on the toolbar.

j. Save the document, preview the document, make any necessary changes, then print the document.

k. Close WordPad and Paint.

3. As the vice-president of Things-That-Fly, a kite and juggling store, you need to design a new type of logo, consisting of three simple circles, each colored differently. You'll use Paint to design the logo, and then paste it into a WordPad document.

To complete this independent challenge:

a. Start Paint and create a small circle using [Shift] and the Ellipse tool.

b. Use the Select tool to select the circle, click the Edit menu, then click Copy. Now you can paste the circle so you don't have to try to re-draw the exact same shape.

c. Click Edit on the menu bar, click Paste, then use the mouse to move the second circle below the first and slightly to the right of the first.

d. Click Edit on the menu bar, then click Paste to paste another copy of the circle. Use the mouse to move the third circle below the first and slightly to the left of the first.

e. For each circle, click the Fill tool, click the color you want the circle to be, then click inside the circle you want filled with that color.

f. Using the Select tool, select the completed logo, click Edit on the menu bar, then click Copy.

g. Open WordPad and click the Center button on the toolbar.

h. Click the Paste button on the toolbar, click to the right of the logo to deselect it, press [Enter] twice, then type *Things-That-Fly*.

i. Using the Format Bar, change the text to 18-point, bold.

j. Save the document as *Stationery* to your Project Disk.

k. Preview the document, make any necessary changes, then print the document.

l. Close WordPad and Paint.

4. As the creative director at Digital Arts, a computer music company, you need to find sample sounds to include on a demo CD. You'll use Windows Media Player to open sound files located on your computer and play each one. You'll also use WordPad to keep track of the sounds you listened to and which ones you liked the best.

To complete this independent challenge:

a. Open Windows Media Player.

b. Open all the sound files in the Media folder (in the Windows folder) on your computer.

c. Play each sound file.

d. In WordPad, create a list of the sound files that you played, and indicate the sounds you liked the best.

e. Save the list as *Sound List* to your Project Disk.

f. Print the list, then close Windows Media Player.

► Visual Workshop

Re-create the screen shown in Figure B-19, which shows the Windows desktop with more than one program window open. You can use the file Win B-2 for the coffee cup logo (save it as *A Cup of Coffee* to your Project Disk). Create a new WordPad document, save it as *Good Time Coffee Club* to your Project Disk, and enter the text as shown in the figure. Print the Screen (Press the Print Screen key to make a copy of the screen, open Paint, click Edit on the menu bar, click Paste to paste the screen into Paint, then click Yes to paste the large image if necessary. Click File on the menu bar, click Print, then click Print.)

FIGURE B-19

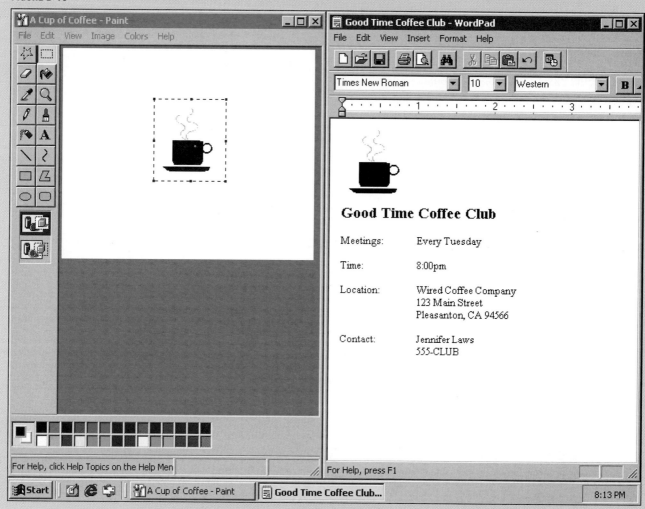

Windows 2000 — Unit C

Managing
Files Using My Computer

Objectives

- ► Understand file management
- ► Open and view My Computer
- ► View folders and files
- ► Create a folder
- ► Move files and folders
- ► Delete and restore files and folders
- ► Create a shortcut to a file
- ► Display drive information

An important Windows 2000 skill is **file management**, organizing and keeping track of files and folders. Windows 2000 provides you with two file management programs: My Computer and Windows Explorer. You can use both of these tools to view the files on your computer or computer network, and how they are arranged. You can also use either tool to rearrange the files by creating new folders, and by moving, renaming, and deleting files and folders. A **folder** is an electronic collection of files and other folders. This unit concentrates on My Computer, the simplest file management tool in Windows 2000; the next unit focuses on Windows Explorer, which contains more powerful features for accomplishing the same tasks. In this unit, John Casey will use My Computer to organize the files on his computer.

Understanding File Management

Managing folders and files enables you to quickly locate any file that you have already created and need to use again. Working with poorly managed files is like looking for a needle in a haystack—it's frustrating and time-consuming to search through several irrelevant, misnamed, and out-of-date files to find the one you want. ✐ Figure C-1 shows the files and folders that John uses in the course of running his business.

As you examine the figure, note that file management can help you do the following:

 Organize folders and files in a file hierarchy, so that information is easy to locate and use
A file hierarchy is a logical structure of files and folders, so that files are located in appropriate folders, and folders are located in other folders as necessary, to make everything easy to find. For instance, John stores all of his correspondence files in a folder called Letters. Within that folder are two more folders. One is named Business Letters and holds all business correspondence. The other is named Personal Letters and holds all of John's personal correspondence.

 Save files to the folder in which you want to store them for future use
John has a folder named Sales in which he stores all information about sales for the current year. He also places files related to accounting information in this folder.

 Create a new folder so you can reorganize information
Now that John is doing more advertising for Wired Coffee Company, he wants to create a new folder to store files related to these marketing efforts.

 Delete files and folders that you no longer need
John deletes files once he's sure he will no longer use them again, to free up disk space and keep his disk organized.

 Create shortcuts
If a file or folder you use often is located several levels down in a file hierarchy (for example, if it is in a file within a folder, within a folder), it might take you several steps to access it. To save you time in accessing the files and programs you use most frequently, you can create shortcuts to them. A shortcut is a link that you can place in any location that gives you instant access to a particular file, folder, or program on your hard disk or on a network. John created a shortcut on the desktop to the Wired Coffee folder. To view or access the contents of his folder all he has to do is double-click the shortcut icon on the desktop.

 Find a file when you cannot remember where it is stored
John knows he created a letter to a supplier earlier this week, but now that he is ready to revise the letter, he cannot find it. Using the Search command on the Start menu, he can quickly find that letter and revise it in no time.

 Open a file when you don't know the type of program in which it was created
If John wants to open a file but doesn't know which program to use to open it, he can use the Open With command. To open a file of unknown type, John can right-click the file icon, point to Open With, and then click one of the programs that are known to open that type of file, or he can click Any Program to open the Open With dialog box, where he can select a program to open the file.

FIGURE C-1: How John uses Windows to reorganize his files

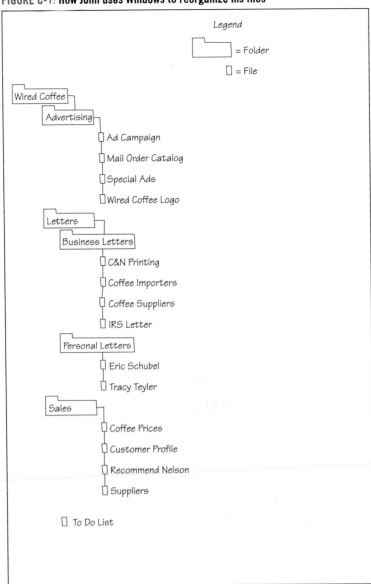

Legend

☐ = Folder

☐ = File

Wired Coffee
  Advertising
    ☐ Ad Campaign
    ☐ Mail Order Catalog
    ☐ Special Ads
    ☐ Wired Coffee Logo
  Letters
    Business Letters
      ☐ C&N Printing
      ☐ Coffee Importers
      ☐ Coffee Suppliers
      ☐ IRS Letter
    Personal Letters
      ☐ Eric Schubel
      ☐ Tracy Teyler
  Sales
    ☐ Coffee Prices
    ☐ Customer Profile
    ☐ Recommend Nelson
    ☐ Suppliers
  ☐ To Do List

CLUES TO USE

Planning a file hierarchy

Windows 2000 allows you to organize folders and files into a file hierarchy that imitates the way you would actually store paper document files in real folders. Just as a filing cabinet contains several folders each containing a set of related documents, and several dividers grouping related folders together, a file hierarchy allows you to place files into folders, then folders into other folders, so that your files are neat and organized. When creating a file hierarchy, create folders for top-level categories, such as a business or major project, and create folders within them to hold subcategories, such as departments in the business or major tasks within the project. For example, Figure C-1 shows the file hierarchy of the Wired Coffee folder on your Project Disk. At the topmost level of the hierarchy is the name of the folder, Wired Coffee. This folder contains a file and several folders that are related to the Wired Coffee Business: Advertising, Letters, Business Letters, Personal Letters, and Sales. Within each of these folders are files and any additional folders related to each subcategory.

Opening and Viewing My Computer

The key to organizing folders and files effectively within a hierarchy is storing related things together and naming folders informatively. That way, you can get a good idea of what's on your system just by looking at the higher levels of your file hierarchy, and not having to examine every individual file or memorize a coding system. ◄──── As the previous lesson showed, the file hierarchy on John's disk contains several folders and files organized by topic. Now he is ready to use My Computer to review this organization and see if it needs to be changed.

Steps

Trouble?

To prevent unwanted changes to your Project Disk, make sure you have made a copy of it. If you need assistance, see your instructor or technical support person.

1. Make sure a copy of your Project Disk is in the appropriate drive, then double-click the **My Computer icon** 🖥

This icon is usually located in the upper-left corner of the desktop. My Computer opens, displaying the contents of your computer, including all the disk drives and printers, as shown in Figure C-2. Because computers differ, your My Computer window will probably look different. There are icons that represent drives and icons that represent folders. As with most other windows, there is a toolbar, a status bar providing information about the contents of the window, a menu bar, and a list of contents in the My Computer window.

Trouble?

If the toolbar is not visible, click View on the Menu bar, point to Toolbar, then click Standard Buttons.

2. If necessary, click the **Maximize button** 🔲 in the My Computer window

This enables you to see the entire toolbar as you work. The toolbar contains a set of buttons that makes using My Computer easier. Table C-1 lists what each of these buttons does and how they are used.

3. Double-click the **drive that contains your Project Disk**

You can see the files and folders that are contained on the disk drive. When you open a disk drive or folder, the Address bar changes to indicate the new location. Notice that the Address bar and the title bar have changed from My Computer to 3½ Floppy (A:).

4. Double-click the **Unit C folder**, then double-click the **Wired Coffee folder**

Now you can see the folders that are contained in the Wired Coffee folder.

QuickTip

To open Windows Explorer from My Computer, right-click any disk or folder icon, then click Explore.

5. Double-click the **Sales folder**

You can now see the files contained in the Sales folder. These are files that John created using WordPad and saved in the Sales folder.

FIGURE C-2: **My Computer window**

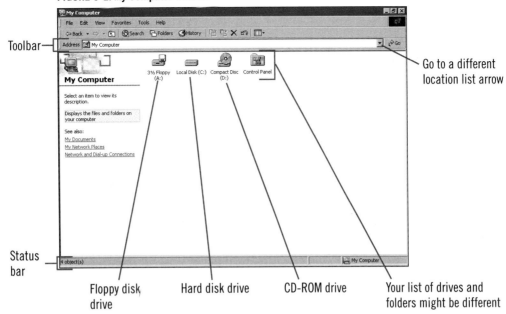

Toolbar

Status
bar

Go to a different
location list arrow

Floppy disk
drive

Hard disk drive

CD-ROM drive

Your list of drives and
folders might be different

TABLE C-1: **My Computer toolbar buttons**

button	name	function
⇐ Back ▾	Back	Moves to the last previous location you visited
⇨ ▾	Forward	Once you have moved back, moves to the location you visited before moving back
⬆	Up	Moves up one level in the file hierarchy
🔍	Search	Lets you search for folders or files
🗂	Folders	Displays a list of folders on your computer
🕑	History	Displays a list of recently used folders and files
📂	Move To	Moves a folder or file to another folder
📑	Copy To	Copies a folder or file to another folder
✕	Delete	Deletes a folder or file
↩	Undo	Undoes the most recent My Computer operation
▦▾	Views	Displays the contents of My Computer in different views

CLUES TO USE

Formatting a disk

All disks have to be formatted before they can be used. Often, new disks come preformatted, but if not, you can easily perform this function yourself. You can also format a disk that already contains data to quickly erase its files and folders. To format a floppy disk, select the disk drive in My Computer that contains the disk, click File on the menu bar, then click Format, or right-click the disk drive, then click Format. Specify the size of the disk and format type, then click Start. If you are formatting a disk that has never been formatted, select the Full format type. If the disk has already been formatted and you simply want to clear its contents, select the Quick format type to reduce the time it takes. Be absolutely certain you want to format a disk before doing so, because formatting removes all the data from a disk.

Viewing Folders and Files

Once you have opened one or more folders, you can use buttons on the toolbar to help you move among folders quickly in My Computer. If you want to move up one step in the hierarchy, you can click the Up One Level button. Each time you open a folder, Windows 2000 keeps track of where you have been. If you want to go back or forward to a folder you have already visited, you can click the Back button or the Forward button. Each time you click the Back or Forward button, you go back or forward to the folder you previously visited. If you want to go to a folder you visited two or more locations ago, you can click the list arrow next to the button to display a menu of places you have been, and then click the place you want to go. When you view a folder in the My Computer window, you can use the Views button on the toolbar to change the way folder and file icons appear. As he works with My Computer, John moves between folders and changes the view depending upon the type of information that he needs.

Steps

QuickTip
You can also click the Address bar list arrow to move to another location up or down the file hierarchy.

holson he norny

Trouble?
If Microsoft Word is installed on your computer, the Word icon will appear in Figure C-4. If not, the WordPad icon will appear.

QuickTip
The target location of the Back and Forward buttons change frequently as you navigate files and folders. To see the target location of either button, point to it and read the ScreenTip.

1. Click the **Up button** on the toolbar
The Wired Coffee folder and its contents appear in the Wired Coffee window. Each time you click the Up button, you move up one step in the hierarchy to the folder that contains the folders and files you currently see on the screen.

2. Click again
You should now be at the topmost level of your disk drive file hierarchy showing several folders and files. See Figure C-3. Instead of double-clicking the Wired Coffee folder icon again to reopen the folder, you can click the Back button on the toolbar to go back to the previous folder (Wired Coffee) you visited.

3. Click the **Back button** ⇐ Back ▾ on the toolbar
Clicking the Back button displays the last folder you visited. The Wired Coffee folder and its contents appear in the My Computer window.

4. Double-click the **Advertising folder**
The Advertising folder and its contents appear in the My Computer window. Instead of using the Up button to go back to the Wired Coffee folder and then clicking the Sales folder, you can click the list arrow next to the Back button to display a menu of places you have been, and then select the Sales folder.

5. Click the **Back button list arrow** ⇐ Back ▾ on the toolbar, then click **Sales**
The Back button list arrow, as shown in Figure C-4, displays the last several locations you opened. You can click any place in the list to return to that location.

6. Click the **Forward button** ⇒ ▾ on the toolbar
Once you have returned to a previously opened folder or drive, clicking the Forward button on the toolbar opens the location you visited just prior to the return. The Wired Coffee folder opens in the My Computer window because this is the location that was open before you clicked the Back button list arrow and then clicked Sales.

7. Click the **Views button** on the toolbar, then click **Details**
In the Details view, the name, size of the object, type of file, and date on which each folder or file was last modified appear, as shown in Figure C-5. This might be the most useful view because it includes a great deal of information about the folder or file, in addition to the icon of the application that was used to create the file.

8. Click the **Views button** on the toolbar, then click **Large Icons**
The files appear as large icons, without additional file information.

FIGURE C-3: Viewing folders and files

Click to view the next level up in the folder hierarchy

Click to view the previous folder

Address bar changes to reflect new location

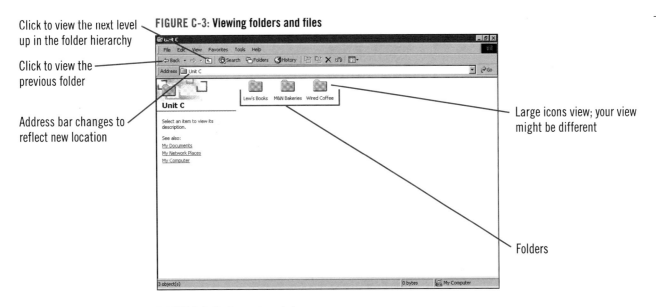

Large icons view; your view might be different

Folders

FIGURE C-4: My Computer window

Click to view list of recently opened locations

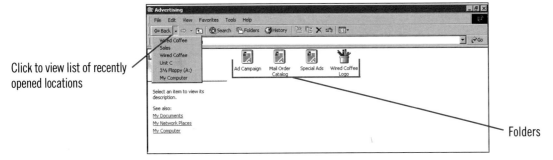

Folders

FIGURE C-5: Viewing folders and files in Details view

Click to change views

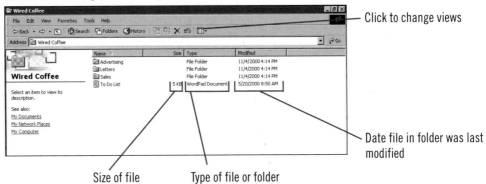

Date file in folder was last modified

Size of file   Type of file or folder

CLUES TO USE

Viewing image and picture files

The My Pictures folder does the same thing for images and pictures as the My Documents folder does for documents—it provides a consistent storage location. The My Pictures folder is the default location for storing images from digital cameras, scanners, and other digital imaging devices. If you store your images and pictures in the My Pictures folder, you can see a preview of a file in the My Computer or Windows Explorer window without having to open the file in an editing program. In the My Computer or Windows Explorer window, the right pane contains a file list, which you can view in a number of different formats, including large icons or **thumbnails** (miniature views), and a preview area. Above the preview area is the selected image or picture. Along the top of the preview area is a row of buttons that allows you to zoom in and out, view the image or picture in actual size ⊞, best fit size ⊡, or full screen ▣, and print the image or picture ⎙. If you want to open the image or picture, you can double-click the file.

Windows 2000

Creating a Folder

You can create one or more new folders to store files and even other folders. Creating and informatively naming new folders makes it easy to organize files and other folders in a logical hierarchy. To create a folder in Windows 2000, you can click the New command on the File menu or you can right-click anywhere in any My Computer window and point to New, then click Folder. ➤ John needs to create two new folders. One will contain his To Do List. The other will contain information about his employees.

Steps

1. Click File on the menu bar, point to New, then click Folder

A new folder appears in the Wired Coffee window, as shown in Figure C-6. All new folders are initially named New Folder. A border appears around the newly created folder, meaning that it is selected and ready to be renamed.

2. Type Important, then press [Enter]

The folder is now named Important, a name that reflects the type of documents it will contain—important files relating to John's work week.

3. Place the mouse pointer anywhere in the Wired Coffee window (except on a file or folder), right-click, then point to New

The pop-up menu opens, as shown in Figure C-7.

4. Click Folder

A new folder appears, named New Folder, where you right-clicked the mouse in the Wired Coffee window.

> **QuickTip**
>
> To rename a folder, right-click the folder you want to rename, click Rename, then type a new name.

5. Type Personnel, then press [Enter]

The Wired Coffee window now has two new folders, Important and Personnel, as shown in Figure C-8. Once you create new folders, you can quickly rearrange them into orderly rows and columns.

6. Click View on the menu bar, point to Arrange Icons, then click By Name

The folder and file icons in the Wired Coffee folder are sorted by name in alphabetical order and automatically moved in line with the other icons. You can change the way individual files and folders are sorted by using other Arrange Icons options on the View menu. Table C-2 describes these options.

FIGURE C-6: Creating a new folder

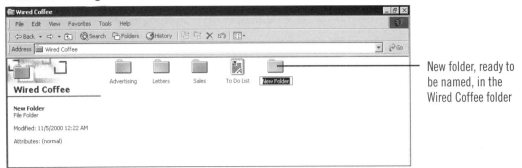

New folder, ready to be named, in the Wired Coffee folder

FIGURE C-7: Right-clicking to create a new folder

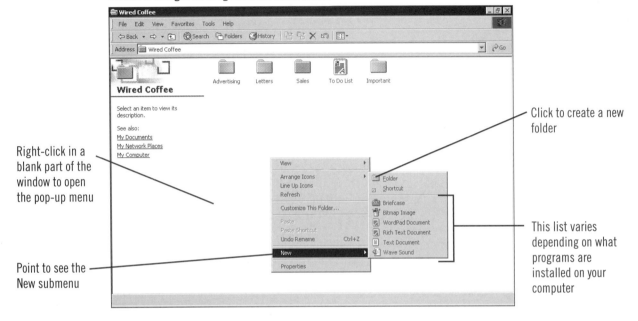

Right-click in a blank part of the window to open the pop-up menu

Point to see the New submenu

Click to create a new folder

This list varies depending on what programs are installed on your computer

FIGURE C-8: Two new folders

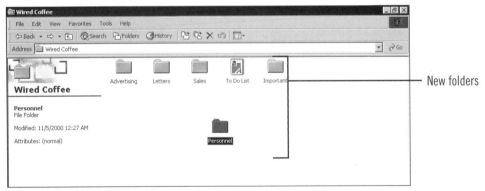

New folders

TABLE C-2: Options on the View menu for arranging files and folders

option	arranges files and folders
By Name	Alphabetically
By Type	By type, such as all documents created using the WordPad program
By Size	By size, with the largest folder or file listed first
By Date	By the date they were last modified with the latest modification being listed last
Auto Arrange	Automatically in orderly rows and columns

Moving Files and Folders

You can move a file or folder from one location to another using a variety of methods in My Computer. See Table C-3 for a description of moving and copying methods. If the file or folder and the location to which you want to move it are visible in a window or on the desktop, you can simply drag the item from one location to the other. When the location is not visible, you can use the Cut, Copy, and Paste commands on the Edit menu or the buttons on the toolbar. Now that John has created the Important folder to store files relating to his weekly tasks, he is ready to move the To Do List file into it. He also needs to move a letter (a recommendation for a new marketing person) currently contained in the Sales folder to the new Personnel folder.

Steps

1. **Drag the To Do List file from the Wired Coffee window to the Important folder**
   The icon representing the To Do List file is removed from the Wired Coffee folder and is placed in the folder named Important. Folders are moved in the same manner. Dragging a file or folder from one place to another on the same disk moves it; whereas dragging it from one disk drive location to another copies it. If you want to copy an item on the same disk by dragging, press and hold [Ctrl] while dragging.

2. **Double-click the Important folder and confirm that the file has been moved**
   The folder named Important now contains John's To Do List.

QuickTip

If you want to perform a file management operation such as moving or copying on more than one file or folder at a time, first select all the files or folders by holding [Ctrl] and clicking each one you want to select. Then perform the operation.

3. **Click the Back button list arrow ⟸ Back ▾ on the toolbar, click Sales, then click the Recommend Nelson file to select it**
   When the folder you want to move a file into is not visible, you can use the Cut and Paste commands to move a file from one folder to another.

4. **Click Edit on the menu bar, then click Cut**
   The file is removed from its original location and stored on the Windows Clipboard. When you cut or copy a file, the file icon turns gray, as shown in Figure C-9.

5. **Click the Back button ⟸ Back ▾ on the toolbar, then double-click the Personnel folder**

QuickTip

To move or copy a folder or file, you can click the Move To button or Copy To button on the toolbar, select the folder in which you want to place the folder or file, then click OK.

6. **Click Edit on the menu bar, then click Paste**
   The file is now pasted into the Personnel folder, as shown in Figure C-10.

7. **Click ⟸ Back ▾**
   You return to the Wired Coffee folder.

FIGURE C-9: Preparing to move a file

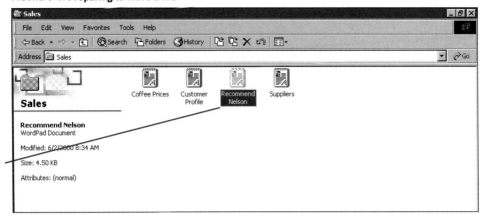

Grayed-out icon indicates file has been cut

FIGURE C-10: Relocated file

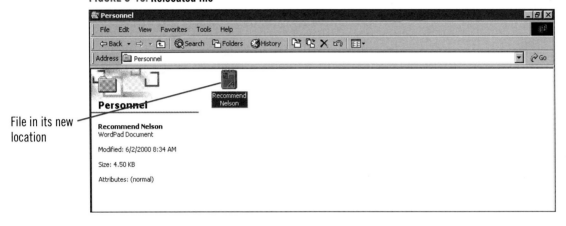

File in its new location

TABLE C-3: Methods for moving and copying files

action	methods
Move	Drag the file or folder to new location on the same disk
	Right-click the file or folder, drag to folder or drive, then click Move Here
	Select the file or folder, click the Move To button on the toolbar, click a folder or drive, then click OK
	Select the file or folder, click File on the menu bar, click Cut, display a folder or drive, click File on the menu bar, then Paste
Copy	Press and hold [Ctrl], then drag the file or folder to new location
	Right-click the file or folder, drag to folder or drive, then click Copy Here
	Select the file or folder, click the Copy To button on the toolbar, click a folder or drive, then click OK
	Select the file or folder, click File on the menu bar, click Copy, display a folder or drive, click File on the menu bar, then Paste

Sending files and folders

The Send To command, located on the pop-up menu of any desktop object, lets you "send" (or move) a file or folder to a new location on your computer. For example, you can send a file or folder to a floppy disk for a quick backup copy of the file or folder, a mail recipient for receiving electronic messages, or the desktop for creating a shortcut. You can also use the Send To command to move a file or folder from one folder to another. To send a file or folder, right-click the file or folder you want to send, point to Send To on the pop-up menu, and then click the destination you want. You can determine the options that appear in the Send To command by creating a shortcut to the program or folder you want included and moving it to the SendTo folder, located within the Windows folder.

Deleting and Restoring Files and Folders

When you organize the contents of a folder, disk, or the desktop, you might find files and folders that you no longer need. You can **delete** these items, or remove them from the disk. If you delete a file or folder from the desktop or from the hard disk, it goes into the Recycle Bin. The **Recycle Bin**, located on your desktop, is a temporary storage area for deleted files. If you delete a file that you still need, you can restore it by moving it from the Recycle Bin to another location. Be aware that if you delete a file from your floppy disk it will not be stored in the Recycle Bin—it will be permanently deleted. See Table C-4 for a summary of the deleting and restoring options. To demonstrate how the Recycle Bin works, John first moves a file to the desktop, deletes that file, and then restores it.

Trouble?
If you cannot find the Recycle Bin, click the title bar in the My Computer window, then drag the window to the right to see the Recycle Bin.

QuickTip
To quickly move files or folders from one disk to another, select the files or folder, press and hold [Shift], then drag the selected items to the new location.

Trouble?
If you are unable to find the deleted file in the Recycle Bin, it may be because your Recycle Bin is full or too small (so that files are deleted right away rather than being stored in the Recycle Bin). See your instructor or technical support person for assistance.

QuickTip
Your deleted files remain in the Recycle Bin until you empty it. To empty the Recycle Bin, right-click the Recycle Bin icon, then click Empty Recycle Bin. This permanently removes the contents of the Recycle Bin from your hard disk.

1. Double-click the **Advertising folder**, then click the **Restore Down button** in the Advertising window
   The Advertising folder and its contents appear in the Advertising window. Before you can delete a file from a floppy disk to the Recycle Bin, you need to move it to the desktop or hard drive. If you want to delete a file directly from a floppy disk without the possibility of restoring it, you can drag the file directly to the Recycle Bin or press [Delete].

2. Right-click and hold the **Ad Campaign file**, drag it to the desktop from the Advertising folder on your Project Disk, then click **Move Here**
   The file now appears on the desktop and can be moved to the Recycle Bin, as shown in Figure C-11.

3. Drag the **Ad Campaign file** from the desktop to the Recycle Bin (you might have to move the Advertising folder window), then click **Yes** if necessary
   The Recycle Bin icon should now look like it contains paper.

4. Double-click the **Recycle Bin icon**
   The Recycle Bin window opens. It contains the file that was deleted. The Recycle Bin window is like most other windows in that it contains a menu bar, a toolbar, and a status bar. Because John still needs this file he decides to restore it. The windows overlap, making it difficult for John to see the contents of both folders.

5. Right-click an empty area of the **taskbar**, then click **Tile Windows Vertically**
   This option allows you to see all open windows on the desktop at one time. The Recycle Bin window and the Advertising window appear side-by-side, as shown in Figure C-12.

6. Select the **Ad Campaign file** in the Recycle Bin window, then drag it back to the Advertising folder window
   The file is restored—it is intact and identical to the form it was in before you deleted it.

7. Click the **Close button** in the Recycle Bin window

FIGURE C-11: Selecting files to drag to the Recycle Bin

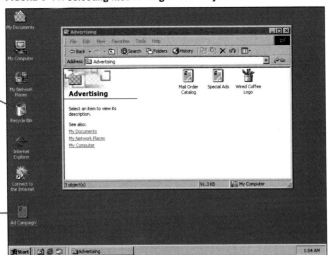

Drag the selected icon here to delete the file

The selected file moved from the Advertising folder to the desktop

FIGURE C-12: Deleted file from the Advertising folder in the Recycle Bin

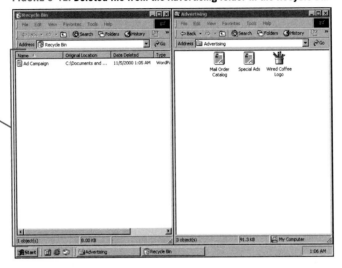

The contents of your Recycle Bin might be different

TABLE C-4: Deleting and restoring files

ways to delete a file	ways to restore a file from the recycle bin
Select the file, then click the Delete button on the toolbar	Click the Undo button on the Recycle Bin toolbar
Select the file, then press [Delete]	Select the file, click File on the menu bar, then click Restore
Right-click the file, then click Delete	Right-click the file, then click Restore
Drag the file to the Recycle Bin	Drag the file from the Recycle Bin to any location

CLUES TO USE

Recycle Bin properties

You can adjust several Recycle Bin settings by using the Properties option on the Recycle Bin pop-up menu. For example, if you do not want files to go to the Recycle Bin when you delete them, but, rather, want them to be immediately deleted, right-click the Recycle Bin, click Properties, then click the Do Not Move Files to the Recycle Bin check box to select the option. Also, if you find that the Recycle Bin is full and cannot accept any more files, you can increase the amount of disk space devoted to the Recycle Bin by moving the Maximum Size of Recycle Bin slider to the right. The percentage shown represents how much space the contents of the Recycle Bin takes up on the drive.

Creating a Shortcut to a File

If a file or folder is buried several levels down in a file hierarchy, it could take you a while to access it. To save you time in getting to the items you use frequently, you can create shortcuts. A shortcut is a link between two points: a "home" folder where a file, folder, or program is actually stored and any other location where you want to access that file or program. The actual file, folder, or program remains stored in its original location, but you place the icon representing the shortcut in a convenient location, whether that is a folder or the desktop. ✒ John always uses his Wired Coffee logo on stationery, in flyers and in general advertising materials. Rather than having to go through the steps to start Paint and then open the file, he simply places a shortcut for this Paint file on the desktop.

1. **In the Advertising folder, right-click Wired Coffee Logo, then click Create shortcut**
   An icon for a shortcut to the Wired Coffee Logo now appears in the Advertising window. Compare your screen to Figure C-13. All shortcuts are named the same as the file on which they are based, with the words "Shortcut to" in front of the original name.

> **Trouble?**
> If you can't see an empty area of your desktop, your My Computer window is maximized. Click the Restore Down button to resize it.

2. **Click the Shortcut to Wired Coffee Logo file, click the Move To button 📇 on the toolbar, click Desktop, then click OK**
   The shortcut appears on the desktop, as shown in Figure C-14. A shortcut can be placed anywhere on the desktop.

3. **Double-click the Shortcut to Wired Coffee Logo icon**
   The Paint program opens with the file named Wired Coffee Logo.

4. **Click the Close button ✕ in the Paint window**
   The logo file and the Paint program close. The shortcut to Wired Coffee Logo remains on the desktop until you delete it, so you can use it again and again. If you are working in a lab environment, you should delete this shortcut.

5. **Right-click the Shortcut to Wired Coffee Logo icon**
   When you right-click folders and files (as opposed to the blank area in a window), a pop-up menu opens that offers several file management commands, as described in Table C-5. The commands on your pop-up menu might be different depending on the Windows 2000 features installed on your computer.

6. **Click Delete on the pop-up menu, then click Yes in the Confirm File Delete dialog box**
   The shortcut is deleted from the desktop and placed in the Recycle Bin, where it will remain until John empties the Recycle Bin or restores the shortcut. When you delete a shortcut, only the shortcut is removed. The original file remains intact in its original location.

7. **Click the Maximize button 🔲 in the Advertising window**

Placing shortcuts on the Start menu or taskbar

You can place shortcuts to your favorite files and programs on the Start menu or on a toolbar on the taskbar. To do this, simply drag the folder, file, or program to the Start button or a toolbar on the taskbar, and the item will appear on the first level of the Start menu or on the toolbar.

FIGURE C-13: **Creating a shortcut**

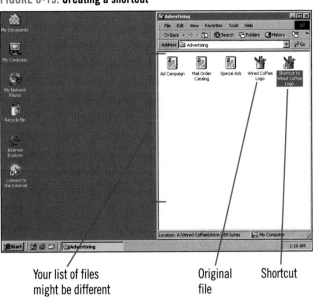

FIGURE C-14: **Dragging shortcut to a new location**

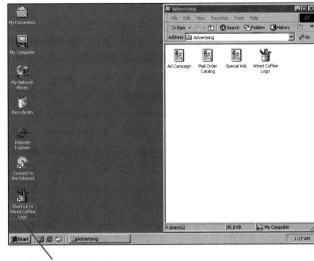

Your list of files
might be different

Original
file

Shortcut

Relocated shortcut on
the desktop

TABLE C-5: **Shortcut menu options for files and folders**

option	description
Copy	Copies the file or folder to the Windows Clipboard
Create Shortcut	Creates a shortcut to the file or folder
Cut	Cuts the file or folder from its original location to the Windows Clipboard
Delete	Deletes the file or folder
Explore	Opens a folder or drive in Windows Explorer
Open	Opens the selected file or folder
Open with	Opens the file with a designated program
Paste	Pastes the file or folder from the Windows Clipboard to a new location
Preview	Previews the selected file
Print	Prints the selected file
Properties	Displays the properties of the file or folder
Rename	Renames the file or folder
Search	Searches for files in a folder or drive
Send To	Sends the selected file or folder to new location
Sharing	Displays the sharing properties of the folder

Displaying Drive Information

You should know as much about your system as possible. You might have to tell your instructor or system administrator certain information if you encounter a problem with your computer, or you might want to know how much space is left on a disk or change a **disk label** (a name you can assign to a hard or floppy disk). When you label a hard disk, the label will appear in the My Computer and Windows Explorer windows. Besides checking hard drive or floppy disk information, you can also use Windows 2000 tools to check your disks for damage, optimize your disk for better performance, make copies of your disks for safe keeping, and share your disk contents with others. You can perform these activities by using the Properties command. John wants to find out how much free space is available on his floppy disk.

QuickTip

To display drive information in the My Computer window, display the My Computer window, then click an icon.

1. Click the **Back button list arrow** `⇐ Back ▼` on the toolbar, then click **My Computer**

2. Right-click the **icon in the My Computer window for the drive that contains your Project Disk**

The icon representing the 3½ disk drive is highlighted. Now John can examine the property information for this disk. In the left pane, you can see a graphical representation of the amount of space being used relative to the amount available in the pie chart for the floppy disk. John reviews the chart and determines that the floppy disk contains plenty of free space.

3. Click **Properties** on the pop-up menu

The 3½ Floppy (A:) Properties dialog box opens with the General tab in front, as shown in Figure C-15. Click the General tab if it is not the frontmost tab.

4. Click the **Label text box** if necessary, then type **ProjectDisk**

A disk label can contain up to 11 characters but no spaces.

5. Click the **Tools tab**

The Tools tab becomes the frontmost tab, as shown in Figure C-16, showing you three utilities that can make Windows work more efficiently: error-checking, backup, and defragmentation. You can use the Defragmentation feature to speed up the performance of a disk. **Defragmenting** means that files will be rewritten to the disk in contiguous blocks rather than in random blocks. When you click any one of these options, Windows will update you as to when that tool was last used on the currently selected disk. Although these tools are mostly used for keeping a hard disk healthy, they can be used on a floppy disk as well. Table C-6 describes what each tool does.

6. Click **OK**

The Properties dialog box closes.

7. Click the **Close button** ☒ in the My Computer window

FIGURE C-15: General tab options in the 3½ Floppy (A:) Properties dialog box

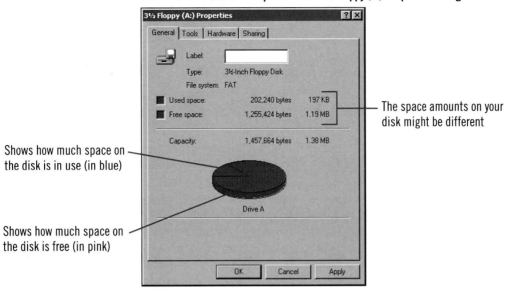

The space amounts on your disk might be different

Shows how much space on the disk is in use (in blue)

Shows how much space on the disk is free (in pink)

FIGURE C-16: Tool tab options in the 3½ Floppy (A:) Properties window dialog box

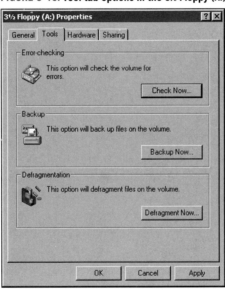

TABLE C-6: Tools in the Properties dialog box

tool	action
Error-checking	Checks for the last time you checked the disk for damage and, if you want, attempts to correct files that are damaged
Backup	Displays the last time you have backed up the contents of the disk, and if you want, starts the Windows 2000 backup program
Defragmentation	Checks for the last time you optimized the disk, and if you want, starts the Windows 2000 Defragmentation procedure

CLUES TO USE

Backing up files

The more you work with a computer, the more files you'll create. To protect yourself from losing critical information, it's important to **back up** your files (make copies on a separate disk) frequently. The Backup option in the disk drive Properties dialog box walks you through a series of dialog boxes to help you back up the files on your hard disk to a floppy or tape drive. You can back up the contents of an entire disk, or only certain files.

Windows 2000 Practice

► Concepts Review

Label each of the elements of the screen shown in Figure C-17.

FIGURE C-17

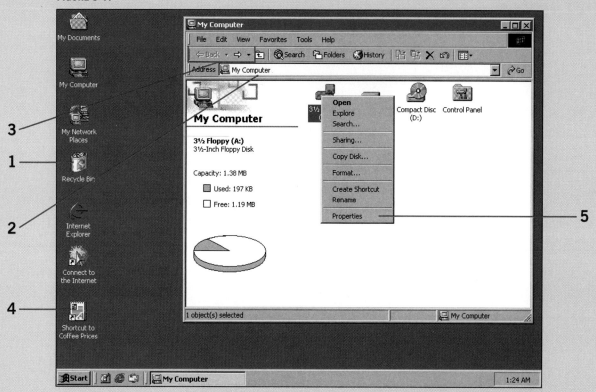

Match each of the terms with the statement that describes its function.

6. My Computer
7. Shortcut
8. File
9. Recycle Bin
10. Folder

a. A collection of files and folders
b. Location of deleted files
c. A file and folder management tool
d. A collection of information
e. A link to a file or folder

Select the best answer from the list of choices.

11. **When a file is deleted, it is placed in**
    a. My Computer.
    b. My Documents.
    c. the Recycle Bin.
    d. the Desktop Container.

12. **My Computer is used to**
    a. manage files and folders.
    b. delete files.
    c. add folders.
    d. all of the above.

13. **Which of the following is not an option for viewing files and folders?**
    a. Large icons
    b. Small icons
    c. File names
    d. Details

14. **When files and folders are arranged by date, they are arranged by**
    a. the current date.
    b. the date they were last modified.
    c. the date they were created.
    d. the date they were last opened.

15. **When right-clicking on a folder, which of the following cannot be done?**
    a. Explore the folder
    b. Find a file
    c. Print the contents of the folder
    d. Create a shortcut

16. **Which of the following is NOT an option for arranging files and folders?**
    a. By Name
    b. By Size
    c. By Location
    d. By Date

17. **Which of the following is NOT disk property information?**
    a. Used space
    b. File type
    c. Capacity
    d. Free space

▶ Skills Review

1. **Open and view My Computer.**
   a. Insert your Project Disk in the appropriate disk drive.
   b. Double-click My Computer.
   c. Click the Maximize button in the My Computer window.
   d. Double-click the 3½ Floppy drive (A: or B:) icon.
   e. Double-click the Unit C folder, then double-click the Wired Coffee folder.
   f. Double-click the Sales folder.

2. **View folders and files.**
   a. Click the Views button, then click List.
   b. Click the Up button on the toolbar twice.
   c. Click the Back button on the toolbar.
   d. Open the Personnel folder.
   e. Click the Back button list arrow on the toolbar, then click Sales.
   f. Click the Forward button on the toolbar.
   g. Click View on the menu bar, then click Details.
   h. Click View on the menu bar, then click Large Icons.

3. **Create a folder.**
   a. Right-click a blank area of the window, point to New, then click Folder.
   b. Type **Marketing** and press [Enter].
   c. Click View on the menu bar, point to Arrange Icons, then click By Name.

4. **Move files and folders.**
   a. Double-click the Advertising folder.
   b. Click the Mail Order Catalog file.
   c. Click Edit on the menu bar, then click Copy.
   d. Click the Back button on the toolbar.
   e. Double-click the Marketing folder.
   f. Click Edit on the menu bar, then click Paste.
   g. Click the Back button on the toolbar.

5. Delete and restore files and folders.
  a. Click the Marketing folder.
  b. Click the Restore Down button on the toolbar.
  c. Right-click the Marketing folder, drag it to the desktop, then click Move Here.
  d. Drag the Marketing folder from the desktop to the Recycle Bin, then click Yes, if necessary.
  e. Double-click the Recycle Bin.
  f. Right-click an empty area of the taskbar, then click Title Windows Vertically.
  g. Click File on the Recycle Bin menu bar, click Empty Recycle Bin, then click Yes. (To restore the Marketing folder, you would drag it back to the Wired Coffee folder.)
  h. Click the Close button in the Recycle Bin window.

6. Create a shortcut to a file.
  a. Double-click the Advertising folder.
  b. Right-click the Special Ads file, then click Create Shortcut.
  c. Right-click and drag the Shortcut to Special Ads file to the desktop, then click Move Here.
  d. Right-click the Shortcut to Special Ads file, then click Delete.
  e. Click Yes.
  f. Right-click the Recycle Bin icon, then click Empty Recycle Bin.
  g. Click Yes.

7. Display drive information.
  a. Click the Back button list arrow on the toolbar, then click My Computer.
  b. Right-click the icon representing your Project Disk in the My Computer window, then click Properties.
  c. Write down the capacity of the disk, how much capacity is being used, and how much is available for further use.
  d. Click OK.
  e. Click the Close button in the My Computer window.

► Independent Challenges

1. As a manager at Lew's Books and Cappuccino bookstore, you need to organize the folders and files on the store's computer. These are located on your Project Disk in the folder named Lew's Books.
  To complete this independent challenge:

  a. Open My Computer, and open and view the contents of the folder named Lew's Books in the Unit C folder on your Project Disk.
  b. In the Lew's Books folder, create four new folders named *Q1*, *Q2*, *Q3*, and *Q4*.
  c. Move the quarterly folders in the 2001 and 2002 folders (2001Q1, 2001Q2, etc.) and place them in the respective Q1, Q2, Q3, and Q4 folders, so that there are two quarterly folders in each of these folders.
  d. Create a shortcut for the Collectors' Newsletter file (located in the Letters folder) and place it in the Lew's Books folder.
  e. In the Store Locations folder, create a new folder and name it *New Stores*.
  f. Move the New Store Location file in the Letters folder to the New Stores folder.
  g. Using paper and pencil, draw out the new organization of all the folders and files in the Lew's Books folder.
  h. Close My Computer.

2. You are the vice president of a small carton manufacturing company, Apex Cartons, and need to organize your Windows 2000 folders and files. As with any typical business, you have correspondence (business and personal), contracts, inventory, personnel documents, and payroll information. You may have other folders as well. Your job is to organize these separate folders.

To complete this independent challenge:

a. Open My Computer and create a new folder named *Apex Cartons* in the Unit C folder on your Project Disk, within which the rest of the organization of files and folders will be created.
b. Create a folder in the Apex Cartons folder named *Manufacturing*.
c. Create another folder in the Apex Cartons folder named *Material Suppliers*.
d. Create two more folders in the Apex Cartons folder; one named *East Coast* and one named *West Coast*.
e. Move (do not copy) the East Coast and West Coast folders into the Material Suppliers folder.
f. Create a file using WordPad (it doesn't need to contain any text) and save it as *Suppliers Bid* to the Manufacturing folder.
g. Move the Suppliers Bid file into the Materials Suppliers folder.
h. Using paper and pencil, draw out the new organization of all the folders and files in your Apex Cartons folder.
i. Close My Computer.

3. You and your college roommate have decided to start a mail order PC business called MO PC, and you decide to use Windows 2000 to organize the business. Your job is to organize the following folders and files, as well as create shortcuts.

To complete this independent challenge:

a. Open My Computer and create a new folder named *MO PC* in the Unit C folder on your Project Disk, within which the rest of the organization of files and folders for this Independent Challenge will appear.
b. Create a new folder in the MO PC folder named *Advertising*.
c. Create another new folder in the MO PC named *Customers*.
d. Use WordPad to create a form letter welcoming new customers (one paragraph long), then save it in the Customers folder as *Customer Letter*.

e. Use WordPad to create a list of tasks that need to get done before the business opens (at least five items), and save it as *Business Plan* in the MO PC folder.

f. Use Paint to create a simple logo, then save it as *MO Logo* to the Advertising folder.

g. Create a shortcut to the MO Logo file.

h. Delete the Business Plan file and then restore it.

i. Using paper and pencil, draw out the new organization of all the folders and files in your MO PC folder.

j. Close My Computer.

4. M & N Bakeries just opened. You have been hired to help the owners sort their recipes into different categories and work on the design of their company logo. For this independent challenge, use the files Icing 1, Icing 2, Brownies, Passover & Easter Torte, located in the M&N Bakeries folder on your Project Disk.

To complete this independent challenge:

a. Open My Computer and open the folder called M&N Bakeries in the Unit C folder on your Project Disk, within which the rest of the organization of files and folders for this Independent Challenge will appear.

b. Create a folder in the M&N Bakeries folder named *Cakes*.

c. Create a folder in the M&N Bakeries named *Flourless Cakes*, and move it into the Cakes folder.

d. Create a folder in the M&N Bakeries named *Flour Cakes*, and move it into the Cakes folder.

e. In the M&N Bakeries folder, create a folder named *Cookies & Bars*.

f. Move the Brownies file to the Cookies & Bars folder.

g. Move the file named Passover & Easter Torte into the Flourless Cakes folder.

h. Move the Icing 1 recipe file to your desktop, then drag the file to the Recycle Bin.

i. Double-click to open the Recycle Bin and restore the Icing 1 recipe to the M&N Bakeries folder on your Project Disk.

j. Using paper and pencil, draw out the new organization of all the folders and files in your M&N Bakeries folder.

k. Close My Computer.

► Visual Workshop

Re-create the screen shown in Figure C-18, which displays the My Computer window for the floppy disk drive with the Project Disk. Use Figure C-1 to help you located the Coffee Price file on your Project Disk. Print the screen (Press the Print Screen key to make a copy of the screen, open Paint, click Edit on the menu bar, click Paste to paste the screen into Paint, then click Yes to paste the large image if necessary. Click File on the menu bar, click Print, then click Print in the Print dialog box.)

FIGURE C-18

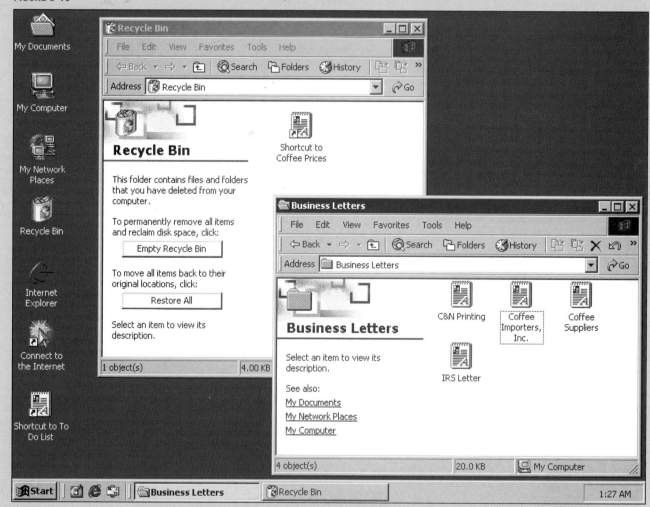

Managing

Folders and Files Using Windows Explorer

Objectives

- ▶ View the Windows Explorer window
- ▶ Open and view folders in Windows Explorer
- ▶ Customize the Windows Explorer window
- ▶ Create and rename folders in Windows Explorer
- ▶ Search for a file
- ▶ Move and copy a file to a folder
- ▶ Restore a deleted file using Undo
- ▶ Customize a folder

Windows 2000 offers another useful feature for managing files and folders, named Windows Explorer. Windows Explorer is more powerful than My Computer, offers more features, and most importantly, allows you to work with more than one computer, folder, or file at once. This is because the Windows Explorer window is split into two panes, or frames, so that you can view and compare information from two different locations. You can also use Windows Explorer to copy, move, delete, and rename files and folders, just as you can with My Computer. ◀━━━ In this unit, John will use Windows Explorer to perform some general file management tasks and also to prepare for the upcoming Wired Coffee Spring Catalog.

Viewing the Windows Explorer Window

The most important aspect of the Windows Explorer window is the two panes shown in Figure D-1. The pane on the left side of the screen, known as the **Explorer Bar** (or simply "the left pane"), displays all drives and folders on the computer, and the right pane displays the contents of whatever drive or folder is selected in the Explorer Bar. This arrangement enables you to simultaneously view the file hierarchy (the overall structure of the contents of your computer) and the contents of specific folders within that structure. ◄━━━ In order to manage his files, John needs to start Windows Explorer and view the contents of his computer.

Trouble?

If you do not see the toolbar, click View on the menu bar, point to Toolbars, then click Standard Buttons to place a checkmark next to it and display the toolbar; follow the same procedure if you don't see the Address Bar.

1. **Click the Start button on the taskbar, point to Programs, point to Accessories, click Windows Explorer, then click the Maximize button if necessary**
Windows Explorer opens, displaying the contents of your My Documents folder, as shown in Figure D-1. Note that the contents of your screen will vary depending on the programs and files installed and also depending on where Windows is installed on your hard disk or network. Windows Explorer has its own toolbar. Below the toolbar is the Address Bar, which you can use to change what is selected in the left pane, and therefore what appears in the right pane. Notice that the toolbar and the Address Bar are the same ones used in the My Computer window. Windows 2000 provides a consistent look and feel to make it easier to accomplish your tasks.

2. **In the Explorer Bar, click the Desktop icon**
The icons on the desktop are listed in the right pane. You can change what appears in the right pane by clicking the drive or folder in the Explorer Bar, which is the left pane.

3. **In the Explorer Bar, click the My Computer icon**
The drives and system folders on your computer appear in the right pane.

Trouble?

To prevent any changes to the original disk, be sure you have made a copy of your Project Disk before using it. For assistance, see your instructor or technical support person.

4. **Make sure a copy of your Project Disk is inserted in the appropriate disk drive, click the Address list arrow on the Address Bar, then click 3½ Floppy (A:) or (B:)**
The 3½ floppy drive opens, as shown in Figure D-2. The Address Bar makes it easy to open items on the desktop and the drives and in the folders and system folders in your computer. The contents of the floppy drive appear in the right pane of Windows Explorer. You can open a folder or open a document in the right pane of Windows Explorer. When you double-click a drive or folder icon in the right pane, the contents of that item appear in the right pane of the Windows Explorer. When you double-click a document icon, the program associated with the file starts and opens the document.

5. **Click the Back button** ⬅ Back ▾ **on the toolbar**
The contents of My Computer (the last location you displayed, in Step 3) appear in the right pane of Windows Explorer. You can move back and forth to the last drive or folder you displayed by using the Back and Forward buttons on the toolbar in Windows Explorer just as you do in the My Computer window.

6. **Click the Forward button** ➡ ▾ **on the toolbar**
The contents of the 3½ floppy drive reappear in the right pane of Windows Explorer. Leave Windows Explorer open and move on to the next lesson.

FIGURE D-1: **Viewing the contents of a computer's drives and folders**

Toolbar

Address Bar

Explorer Bar displays your computer's content in a file hierarchy

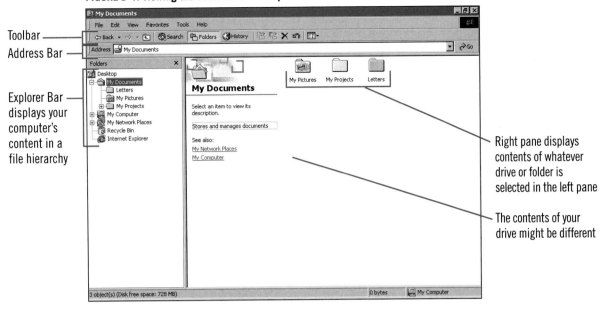

Right pane displays contents of whatever drive or folder is selected in the left pane

The contents of your drive might be different

FIGURE D-2: **Contents of 3½ Floppy disk**

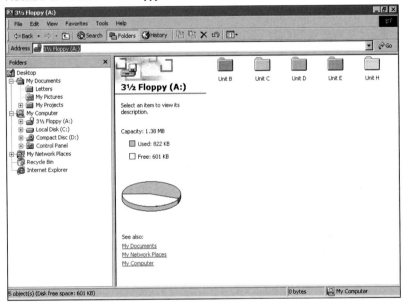

Changing folder options

You can change your view of the current folder in Windows Explorer by changing the folder view settings. You can choose to display the full path of the folder in the Address Bar or title bar, show or hide hidden files and folders in the folder, show the My Documents folder on the desktop, and show pop-up descriptions of folders and desktop items. To change view settings, click Tools on the menu bar, click Folder Options, click the View tab, then click check boxes and

option buttons in the Advanced settings window for the settings you want. If you don't like the options you have set in the Folder Options dialog box, you can restore the dialog box settings back to Windows default settings by clicking Restore Defaults. If you want the new settings to apply to all folders on your computer, click Like Current Folder under Folder views. To restore all folders back to original Windows settings, click Reset All Folders.

Opening and Viewing Folders in Windows Explorer

The Explorer Bar (the left pane of Windows Explorer) displays your computer's contents in a file hierarchy. The top of the file hierarchy is the desktop, followed by the drives, and then the folders. The dotted gray lines indicate the different levels. You can display or hide the different levels by clicking the plus sign (+) or minus sign (−) to the left of an icon in the Explorer Bar so that you don't always have to look at the complicated structure of your entire computer or network. Clicking the + to the left of an icon displays (or expands) the contents of the drive or folder under the icon, and clicking the − hides (or collapses) them. Clicking the icon itself displays the contents of the item in the right pane. When neither a + nor a − appears next to an icon, it means that the item does not have any folders in it (although it may have files, which you could display in the right pane by clicking the icon). Using the + and − in the Explorer Bar allows you to quickly display the file hierarchy on your computer without having to open and display the contents of each folder. John wants to open the Personnel and Letters folders without having to open and display the contents of each folder in the file hierarchy.

QuickTip
To get tips about Windows 2000, click View on the menu bar, point to Explorer Bar, then click Tip of the Day.

1. **Click the − (minus sign) next to the My Documents folder** in the Explorer Bar
The folders in the My Documents folder collapse to display only the My Documents folder icon. The − changes to a + indicating the hard drive contains folders and files. Because you did not click the My Documents folder icon, the right pane still displays the contents of the A: drive as it did before.

2. **Click the + (plus sign) next to the 3½ Floppy drive icon** in the Explorer Bar
The folders on the floppy disk drive, which is where your Project Disk is located, appear in the Explorer Bar.

3. **Click the ⊞ next to the Unit D folder** in the Explorer Bar, then click the **+ next to the Wired Coffee folder icon** in the Explorer Bar
The folders in the Wired Coffee folder appear in the Explorer Bar, as shown in Figure D-3.

4. **Click the Personnel folder** in the Explorer Bar
The contents of Personnel folder appear in the right pane, as shown in Figure D-4. When you click a folder in the Explorer Bar, the contents of that folder appear in the right pane of Windows Explorer.

5. **Click the Letters folder** in the Explorer Bar, then double-click the **Business Letters folder** in the right pane of Windows Explorer
The Business Letters folder opens, as shown in Figure D-5. The folders in the Letters folder are expanded in the Explorer Bar and the contents of the Business Letters folder appear in the right pane.

Opening each folder in its own window

Instead of using the same window to display each folder, you can open each folder in its own window. This can be helpful when you want to use drag and drop to copy or move files. To choose this folder view option, click Tools on the menu bar, click Folder Options, click the General tab, click the Open each folder in its own window option button, then click OK.

FIGURE D-3: Folders on the 3½ Floppy drive

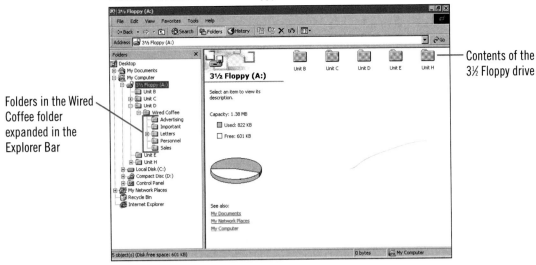

Folders in the Wired Coffee folder expanded in the Explorer Bar

Contents of the 3½ Floppy drive

FIGURE D-4: Personnel folder

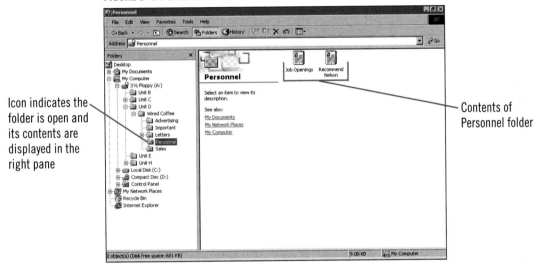

Icon indicates the folder is open and its contents are displayed in the right pane

Contents of Personnel folder

FIGURE D-5: Business Letters folder

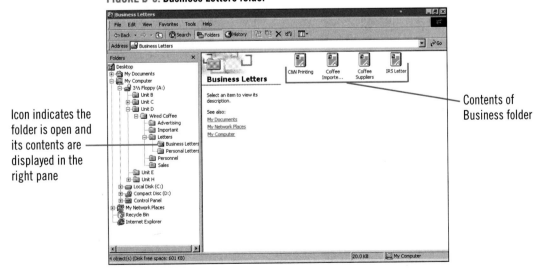

Icon indicates the folder is open and its contents are displayed in the right pane

Contents of Business folder

Customizing the Windows Explorer Window

You can display Windows Explorer and your file hierarchy in a variety of different ways depending on what you want to see and do. For example, if you have a lot of files and folders to display, you can hide the Explorer Bar or status bar to free up more viewing room. If you need to change the way Windows Explorer sorts your files and folders, you can use the column indicator buttons in the right pane in Details view. When you click one of the column indicator buttons, such as Name, Size, Time, or Modified (date) in Details view, the folders and files are sorted by the type of information listed in the column. ► John wants to find out the date he last modified the Coffee Suppliers file, so he decides to sort the files in the Business Letters folder.

1. Point to **Business Letters** in the Explorer Bar
   A ScreenTip appears, displaying the full name of the folder. When you are unable to view the entire folder name in the Explorer Bar, you can point to any part of the folder name to display a ScreenTip.

2. Position the pointer on the vertical bar that separates the two panes of the Explorer window; when the mouse changes to ↔, drag the **vertical bar** to the right until the full name of each folder appears

3. Click the **Views button** 🔲▾ on the toolbar, then click **Details**
   The files and folders on your Project Disk (in the 3½ floppy disk drive) appear in Details view, shown in Figure D-6.

4. Click the **Close button** in the Explorer Bar
   The Explorer Bar closes.

5. Position the pointer between the Name column indicator button and the Size column indicator button; when the pointer changes to ✛, drag to the right until the full name of each file appears
   You know that all file names are completely visible when no ellipses appear after a file name. You can sort by any category listed by clicking the column indicator button located at the top of the folders and files list in the right pane. The files in the Business Letters folder are currently sorted in alphabetical order.

6. Click the **Modified column indicator button**
   The files and folders are sorted by the date they were last modified, from earliest to latest, as shown in Figure D-7.

7. Click the **Name column indicator button**
   The files and folders are sorted by name in alphabetical order. John finds the Coffee Suppliers file and sees the date he last modified the file.

8. Click the **Folders button** 📁 on the toolbar
   The Explorer Bar opens and displays folders. In the Explorer Bar, you can change the view from the file hierarchy to a search feature, list of favorite Web pages, or list of Web pages you've recently visited, known as History.

9. Click the **Views button** 🔲▾ on the toolbar, then click **Large Icons**

FIGURE D-6: Windows Explorer in Details view

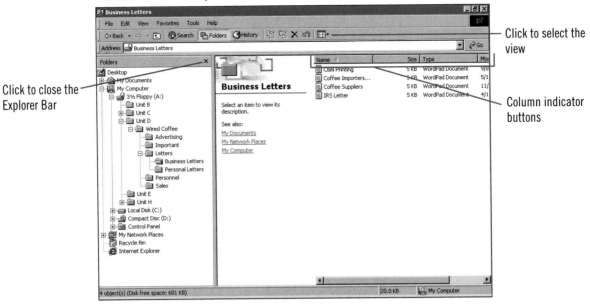

Click to close the
Explorer Bar

Click to select the
view

Column indicator
buttons

FIGURE D-7: Sorting files and folders by date

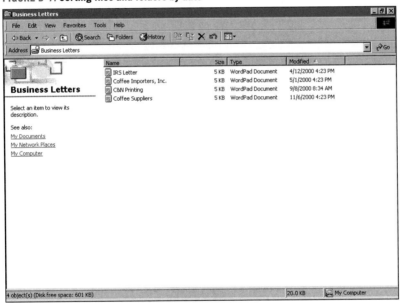

Using the status bar

The status bar at the bottom of the Windows Explorer window gives you information about drives, folders, and files on your computer. You can quickly find out how many items a drive or folder contains, the total size of its contents, where it is located on your com-puter and (for drives) the amount of free disk space. If you don't want to use the status bar, you can turn the status bar off by clicking View on the menu bar and then clicking Status Bar.

Windows 2000

Creating and Renaming Folders in Windows Explorer

To effectively manage all the files on your computer, you need folders in convenient locations to store related files. You should give each folder a meaningful name so that merely glancing at the folder reminds you what is stored there. Creating a new folder in Windows Explorer is much like doing so in My Computer. First, select the location where you want to store the new folder, then create the folder, and finally, name the folder. You can create a folder in Windows Explorer by using the New command on the File menu, or by right-clicking in the right pane, clicking New, then clicking Folder. You can rename a folder or file in Windows Explorer using the Rename command. John wants to create a set of new folders that will hold the files related to the creation of the Wired Coffee Spring Catalog.

1. Click the **Wired Coffee folder** in the Explorer Bar

To create a new folder, you must first select the drive or folder where you want the folder, which in this case is the Wired Coffee folder.

2. Click **File** on the menu bar, point to **New**, then click **Folder**

A new folder, temporarily named New Folder, appears highlighted with a rectangle around the title in the right pane of Windows Explorer, as shown in Figure D-8.

> **Trouble?**
>
> If nothing happens when you type the name, you pressed [Enter] or clicked outside the new folder. Select the folder, click the name "New Folder" so a rectangle surrounds it (with the insertion point inside), then repeat Step 3.

3. Type **Spring Catalog**, then press **[Enter]** or click an empty area in the right pane

The name of the folder changes to Spring Catalog, as shown in Figure D-9.

4. In the right pane, double-click the **Spring Catalog folder**

Nothing appears in the right pane because the folder is empty; there have been no new files or folders created or moved here. Because Spring Catalog is the currently selected folder, any folders you create will be located here.

5. Right-click anywhere in the right pane, point to **New** on the pop-up menu, then click **Folder**

A new folder, named New Folder, appears in the right pane of Windows Explorer.

6. Type **Catalog Text**, then click an empty area in the right pane

The new folder is named Catalog Text. Notice also that there is a + (or a – if the folder is expanded) next to the Spring Catalog folder in the left pane, indicating that this folder contains other folders or files.

> **QuickTip**
>
> To rename a file, you can also select the item, click the name so a rectangle surrounds it, type the new name, and then press [Enter].

7. Right-click the **Catalog Text folder** in the right pane, then click **Rename** on the pop-up menu

The folder appears highlighted with a rectangle around the title in the right pane of Windows Explorer.

8. Type **Catalog Pages**, then press **[Enter]**

The folder is renamed from Catalog Text to Catalog Pages.

FIGURE D-8: **Newly created folder**

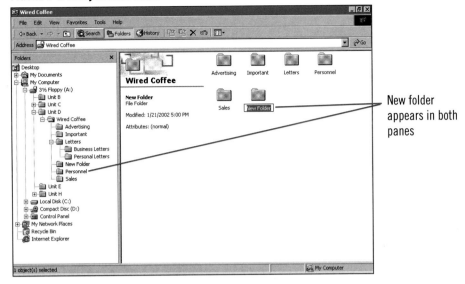

New folder
appears in both
panes

FIGURE D-9: **Creating a new folder using the right-click method**

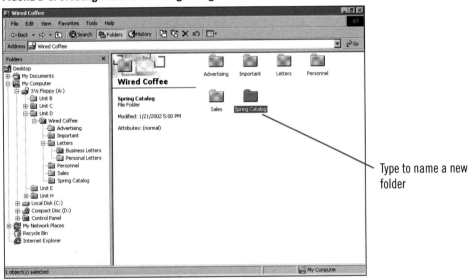

Type to name a new
folder

FIGURE D-10: **Renaming a folder using the right-click method**

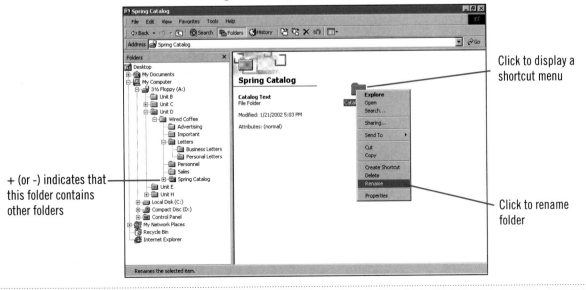

Click to display a
shortcut menu

+ (or -) indicates that
this folder contains
other folders

Click to rename
folder

MANAGING FOLDERS AND FILES USING WINDOWS EXPLORER

Searching for a File

Sometimes it is difficult to remember precisely where you stored a file. Windows Explorer provides a Search feature located in the Explorer Bar to help you find files or folders on your computer or network, computers on your network, and people and information on the Internet. The Search feature also gives you advanced options to find a file or folder by name, location, size, type, and the date on which it was created or last modified. The Search feature is also available on the Start menu to help you locate the information you are looking for when you are not using Windows Explorer. ◢━━━ John wants to find a file he created several months ago with a preliminary outline for the Spring Catalog. He cannot remember the exact name of the file or where he stored it, so he needs to do a quick search.

Steps

1. Click the **Search button** 🔍 on the toolbar
The Spring Catalog window opens, as shown in Figure D-11.

2. Type **Catalog** in the Search for files or folders named text box
You can supply the full name of the folder or file you want to find, or only the part you're sure of. If, for example, John were unsure as to whether he had saved the file as Spring Catalog or Catalog Outline, he could type "Catalog," because he's sure of that much of the name. If John didn't know the name of the file but did know some text contained in the file, he could enter the text in the Containing text box. Before you can start the search, you need to indicate where you want the Search feature to search. The Search feature initially enters the currently displayed folder in Windows Explorer, but you can choose the location you want.

> **QuickTip**
>
> Insert the * (asterisk) wild-card symbol in a file name when you're unsure of the entire name. For example, type "S*rs" to find not only the file named Suppliers, but also all other files beginning with S and ending with rs (such as Stars and Sportscars).

3. Click the **Look in list arrow**, then click the **drive that contains your Project Disk**
Before you start the search, you can set additional search criteria. Table D-1 describes the additional search options available using the Search feature.

> **QuickTip**
>
> To perform a new search, click the New button in the Explorer Bar.

4. Click **Search Now**
The Search feature searches all the folders and files on your Project Disk and lists those folders and files whose names contain the word "Catalog" in the box at the bottom of the Search Results window. The full names, locations, sizes, types, and the dates on which the folders or files were created or last modified are listed.

5. Position the pointer between the In Folder column indicator button and the Relevance column indicator button; when the pointer changes to ↔ , drag to the right to display the location of the files, as shown in Figure D-12
At this point, John can either double-click the file to start the associated program and open the file, or he can note the file's location and close the Search Results window.

6. Click the **Folders button** 🗂 on the toolbar, then click the **Spring Catalog folder** in the Explorer Bar

TABLE D-1: Search options in Explorer Bar

option	use to search for
Files or Folders	File or folders on your computer or network
Computers	Other computers on your network
People	People and groups on the Internet or in your organization
Internet	Information on the Internet

FIGURE D-11: The search for Files and Folders in the Explorer Bar

Enter name or partial name of the file you are looking for here

Enter text contained in the file here

Specify where you think the file is here

Options for searching using criteria

Different search types

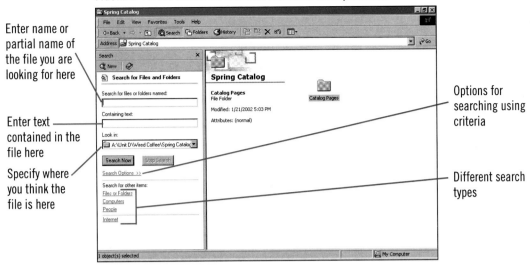

FIGURE D-12: Results of search for Suppliers file

Click to start a new search

Files that matched your search

Drag to resize column size

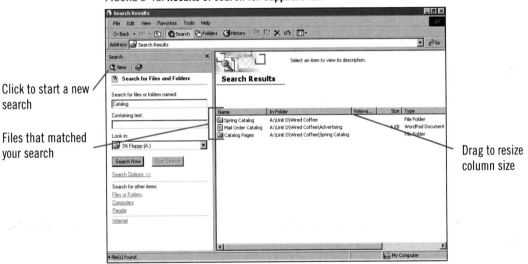

Performing an advanced search

You can also complete an advanced search in Windows Explorer that uses **criteria**, or information, beyond just the name or partial name of a file. If you have no idea what the name or content of the file is, but can recall the type of file (such as a WordPad document), then click the Search button on the toolbar, click Search Options, and then click the Type check box, as shown in Figure D-13. When you click Search Now, Windows will search for and display all the files for the type you specified. This can take a long time, although probably less time than it would take to re-create the missing file. You can also search for files and folders by date and size.

FIGURE D-13: Using Advanced Search features

Search Options <<

☐ Date

☑ Type

(All Files and Folders)

☐ Size

☐ Advanced Options

Indexing Service has finished building an index of all the files on your local hard disks and is monitoring changes.

Moving and Copying a File to a Folder

You should always store your files in the appropriate folders. Sometimes this involves moving a file from one folder to another (removing it from the first and placing it in the second) and sometimes it involves copying a file from one folder to another (leaving it in the first but placing a copy of it in the second). You can move and copy files and folders in several different ways in Windows Explorer. You can use the Cut, Copy, and Paste buttons on the Windows Explorer tool-bar, use the drag and drop method, or right-click the file or folder and click the appropriate command in the pop-up menu. ◢▬▬ John plans to use text from the Mail Order Catalog file (currently located in the Advertising folder) in the Spring Catalog, so he wants to move the Mail Order Catalog file from the Advertising folder to the Catalog Pages folder. He also wants to make a copy of the Wired Coffee Logo file and place it in the Spring Catalog folder.

Steps 1 2 3 4

1. Click the **+ (plus sign)** next to the Spring Catalog folder in the Explorer Bar
The Spring Catalog folder expands, displaying the folder it contains.

2. Click the **Advertising folder** in the Explorer Bar
The contents of the folder appear in the right pane of Windows Explorer. When moving or copying files or folders in Windows Explorer, make sure the file or folder you want to move or copy appears in the right pane.

QuickTip

To select files or folders that are not consecutive, press and hold [Ctrl], then click each item.

3. Drag the **Mail Order Catalog file** across the vertical line separating the two panes to the Catalog Pages folder, as shown in Figure D-14, then release the mouse button
Once you release the mouse button, the Mail Order Catalog file is relocated in the Catalog Pages folder. If you decide that you didn't want the file moved, you can move it back easily using the Undo button on the toolbar.

4. Point to the **Wired Coffee Logo file**, press and hold down the **right mouse button**, drag the file across the vertical line separating the two panes to the Spring Catalog folder, then release the mouse button
As Figure D-15 shows, the pop-up menu offers a choice of options. The Copy Here option is listed first. You can also right-click a file in the right pane to open a pop-up menu—another way to copy or move the file to a new location.

QuickTip

To quickly copy a file from one folder to another on the same disk, select the file, press and hold down [Ctrl], then drag the file to the folder. You can also copy a file from a hard disk to a floppy disk by right-clicking the file, pointing to Send To, and clicking the appropriate disk drive icon.

5. Click **Copy Here**
The original file named Wired Coffee Logo remains in the Advertising folder and a copy of the file has been placed in the Spring Catalog folder.

6. Click the **Spring Catalog folder** in the Explorer Bar
The Wired Coffee Logo file was copied from the Advertising folder (where the original is still located) to the Spring Catalog folder (where the copy is located).

7. Click the **Catalog Pages folder** in the Explorer Bar
The folder opens, and the Mail Order Catalog file appears in the right pane.

2

n score

FIGURE D-14: Copying a file

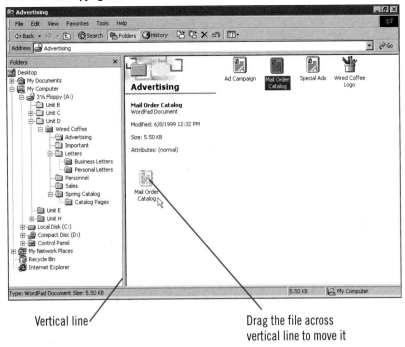

Vertical line

Drag the file across
vertical line to move it

FIGURE D-15: Copying or moving a file

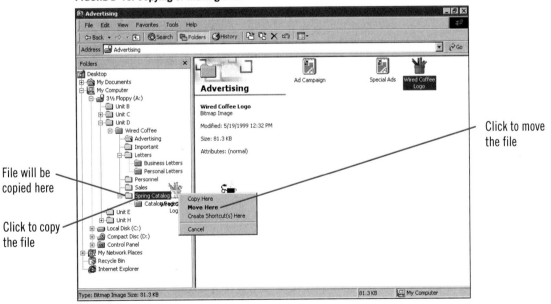

File will be
copied here

Click to copy
the file

Click to move
the file

Finding files or folders using the History folder

Windows 2000 keeps a list of your most recently used files, folders, and network computers in the History folder. To display the History folder, click the History button on the toolbar. You can view the History folder is several ways: by date, by size, by most visited, and by order visited today. In the Explorer Bar, click the View button, then click the view you want.

Restoring a Deleted File Using Undo

To keep your files and folders manageable, you should delete files and folders you no longer need. All the items you delete from your hard disk are stored in the Recycle Bin, so that if you accidentally delete an item, you can move it out of the Recycle Bin window to restore it, or you can use the Undo command. You cannot restore files and folders that you delete from a floppy disk or that you drag from a floppy disk to the Recycle Bin. Windows does not store items deleted from a floppy disk in the Recycle Bin; they are permanently deleted (after a confirmation). See Table D-2 for the various methods of deleting and restoring items.  John wants to delete a file and then restore it using the Undo command. Because you cannot restore files deleted from a floppy disk, you will start by moving a file from your Project Disk to the desktop.

1. Click the **Spring Catalog folder** in the Explorer Bar
The contents of the Spring Catalog folder appear in the right pane.

2. Right-click the **Wired Coffee Logo file** in the right pane, hold down the right mouse button, drag the file to the My Documents folder in the Explorer Bar, then click **Move Here**
The Wired Coffee file is now moved to the My Documents folder.

3. Click the **My Documents folder** in the Explorer Bar
The My Documents folder is a general folder where you can store files and folders.

4. Drag the **Wired Coffee Logo file** in the right pane to the Recycle Bin in the Explorer Bar
You can also right-click the file and then click Delete, or select the file and then press [Delete]. The Wired Coffee Logo file is now removed from My Documents and stored in the Recycle Bin.

5. Click the **Recycle Bin icon** in the Explorer Bar
The Recycle Bin window opens, as shown in Figure D-16.

6. Click the **Undo button** 🔄 on the toolbar
The Wired Coffee Logo file is now restored to the My Documents folder. The Undo command also lets you reverse multiple actions, so you can use the Undo command again to return the Wired Coffee Logo file back into the Spring Catalog folder on your Project Disk.

7. Click 🔄 again
The Wired Coffee Logo file is now moved back to the Spring Catalog folder on your Project Disk.

8. Click the **Spring Catalog folder** in the Explorer Bar
The contents of the Spring Catalog folder, including the Wired Coffee Logo file, appear in the right pane.

9. Click **View** on the menu bar, point to **Arrange Icons**, then click **by Name**
The items are arranged by name in the right pane, as shown in Figure D-17.

FIGURE D-16: **Recycle Bin window**

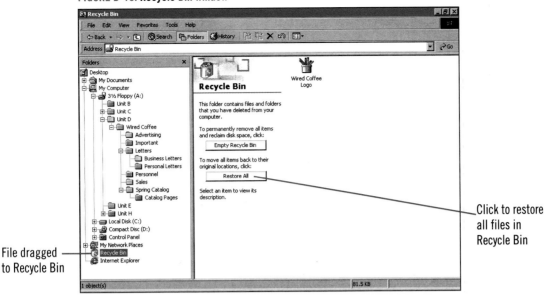

File dragged
to Recycle Bin

Click to restore
all files in
Recycle Bin

FIGURE D-17: **Results of using Undo to restore a file to its original location**

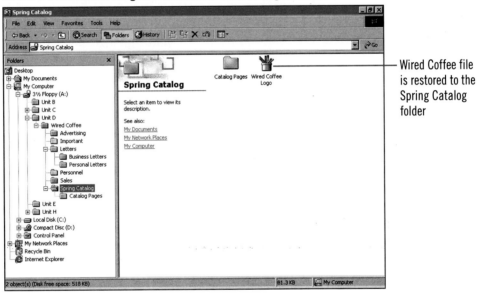

Wired Coffee file
is restored to the
Spring Catalog
folder

TABLE D-2: **Methods for deleting and restoring files in Windows Explorer**

action	methods
Delete	• Right-click the file or folder you want to delete, then click Delete
	• Drag the file or folder to the Recycle Bin
	• Select the file or folder, click File on the menu bar, then click Delete
	• Select the file or folder you want to delete, then press [Delete]
Restore	Open the Recycle Bin, then
	• Select the file or folder you want to restore, click File, then click Restore
	• Right-click the file or folder you want to restore, then click Restore
	• Drag the file or folder to a new location on the desktop

Customizing a Folder

To make working in Windows Explorer more interesting and appealing, you can customize the way a folder looks when it is open (when its contents are displayed in the right pane). As you have seen, by default, folders appear against a white background. However, you can change the background color, select a picture to use as a background, or even create your own Web page view of the folder. Windows Explorer comes with a **wizard** (a series of dialog boxes) that walks you through the steps of customizing a folder. John wants to customize the background of the Wired Coffee folder to display the Wired Coffee logo.

1. **Click the Wired Coffee folder in the Explorer Bar**
   The contents of Wired Coffee folder appear in the right pane of Windows Explorer.

2. **Click View on the menu bar, click Customize This Folder, then click Next**
   The Customize This Folder Wizard opens, as shown in Figure D-18. This wizard helps you change the background appearance of the currently displayed folder. See Table D-3 for a description of the wizard options.

3. **Click the Choose or edit on HTML template for this folder check box to clear it if necessary**

4. **Click the Modify background picture and filename appearance check box to select it if necessary, then click Next**
   Now you need to select a background picture for the Wired Coffee folder. You can select a picture from the list provided, or you can click the Browse button to select a picture stored elsewhere on your computer.

   > **QuickTip**
   > To remove a background picture, follow Steps 1 through 4, click None, click Next, then click Finish.

5. **Click Browse**
   The Open dialog box opens, displaying the My Documents folder.

6. **Click the Look in list arrow, click the drive that contains your Project Disk, double-click the Unit D folder, double-click the Wired Coffee folder, double-click the Advertising folder, then double-click Wired Coffee Logo**
   The Wired Coffee Logo file appears in the left pane of the Customize this Folder dialog box and is selected in the list of available background pictures.

7. **Click Next**
   The wizard displays the file name and location of the background picture you have selected. You can click the Back button to change the picture you have selected or click the Finish button to complete the wizard with the selected picture.

8. **Click Finish**
   The right pane of Windows Explorer displays the Wired Coffee logo in the background, as shown in Figure D-19.

9. **Click the Close button ☒ in Windows Explorer**
   Windows Explorer closes.

FIGURE D-18: Customize This Folder Wizard

Click to choose a
background picture

Click to continue

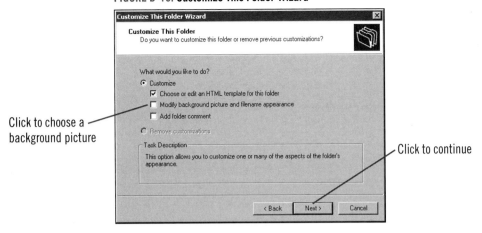

FIGURE D-19: Customized Wired Coffee folder

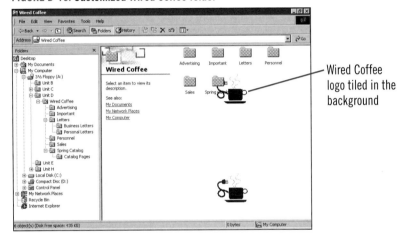

Wired Coffee
logo tiled in the
background

TABLE D-3: Customize This Folder Wizard options

option	allows you to
Choose or edit on HTML template for this folder	Choose or edit an Internet document to view the folder as a Web page (you must know how to use HTML, a computer programming language, to use this option)
Modify background picture and filename appearance	Change the background and file name color or select a picture as a background for the folder
Add folder comment	Add a ScreenTip comment for a folder

Displaying a thumbnail of a graphic

In Windows Explorer you can view a thumbnail version of files in selected folders, as shown in Figure D-20. A thumbnail is a miniature version of an image that is often used for quick browsing through multiple images. Thumbnail versions are available for graphical format only. Click the folder that contains the files you want to view in a thumbnail version. Click View on the menu bar, then click Thumbnails.

FIGURE D-20: Thumbnail of graphic file

Wired Coffee Logo

Practice

► Concepts Review

Label each of the elements of the screen shown in Figure D-21.

FIGURE D-21

address bar

1

explorare bar.

2

minus.

3

colleaps buittons

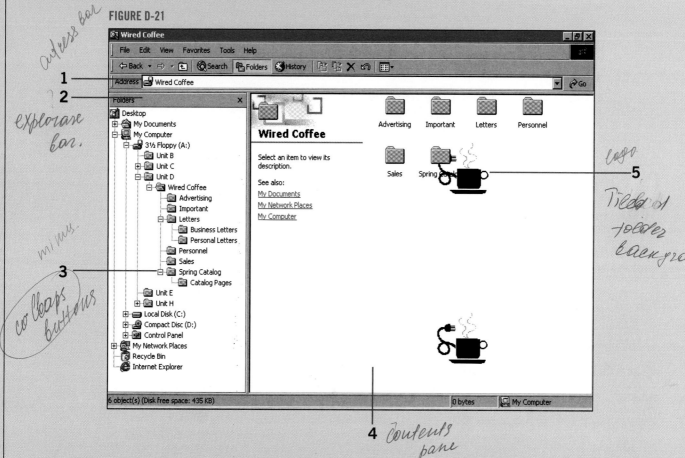

Wired Coffee

| File | Edit | View | Favorites | Tools | Help |

Advertising   Important   Letters   Personnel

Sales   Spring

logo

5

Tiedd of folder background

4 *Contents pane*

Match each of the terms with the statement that describes its function.

c 6. Move a file or folder to the Recycle Bin
e 7. Column indicator
b 8. Pane
a 9. + icon
d 10. Right-click an icon

a. Icon that is clicked to expand folder contents
b. Frames that display information from two different locations
c. Delete selected file or folder
d. Opens pop-up menu
e. Sorts files and folders

Select the best answer from the list of choices.

11. Windows Explorer is different from My Computer in that it allows you to
   a. view the structure of your computer's content.
   b. view the contents of a folder or drive.
   c. change the view.
   d. move between folders.

12. **Where is the Explorer Bar located in Windows Explorer?**
    a. Right pane
    b. Left pane
    c. Folder
    d. Hard drive

13. **In Windows Explorer, which of the following do you click to list the contents of a folder or drive in the Explorer Bar?**
    a. +
    b. -
    c. ⬆
    d. ⬅ Back ▾

14. **To sort files and folders in Windows Explorer, click**
    a. View on the menu bar, then click Sort.
    b. a column indicator button.
    c. the Views button on the toolbar, then click List.
    d. View on the menu bar, then click Arrange.

15. **Which of the following is NOT a valid *search criterion* for a file using the Find program?**
    a. Name
    b. Location
    c. Type
    d. Date opened

16. **To copy a folder or file in Windows Explorer,**
    a. double-click the folder or file.
    b. left-click the folder or file and click Copy.
    c. press [Ctrl] and drag the folder or file.
    d. drag the folder or file.

17. **When a folder or file is moved to another disk,**
    a. the original is moved.
    b. a copy of the original is created.
    c. a copy of the original is created and moved.
    d. a shortcut is created and moved.

18. **Which of the following locations is NOT a valid place from which to delete a file and sent it to the Recycle Bin?**
    a. Hard drive
    b. My Computer
    c. Floppy disk
    d. My Documents folder

19. Which of the following is NOT a Customize This Folder Wizard option?

    a. Choose a background picture

    b. Create and edit an HTML document

    c. Remove customization

    d. Choose a color scheme

▶ Skills Review

1. View the Windows Explorer window.

    a. Insert your Project Disk in the appropriate disk drive.

    b. Click the Start button on the taskbar, point to Programs, point to Accessories, then click Windows Explorer.

    c. In the Explorer Bar, click My Computer

    d. Click the Address list arrow, then click the 3½ Floppy Drive (A:) or (B:).

    e. Click the Back button on the toolbar.

    f. Click the Forward button on the toolbar.

2. Open and view folders in Windows Explorer.

    a. Click the − next to the My Documents folder icon in the Explorer Bar.

    b. Click the + next to the 3½ Floppy drive icon in the Explorer Bar.

    c. Click the ⊞ next to the Unit D folder icon in the Explorer Bar.

    d. Click the + next to the Wired Coffee folder icon in the Explorer Bar.

    e. Click the Personnel folder in the Explorer Bar.

    f. Click the Letters folder in the Explorer Bar.

    g. Double-click the Business Letters folder in the right pane.

3. Customize the Windows Explorer window.

    a. Click the Views button on the toolbar, then click Details.

    b. Click the Close button in the Explorer Bar.

    c. Click the Modified column indicator button.

    d. Click the Name column indicator button.

    e. Click View on the menu bar, point to the Explorer Bar, then click Folders.

    f. Click the Views button on the toolbar, then click Large Icons.

4. Create and rename folders in Windows Explorer.

    a. Click the Wired Coffee folder in the Explorer Bar.

    b. Right-click in a blank area of the right pane of Windows Explorer.

    c. Point to New on the pop-up menu, then click Folder.

    d. Name the folder *Money*, press [Enter], then click in a blank area of the right pane.

    e. Click File on the menu bar, point to New, then click Folder.

    f. Name this folder *Legal*, then press [Enter].

    g. Right-click the Money folder, then click Rename.

    h. Rename this folder *Financial*, then press [Enter].

5. Search for a file.

    a. Click the Search button on the toolbar.

    b. Type **IRS** in the Search for files or folders named text box.

    c. Click the Look in list arrow, then click 3½ Floppy (A:) or (B:).

    d. Click Search Now.
    e. Write down the location of the IRS Letter file.
    f. Click the Folders button on the toolbar.

6. Move and copy a file to a folder.
    a. Drag the IRS Letter file in the right pane to the Financial folder in the Explorer Bar.
    b. Click the Business Letters folder in the Explorer Bar.
    c. Right-click and then drag the Coffee Importers, Inc. file from the Business Letters folder in the right pane to the Legal folder in the Explorer Bar.
    d. Click Copy Here on the pop-up menu.
    e. Click the Legal folder in the Explorer Bar.

7. Restore a deleted file using Undo.
    a. Right-drag the Coffee Importers, Inc. file (right-click and hold down the right mouse button while dragging) from the Legal folder in the right pane to the My Documents folder in the Explorer Bar, then click Move Here.
    b. Click the My Documents folder in the Explorer Bar.
    c. Drag the Coffee Importers, Inc. file from the My Documents folder in the right pane to the Recycle Bin in the Explorer Bar.
    d. Click the Recycle Bin in the Explorer Bar.
    e. Click the Undo button on the toolbar.
    f. Click the Undo button on the toolbar again.
    g. Click the Legal folder in the Explorer Bar.

8. Customize a folder.
    a. Click the Wired Coffee folder in the Explorer Bar.
    b. Click View on the menu bar, click Customize This Folder, then click Next.
    c. Click the Modify background picture and filename appearance check box to select it.
    d. Click Next, then click None.
    e. Click Next, then click Finish.
    f. Click the Close button in Windows Explorer.

▶ Independent Challenges

1. You have just started Sewing Works, a sewing machine repair business, and want to use Windows 2000 to organize your documents. For this challenge, you will create on your Project Disk a set of files that are relevant to the business and organize them in a set of folders that will make it easy for you to locate what you need when you need it.
    To complete this independent challenge:

a. Create a WordPad file named *Wilson Letter* on your Project Disk thanking Mr. Wilson for his business.
b. On your Project Disk, create another WordPad file named *Suppliers*. List the following suppliers in the file:
Apex Sewing Machine Parts
POB 3645
Tempe, AZ 12345
Jones Sewing Repair
18th and 3rd
Brooklyn, NY 12345

c. On your Project Disk, create a third WordPad file and name it *Bills*. List the following information in the file:

Apex   16453 $34.56
Jones   47354 $88.45
Ott   44412 $98.56

d. On your Project Disk, create a folder named *Sewing Works*.
e. In the Sewing Works folder, create three folders. Name the folders *Letters*, *Contacts*, and *Accounts*.
f. Expand the Sewing Works folder in the Explorer Bar.
g. Move the Wilson Letter file to the Letters folder, the Suppliers file to the Contacts folder, and the Bills file to the Accounts folder.
h. Open the Letters folder.
i. Print the screen. (Press the Print Screen key to make a copy of the screen, open Paint, click Edit on the menu bar, click Paste to paste the screen into Paint, then click Yes to paste the large image if necessary. Click File on the menu bar, click Print, then click Print in the Print dialog box.)
j. Close Windows Explorer.

2. As manager of the summer program at a day camp, you need to keep your folders and files organized so information can be easily and quickly found. Your files fall into two main categories: children and activities. You need to create a folder for each category and place them in a separate folder named Day Camp, to distinguish it from other years you've managed the camp.

To complete this independent challenge:

a. On your Project Disk, create three folders. Name the folders *Camp 2001*, *Campers*, and *Activities*.
b. Create a WordPad file named *Camper Data*. Save the file to your Project Disk. In this file, create information on five campers, including their name, age, bunk, and favorite sports. Here's a sample of two:

Name	Age	Bunk #	Sports
Bill Moore	11	3	Swimming, Horseshoes
Michael Morley	12	4	Basketball

c. Move the Camper Data file into the Campers folder.
d. Create a WordPad file named *Activities Overview*. Save the file to your Project Disk. In this folder, create information on five camp activities, including the name, equipment or supplies the children need to supply, number of children, and name of the activity leader. Here's a sample of two:

Activity	Children provide	Number allowed	Leader
Swimming	Swimsuit, water wings if needed	18	John Lee
Soccer	Shoes, shin guards	24	Madeline Harman

e. Move the Activities Overview file into the Activities folder.
f. Move the Activities folder and the Campers folder into the Camp 2001 folder.
g. Expand the Camp 2001 folder in the Explorer Bar.
h. Open the Campers folder.
i. Copy the Camper Data file to the Activities folder.
j. Open the Activities folder.
k. Print the screen. (See Independent Challenge 1, Step K for screen printing instructions.)
l. Close Windows Explorer.

3. The summer fine arts program that you manage has different categories of participation for young adults, including two-week and four-week programs. In order for you to keep track of who is participating in each program, you have to organize the files with program information into folders. For this challenge, you'll have to create new folders, create a list of participants, and then move the document lists into folders.

To complete this independent challenge:

a. On your Project Disk, create a folder named *Summer Program*.
b. Within the Summer Program folder, create a folder named *Arts*.
c. Within the folders you created named Arts, create two other folders named *2 Weeks* and *4 Weeks*.
d. Create a WordPad file named *2 Weeks Art* on your Project Disk with the following:

Leni Welitoff	2 weeks painting
Tom Stacey	2 weeks ceramics and jewelry

e. Create a WordPad file named *4 Weeks Art* on your Project Disk with the following:

Kim Dayton	4 weeks painting and landscape design
Sara Jackson	4 weeks set construction

f. Move the files you created into their respective folders named 2 Weeks and 4 Weeks.
g. Rename the Arts folder to *Fine Arts*.
h. Collapse and expand the Summer Program 2001 folder.
i. Expand the Fine Arts folder.
j. Open the 4 Weeks folder located in the Fine Arts folder.
k. Print the screen. (See Independent Challenge 1, Step K for screen printing instructions.)
l. Find the files on your Project Disk that contain "painting" in the text (not the title).
m. Print the screen. (See Independent Challenge 1, Step K for screen printing instructions.)
n. Close Windows Explorer.

4. As the head of the graphics department in a small design firm, one of your jobs is to organize the clip art images used by the company. The two categories in which you can place an image are Lines and Shapes. You can place clip art images in more than one category as well. For this challenge, you'll have to create several folders and Paint images and move and copy them to different folders.

To complete this independent challenge:

a. On your Project Disk, create two different small Paint images and save them using the following names: *Ellipses* and *Lines*.
b. On your Project Disk, create two folders named *Lines* and *Shapes*.
c. Move the Lines file to the Lines folder.
d. Move the Ellipses file to the Shapes folder.
e. Copy the Curves file into the Shapes folder.
f. Rename the Ellipses file to *Ovals*.
g. Customize the Lines folder with the Curves file as a background.
h. Open the Lines folder.
i. Print the screen. (See Independent Challenge 1, Step K for screen printing instructions.)
j. Close Windows Explorer.

▶ Visual Workshop

Re-create the screen shown in Figure D-22, which displays the Windows Explorer window. Print the screen. (See Independent Challenge 1, Step K for screen printing instructions.)

FIGURE D-22

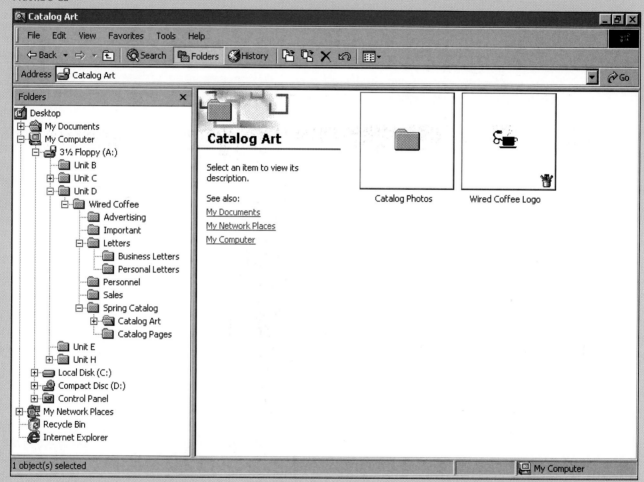

Customizing

Windows Using the Control Panel

- ► **Customize the Active Desktop**
- ► **Change the desktop background and screen saver settings**
- ► **Change the desktop scheme**
- ► **Set the date and time**
- ► **Work with fonts**
- ► **Manage power options**
- ► **Add a scheduled task**
- ► **Customize the taskbar**
- ► **Customize the Start menu**

In this unit, you will learn how to customize Windows 2000 to suit your personal needs and preferences. Most Windows features can be adjusted through the **Control Panel**, a central location where you can change Windows settings. The Control Panel contains several icons, each of which opens a dialog box for changing the **properties**, or characteristics, of a specific element of your computer, such as the desktop, the taskbar, or the Start menu. John wants to customize some Windows 2000 settings. *If you are concerned about changing the aspects of Windows 2000 at your location, or your instructor or technical support person does not wish you to customize, simply read through this unit without completing the steps, or click the Cancel button in any dialog box where a change could be made.*

Customizing the Active Desktop

Because more and more people are using the Internet, Windows 2000 includes Active Desktop, a feature that allows you to view Web content, or Active Desktop items, on your desktop as you would a document on the Internet, known as a **Web page**. **Active Desktop items** are elements you can place on the desktop to access or display information from the Internet. For example, you can add an Active Desktop item to continuously display Web information such as a home page, stock prices, or weather information. Using the Control Panel Display Properties dialog box, you can customize the desktop to display the Active Desktop items you want to use. John wants to learn how to customize the Active Desktop.

Steps

Trouble?

In order for Web content to appear when you click Show Web Content, you need to be connected to the Internet.

1. Right-click in an empty area on the **desktop**, point to **Active Desktop**, then click **Show Web Content**

All Active Desktop items, such as a home page, that are turned on are retrieved from the Internet and displayed on the desktop, as shown in Figure E-1. A **home page** is the Web page that opens when you start your Web browser.

QuickTip

You can change the way you click on desktop icons from double-clicking to open an item to single-clicking (like a document on the Internet). Double-click the Mouse icon ⟶ in the Control Panel, click the Single-click to open an item option button on the Buttons tab, then click OK.

2. Right-click in an empty area on the **desktop** (to the left of the Web page), point to **Active Desktop**, then click **Customize My Desktop**

The Display Properties dialog box opens with the Web tab in front, as shown in Figure E-2. The Web tab displays a list of Active Desktop items and a preview of the items. To turn on or turn off items on the Active Desktop, you select or deselect the Active Desktop item check boxes.

3. Click the **My Current Home Page check box** to deselect it

The My Current Home Page is removed from the preview display. You can turn off all Active Desktop items by clicking the Show Web content on my Active Desktop check box to deselect the option.

4. Click **Apply**

The My Current Home Page is removed from the Active Desktop.

5. Click the **My Current Home Page check box** to select it

The My Current Home Page appears in the preview display.

QuickTip

You can quickly turn off all Active Desktop items from the desktop by right-clicking the desktop, pointing to Active Desktop, and then clicking Show Web Content to remove the checkmark.

6. Click the **Show Web content on my Active Desktop check box** to deselect it

The Show Web Content feature is turned off.

7. Click **Apply**

The Display Properties dialog box remains open.

FIGURE E-1: Active Desktop with Web content

Web content on the
Active Desktop

FIGURE E-2: Display Properties dialog box

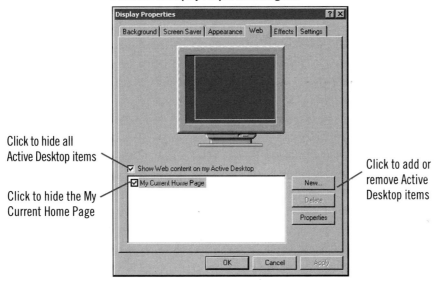

Click to hide all
Active Desktop items

Click to hide the My
Current Home Page

Click to add or
remove Active
Desktop items

Adding a new Web item to the Active Desktop

You can add new desktop items, live Web content,
or pictures to your Active Desktop. Right-click in
an empty area on the desktop, point to Active
Desktop, then click Customize My Desktop. Click
the Show Web content on my Active Desktop check
box to select it, then click New. The New Active
Desktop Item dialog box opens, as shown in E-3.
To add a Web page or picture from the Internet,
type its Web address in the Location box. To add a
new desktop item, click Visit Gallery to access and
display Microsoft's Active Desktop Gallery on the
Internet, then select the item in which you want to
add. To access and display a Web page, you need to
be connected to the Internet.

FIGURE E-3: Creating a new Active Desktop item

Windows 2000

Changing the Desktop Background and Screen Saver Settings

You can change the look of your Windows desktop using the Display Properties dialog box. You can adjust your screen's **background**, the basic surface on which icons and windows appear. You can use a **screen saver**, a moving display that protects your monitor from burn-in, which can occur when there is no movement on your screen for a long time. You can also assign a password to your screen saver to prevent others from using your computer. ✎ John wants to choose a new background for his desktop and set one of the standard screen savers to start when his computer is idle for more than five minutes.

QuickTip

You can also open the Display Properties dialog box by right-clicking an empty area of the desktop, then clicking Properties.

1. In the Display Properties dialog box, click the **Background tab**

The Background tab appears, as shown in Figure E-4. Table E-1 describes the tabs in this dialog box.

2. In the Wallpaper section, click the **up** or **down scroll arrow**, then click **Coffee Bean** (or a wallpaper of your choosing if this one is not available on your system)

The preview window shows how the wallpaper will look on your screen. **Wallpaper** is a picture that serves as your desktop's background. Acceptable formats for wallpaper files are Bitmap (the format of a Paint file) or JPEG (the format of an Internet document). You can use Paint to create new wallpaper designs or change existing ones. Besides the wallpaper, you can also choose a desktop **pattern**, a design that can be modified by clicking the None Wallpaper icon and then clicking the Pattern button.

3. Click the **Picture Display list arrow**, then click **Tile**

You can determine how a wallpaper or pattern appears on the screen using the Picture Display list arrow. **Tile** displays the wallpaper picture or pattern consecutively across the screen; **Center** displays the picture or pattern in the center of the screen; and **Stretch** displays the picture or pattern enlarged in the center of the screen.

4. Click **Apply**

The new wallpaper appears on the desktop.

5. Click **(None)** in the Wallpaper section, then click **Apply**

6. Click the **Screen Saver tab**

The default setting is for no screen saver, meaning that your screen will not be replaced by a constantly changing image no matter how long your computer remains idle. If someone else used this machine before you, a screen saver might already be set.

QuickTip

To assign a password to your screen saver, click the Password protected check box to select it, then click Apply.

7. Click the **Screen Saver list arrow**, then click **3D Flying Objects**

The 3D Flying Objects screen saver appears in the preview window, as shown in Figure E-5.

8. In the Wait box, click the **up arrow** (or **down arrow**) until it reads 5 minutes

This is the amount of time between when your computer detects no mouse or keyboard activity and when the screen saver begins.

9. Click **Preview**, move the mouse or press any key to stop the preview, then click **Apply**

The entire desktop previews the screen saver pattern.

FIGURE E-4: Background tab of Display Properties dialog box

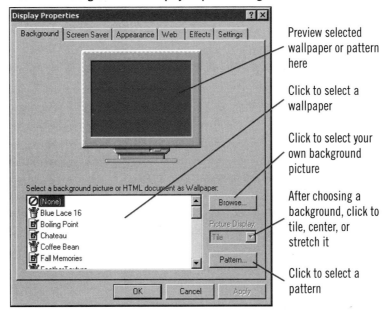

Preview selected wallpaper or pattern here

Click to select a wallpaper

Click to select your own background picture

After choosing a background, click to tile, center, or stretch it

Click to select a pattern

FIGURE E-5: Screen Saver tab of Display Properties dialog box

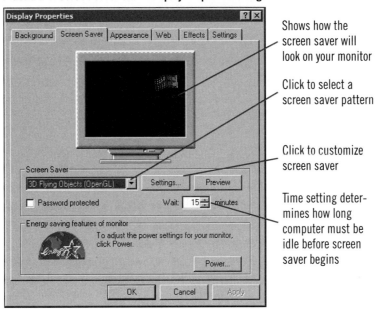

Shows how the screen saver will look on your monitor

Click to select a screen saver pattern

Click to customize screen saver

Time setting determines how long computer must be idle before screen saver begins

TABLE E-1: Display Properties tab description

display tab	allows you to
Background	Choose a picture or pattern to display on the desktop
Screen Saver	Choose and preview a screen saver pattern, set pattern characteristics, and adjust some power settings depending on your monitor
Appearance	Choose colors, sizes, and fonts for Windows screen items such as title bars, icons, etc., or choose a coordinated Windows Scheme for these items
Web	Choose whether to view the desktop as a Web page, and add or delete Active Desktop items
Effects	Change appearance of desktop icons and set visual effects such as large icons
Settings	Set the maximum number of colors viewable at one time, change the screen resolution, and change advanced settings such as monitor settings

Windows 2000

Changing the Desktop Scheme

You can change the appearance of colors, fonts, and sizes used for major window elements such as title bars, icons, menus, borders, and the desktop itself. You can change each item individually, or use a **scheme**, a predefined combination of settings that assures all items are visually coordinated. Windows includes many predefined schemes, and you can also create your own. When you create a custom scheme or modify an existing scheme, you save the changes you've made with a unique name. ◢▬▬ Ray Adams, an employee of Wired Coffee, is visually impaired and needs a display configuration in which the window elements are larger than the standard size and in which the background color provides greater contrast with window elements. John decides to create a scheme for Ray, who can switch to the scheme whenever he uses the computer.

1. Click the **Appearance tab** in the Display Properties dialog box
   The Appearance tab, as shown in Figure E-6, allows you to change the appearance of individual desktop elements, such as the menu bar, message box, and selected text, or to select one of several predefined schemes that Windows provides, and modify it as necessary.

2. Click the **Scheme list arrow**, then click **Windows Standard (large)**
   In Figure E-7, you can see that the size of everything in the Preview box is increased from standard size to extra large.

3. Click the **Item list arrow**, then click **Desktop** if necessary
   The desktop color can now be changed. Notice that the Item size option and Font option are grayed out, indicating that these options do not apply to the desktop.

4. Click the **Color list arrow**, then click the **black color box** in the first row
   You can select from a matrix of different colors. Before you save the scheme, you can apply the scheme to the desktop to see how it looks.

5. Click **Apply**
   The desktop changes, but the dialog box remains open. Use the Apply button when you want to test your changes and the OK button when you want to keep your changes and close the dialog box.

6. Click **Save As**, type **Ray**, and then click **OK**
   The scheme is saved with the name Ray. Now, anytime Ray wants to use the computer, he can easily switch to this scheme.

7. Click **Delete** to remove the Ray scheme, click the **Scheme list arrow**, click **Windows Standard**, then click **Apply**

8. Click the **Screen Saver tab**, click the **Screen Saver list arrow**, then click **None**
   The screen saver is turned off.

9. Click **OK**

FIGURE E-6: Appearance tab of the Display Properties dialog box

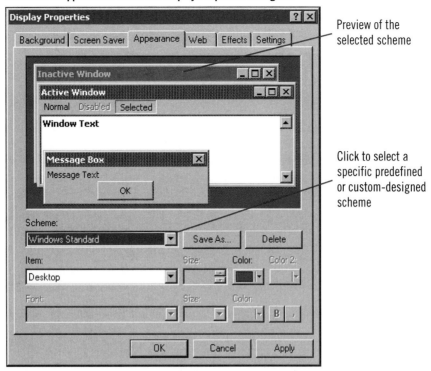

Preview of the
selected scheme

Click to select a
specific predefined
or custom-designed
scheme

FIGURE E-7: Changing the desktop color scheme

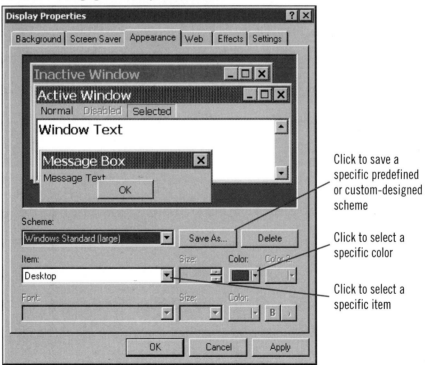

Click to save a
specific predefined
or custom-designed
scheme

Click to select a
specific color

Click to select a
specific item

Changing the size of the desktop

You can change the size of the desktop that appears on your monitor. In the Display Properties dialog box, click the Settings tab, then drag the Screen Area slider. The settings available depend upon the hardware that Windows detects when it is installed. In some cases, you might even have higher settings than 640 × 480 or 800 × 600 (such as 1024 × 768) available. A higher setting means higher resolution, so more information can fit on the screen.

Setting the Date and Time

The date and time you set in the Control Panel appears in the lower-right corner of the taskbar and is used by programs to establish the date and time that files and folders are created and modified. To change the date and time, you modify the date and time settings in the Date/Time Properties dialog box. In addition to changing the date and time, you can also change how the date and time appear. This can be handy if you are working on documents from a different country or region of the world. To change the date and time display, you modify the date or settings on the Date/Time tab in the Regional Settings Properties dialog box. ➤ John is working on an international document and wants to change his date and time settings.

Steps

1. **Click the Start button** on the taskbar, point to **Settings**, then click **Control Panel**
   The Control Panel window opens, as shown in Figure E-8. Each icon represents an aspect of Windows that can be adjusted to fit your own working habits and personal needs.

2. Double-click the **Date/Time icon** 🕒 in the Control Panel window
   The Date/Time Properties dialog box opens with the Date & Time tab in front, as shown in Figure E-9. To change the date, you choose the month and year you want in the Date section, and then click the day you want in the calendar. To change the time, you choose the hours, minutes, or seconds you want in the text box in the Time section, and then type a new number or click the up or down arrow to select the new time.

3. Double-click the **current hour** in the text box in the Time section, then click the **up arrow** three times
   The new time appears in the running clock.

4. Click **Apply**
   The new time appears in the right corner of the taskbar.

5. Double-click the **current hour**, click the **down arrow** three times to restore the correct time, then click **OK**

6. Double-click the **Regional Options icon** 🌐 in the Control Panel window
   The Regional Settings dialog box opens, displaying tabs for General, Number, Currency, Time, Date, and Input Locales (for international keyboard support). Using these tabs, you change the format, symbols, and international languages used for text, numbers, currency, time, and date in your files and programs.

7. Click the **Date tab**
   The Date tab appears, displaying the current date formats being used. You can click the short date or long date list arrows to change the two date formats, as shown in Figure E-10.

8. Click the **Time tab**
   The Time tab appears, displaying the current time formats being used.

9. Click **OK**

FIGURE E-8: Control Panel window

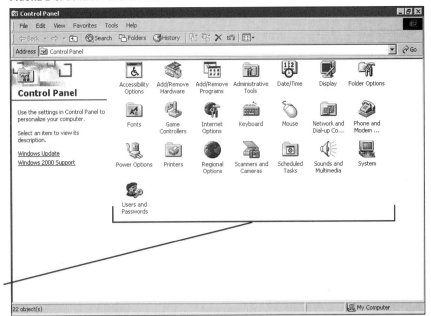

Depending on your computer, your icons might be different

FIGURE E-9: Date/Time Properties dialog box

Click to change time zone

Click to change month

Click to change the day

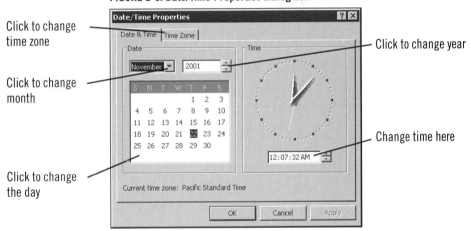

Click to change year

Change time here

FIGURE E-10: Regional Options dialog box

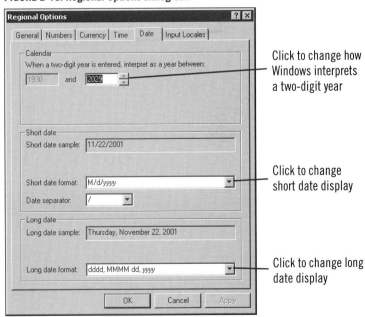

Click to change how Windows interprets a two-digit year

Click to change short date display

Click to change long date display

Windows 2000

Working with Fonts

Everything you type appears in a font, such as Times New Roman, Arial, Courier, or Symbol. A font describes the design of a set of characters, known as a typeface, along with other qualities, such as size and spacing. Windows comes with a variety of fonts that appear and print in programs that are part of Windows, such as WordPad and Paint. Using the Fonts window, you can view these fonts, compare them to each other, see a sample of how a font would appear if printed, and even install new fonts. ✐ John wants to examine different fonts in preparation for an upcoming flyer he wants to make.

Steps

1. **Double-click the Fonts icon** 🖼 **in the Control Panel window, then click the Maximize button** ▣ **in the Fonts window if necessary**
   The Fonts window opens, as shown in Figure E-11. The window displays the fonts available on your system and indicates whether each is an OpenType or a screen font. An **OpenType** font is based on a mathematical equation so the curves are smooth and the corners are sharp. A **screen font** consists of **bitmapped characters**, small dots organized to form a letter. Table E-2 lists the various options on the Font toolbar and describes what they do.

2. **Click View on the menu bar, then click Hide Variations (Bold, Italic, etc.)**
   The main font styles appear in the Font window.

3. **Double-click the Arial font icon**
   As shown in Figure E-12, the window displays information about this font and shows a sample of the font in different sizes.

4. **Click Print in the Arial (OpenType) window, then click Print again**
   A copy of the font information prints.

5. **Click Done**
   The Arial (OpenType) window closes.

6. **Click the Similarity button** 🔲 **on the Fonts toolbar**
   The Similarity tool helps you find fonts that are similar to the selected font. All the fonts are listed by how similar they are to Arial, the font listed in the List fonts by similarity to box. You can choose a different font to check which ones are similar to it by clicking the List fonts by similarity to list arrow, and then selecting the font you want to check.

7. **Click the Large Icons button** 🔲 **on the Fonts toolbar, then click the Back button** ⬅ Back ▾ **on the toolbar**
   You return to the Control Panel.

CLUES TO USE

Installing a font

Windows 2000 might not come with all the fonts you need or want, but you can purchase additional fonts and easily install them. To install a new font, click Install New font on the File menu in the Fonts window, indicate the location of the font you want to install (on the hard drive or a floppy disk), and then click OK. The new font will be installed and will be available in the Fonts window of the Control Panel and in all your Windows programs.

FIGURE E-11: Fonts window

OpenType font

Fonts toolbar

Installed fonts; your list might be different

Screen font

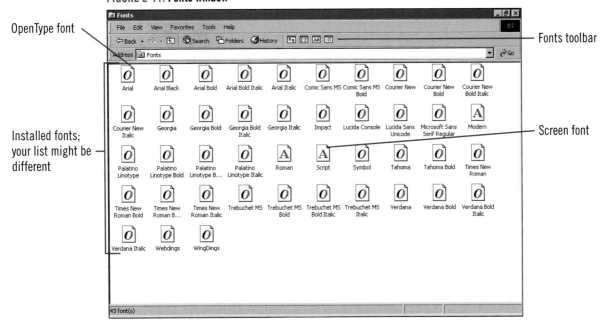

FIGURE E-12: Information on the selected font

Click to print the displayed information

Font information

Sample sizes

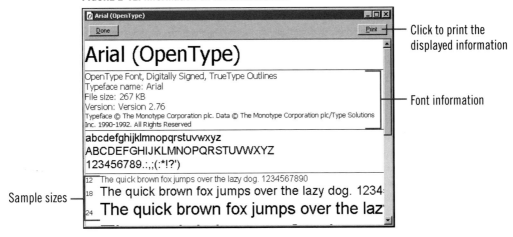

TABLE E-2: Font toolbar options

toolbar icon	name	description
⇐ Back ▾	Back	Moves you back to a previous folder
⇒ ▾	Forward	Moves you forward to a previously opened folder
⬆	Up	Moves to the next level up in the hierarchy of folders
🔍	Search	Searches folder or file
📁	Folders	Displays a list of folders on your computer
🕘	History	Displays a list of recently used folders and files
🔲	Large Icons	Lists fonts by large icon
▤	List	Lists fonts alphabetically
AᴮI	Similarity	Lists fonts by similarity to the selected font
▦	Details	Lists details of fonts, including file name, font name, size, and date last modified

Unit E

Windows 2000

Managing Power Options

You can change power options properties on your computer to reduce the power consumption of your entire system or a specific device. For example, if you are often away from your computer for a short time while working, you can set your computer to go into **standby**, a state in which your monitor and hard disks turn off, after standing idle for a set time. When you bring the computer out of standby, your desktop appears exactly as you left it. Because standby does not save your desktop settings to disk, a power failure while on standby can cause you to lose unsaved information. If you are often away from your computer for an extended time or overnight but like to leave the computer on, you can set it to go into **hibernation**, a state in which your computer shuts down but first saves everything in memory on your hard disk. When you restart the computer, your desktop is restored exactly as you left it. Table E-3 lists common tabs in the Power Options Properties dialog box and describes the power options each offers. During the day, John takes short breaks from his computer to attend meetings, so he wants to change power options for his computer to save power.

Steps

1. **Double-click the Power Options icon in the Control Panel window**

   The Power Options Properties dialog box opens with the Power Schemes tab in front, as shown in Figure E-13. A **power scheme** is a predefined collection of power usage settings. You can choose one of the power schemes included with Windows or modify one to suit your needs. The Power Options you see will vary depending on your computer's hardware configuration. The Power Options feature automatically detects what is available on your computer and shows you only the options that you can control.

2. Click the **Power schemes list arrow**, then click **Portable/Laptop**

   Settings for the Portable/Laptop power scheme appear in the bottom section of the Power Schemes tab.

3. Click the **Turn off monitor list arrow**, then click **After 1 min**

4. Click **Apply**, then wait one minute without moving the mouse or pressing a key

   After a minute, the screen goes on standby (a blank screen). While on standby, your entire computer switches to a low power state where devices, such as the monitor and hard disks, turn off and your computer uses less power.

5. Move the mouse to restore the desktop

   The computer comes out of standby, and your desktop is restored exactly as you left it.

6. Click the **Power schemes list arrow**, then click **Always On**

   The Turn off monitor and Turn off hard disks options change to reflect power settings for this scheme. For the computer shown in Figure E-13, the power settings change to Never, the preset option.

7. Click the **Hibernate tab**

   The Hibernate tab appears, displaying settings for hibernation support, as shown in Figure E-14. In this case, the hibernation support is turned on. When you shut down your computer, the Hibernation option is available for you to select.

8. Click **OK**

QuickTip

To create your own power scheme, click the Power Schemes tab in the Power Options Properties dialog box, select the Turn off monitor and Turn off hard disks power options you want, click Save As, type a name, then click OK.

QuickTip

To show a power option icon in the taskbar, click the Advanced tab, click the Always show icon on the taskbar check box to select it, then click Apply or OK.

Trouble?

If you do not see the Hibernate tab, skip to Step 8. For most laptop computers, other tabs appear instead of the Hibernate tab.

FIGURE E-13: Power Options Properties dialog box

Click to select a different tab and power options (depending on your computer, your tabs might be different)

Click to save a customized power scheme

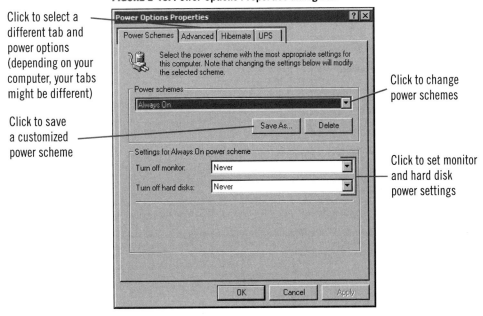

Click to change power schemes

Click to set monitor and hard disk power settings

FIGURE E-14: Hibernate tab of Power Options Properties dialog box

Hibernate support is turned on

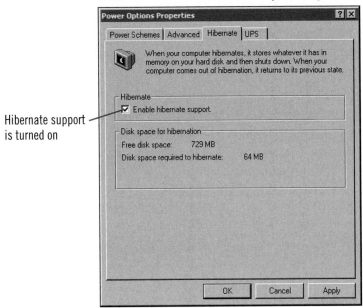

TABLE E-3: Common Power Options Properties tabs

tab	allows you to
Power Schemes	Change power settings for your monitor and hard disks
Advanced	Change user power options
Hibernate	Turn on and off hibernate support
UPS	Select and configure an Uninterruptible Power Supply (UPS) device (availability depends on the specific UPS hardware installed on your computer)
Alarms	Change settings for low battery notification alarms (available on most laptop computers)
Power Meter	Display power usage details for each battery in your computer (available on most laptop computers)
APM	Turn on or turn off Advanced Power Management (APM) support in order to reduce overall power consumption (available on most laptop computers)

Adding a Scheduled Task

Task Scheduler is a tool that enables you to schedule tasks (such as Disk Cleanup, a program that removes unnecessary files) to run regularly, at a time that is convenient for you. Task Scheduler starts each time you start Windows. When Task Scheduler is running on your computer, its icon appears next to the clock on the taskbar. With Task Scheduler, you can schedule a task to run daily, weekly, monthly, or at certain times (such as when the computer starts or is idle), change the schedule for or turn off an existing task, or customize how a task will run at its scheduled time. Before you schedule a task, be sure that the system date and time on your computer are accurate, as Task Scheduler relies on this information to run scheduled tasks. ➤ John schedules a task to back up files on his computer.

QuickTip

To modify a scheduled task, right-click the task you want to modify, and then click Properties.

1. Double-click the **Scheduled Tasks icon** ▣ in the Control Panel window

   The Scheduled Tasks window opens, as shown in Figure E-15.

2. Double-click the **Add Scheduled Task icon** ▣, then in the Scheduled Task Wizard dialog box, click **Next**

   The Scheduled Task Wizard displays a list of programs you can schedule to run. If the program or document you want to use is not in the list, you can click Browse to locate the program on your computer disk drive or network.

3. In the list of programs, click **Backup**, click **Next**, click the **Weekly option button**, then click **Next**

   The next Scheduled Task Wizard dialog box opens, as shown in Figure E-16, asking you to select the time and day you want to the task to start.

4. In the Start time box, change the time to one minute ahead of the current time, click the current day of the week check box to select it, then click **Next**

   The next Scheduled Task Wizard dialog box opens, asking you to enter the name and password of the current user. The task will run as if it were started by that user.

5. In the Enter the password box, type your **password**, press **[Tab]**, then type your password again

QuickTip

To stop a scheduled task that is running, right-click the task that you want to stop, then click End Task.

6. Click **Next**, then click **Finish**

   The scheduled task appears in the Scheduled Task window, as shown in Figure E-17.

7. Wait for the backup to take place, then click the **Close button** ✕ in the Backup Window

QuickTip

To notify you when a scheduled task is missed, click Advanced on the menu bar, then click Notify Me of Missed Tasks to select the option.

8. Right-click the **Backup icon** ▤, click **Delete**, then click **Yes**

   The scheduled task is deleted.

9. Click the **Close button** ✕ on the Scheduled Tasks window

FIGURE E-15: Scheduled Tasks window

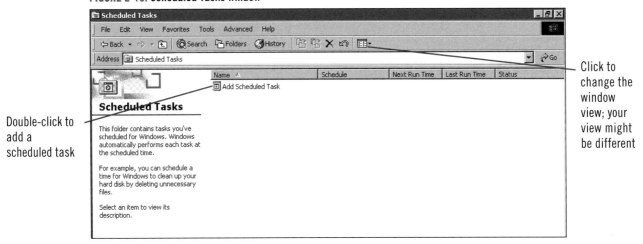

Double-click to add a scheduled task

Click to change the window view; your view might be different

FIGURE E-16: Scheduled Task Wizard

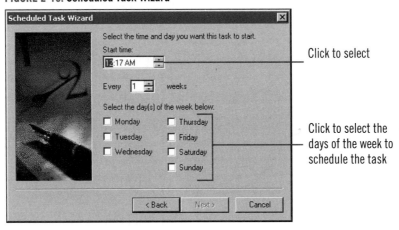

Click to select

Click to select the days of the week to schedule the task

FIGURE E-17: Task added to Scheduled Tasks window

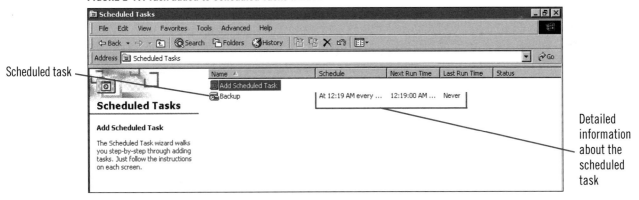

Scheduled task

Detailed information about the scheduled task

CLUES TO USE

Adding new hardware and software to Windows

You can add new hardware, such as a printer, and add or remove programs by using tools on the Control Panel. The Add New Hardware and Add/Remove Programs dialog boxes walk you through the necessary steps. To start the add new hardware procedure, click the Add New Hardware icon in the Control Panel, then click the Next button and follow the prompts. To add or remove a program, click the Add/Remove Program icon, click Install, then follow the prompts. In both cases, Windows 2000 should recognize that there are new hardware needs to be added or that there is an installation file that needs to be executed.

Customizing the Taskbar

The taskbar is most often used for switching from one program or document to another. The taskbar is initially located at the bottom of the Windows desktop. As with other Windows elements, you can customize the taskbar; for example you can change its size and location, or add or remove toolbars to it that help you perform the tasks you need to do. Sometimes you need more room on the screen to display a window, and it would help to hide the taskbar. You can use the **Auto hide** feature to help you automatically hide the taskbar when you don't need it. ➤ John wants to remove and add a toolbar to the taskbar. He also wants to learn how the Auto hide feature works.

QuickTip

You can show the toolbar title or toolbar button names for a toolbar on the taskbar. Right-click an empty area of the toolbar, then click Show Title or Show Text.

1. **Place the mouse pointer in a blank section of the taskbar (not on a button), right-click the taskbar, then point to Toolbars**
   The Toolbars submenu appears, as shown in Figure E-18. You can add or remove a variety of existing toolbars to the taskbar or create a new one.

2. **Click Quick Launch to deselect it**
   The Quick Launch toolbar is removed from the taskbar. Now you have more room on the taskbar for program buttons.

3. **Click the Start button, point to Settings, then click Taskbar & Start Menu**
   The Taskbar and Start Menu dialog box opens, displaying the General tab, as shown in Figure E-19. You can show how items (such as the clock and small icons on the Start menu) appear on the taskbar or how the taskbar appears on the screen.

4. **Click the Auto hide check box to select it**
   The taskbar in the preview box is hidden.

5. **Click OK**
   The taskbar is hidden at the bottom of the screen.

6. **Move the mouse pointer to the bottom of the screen**
   While the mouse pointer is located at the bottom of the screen, the taskbar appears. When you move the mouse pointer up, the taskbar is hidden.

Trouble?

If the Quick Launch toolbar reappears on the right side of the taskbar, position the mouse pointer over the small bar (which changes to ↔ to the left of the Internet Explorer icon, then drag to the left until you reach the Start button.

7. **Right-click in an empty section of the taskbar, point to Toolbars, then click Quick Launch to select it**
   The Quick Launch toolbar is added to the taskbar.

8. **Click the Start button, point to Settings, then click Taskbar & Start Menu**
   The Taskbar and Start Menu dialog box opens.

9. **Click the Auto hide check box to deselect it, then click Apply**

FIGURE E-18: **Removing a toolbar from the taskbar**

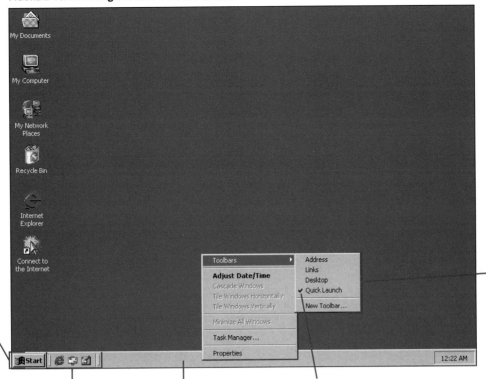

Default position
for the taskbar
is at the bottom
of the screen

Click to add or
remove a
toolbar

Quick Launch toolbar   Right-click a blank area   Checkmark indicates the
                         to open a shortcut menu   toolbar is currently displayed

FIGURE E-19: **Taskbar and Start Menu Properties dialog box**

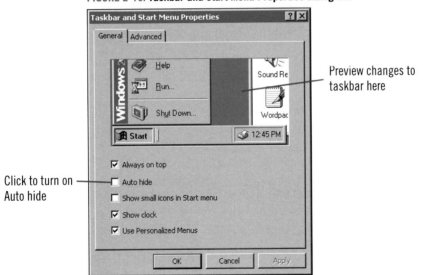

Preview changes to
taskbar here

Click to turn on
Auto hide

Starting a program as a taskbar button

You can change how Windows 2000 displays a program each time you start it using its Start menu shortcut. The program can open in a standard window, in a maximized window, or minimized as a button on the taskbar. Starting a program as a taskbar button is useful for a program you don't need maximized but want quick access to. To set a program to start in minimized form, click the Start button on the taskbar, point to Settings, click Taskbar & Start Menu, click the Advanced tab, then click Advanced. In the Start Menu folder, locate the shortcut to the program you want to start, and then click it. Click File on the menu bar, click Properties, then click the Shortcut tab. Click the Run list arrow, click Minimized, click OK, click File, click Close, then click OK again.

Windows 2000

Customizing the Start Menu

You can add shortcuts to programs, files, or folders to the Start menu, so that instead of having to navigate several levels of the Start menu to start a program or access a file, you can simply click the Start button and then click the item you want on the Start menu. Of course, if you add too many items to the Start menu, you defeat the purpose. To further customize the Start menu, you can display additional menu items on the Start menu, including Favorites, Log Off, and Administrative Tools, or extend a submenu from the Control Panel, Printers, or Dialup and Network Connections menu items on the Settings submenu. When you extend a menu item, a submenu appears with additional menu items. For example, when you extend the Control Panel, a submenu appears with a menu item for each icon in the Control Panel to provide easy access to each one. ◢ Because John uses the Wired Coffee logo so often in his work, he decides to add the file as a menu item to the Start menu.

Steps

QuickTip

To remove all recently used documents on the Documents submenu, click the Advanced tab in the Taskbar and Start Menu Properties dialog box, then click Clear.

1. Click the **Advanced tab** on the Taskbar and Start Menu Properties dialog box
   The Advanced tab appears, as shown in Figure E-20. You can use this tab to add and delete items from the Start menu.

2. Make sure your Project Disk is in the floppy disk drive, click **Add**, then click **Browse**
   The Browse For Folder dialog box opens, where you search for and select a file, folder, or program you want to add to the Start menu.

3. Click the **+ (plus sign) next to the drive containing your Project Disk**, then click the **+ next to the folder containing the Project files for this unit**

4. Click the **Wired Coffee Logo**, click **OK**, then click **Next**

5. Click the **Start Menu folder** in the Select Program Folder dialog box, click **Next** to accept the default name, then click **Finish**
   The shortcut will be placed in the Start Menu with the name Wired Coffee Logo. The Taskbar and Start Menu Properties dialog box appears with the Advanced tab in front.

6. In the Start Menu Settings section of the Advanced tab, click the **Display Favorites check box** to select it, then click **OK**
   This adds the Favorites menu to the Start menu.

QuickTip

You can also add an item to the Start menu by creating a shortcut to it (on the desktop or in Explorer, for example) and dragging the icon to the Start button.

7. Click the **Start button** on the taskbar
   Notice that the Favorites menu item appears below Programs, and the Wired Coffee logo appears at the top of the Start menu, as shown in Figure E-21. To open the Wired Coffee logo file, all you need to do is click the icon on the Start menu.

8. Press [Esc] to close the Start menu, right-click an empty area on the **taskbar**, click **Properties**, click the **Advanced tab**, then click **Remove**
   The Remove Shortcuts/Folders dialog box opens.

QuickTip

To start a program each time you start Windows 2000, click the Advanced tab, click Advanced, find the shortcut to the program you want to start each time you start Windows, then drag it to the Startup folder.

9. Click **Wired Coffee Logo** in the list of shortcuts and folders, click **Remove**, click **Yes** to confirm the deletion, click **Close**, click the **Display Favorites check box** to deselect it, then click **OK**
   The Taskbar and Start Menu Properties dialog box closes, and the menu items are removed from the Start menu.

FIGURE E-20: **Advanced tab of the Taskbar and Start Menu Properties dialog box**

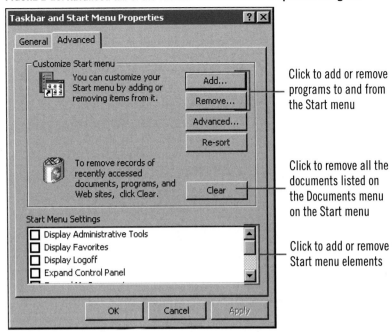

Click to add or remove programs to and from the Start menu

Click to remove all the documents listed on the Documents menu on the Start menu

Click to add or remove Start menu elements

FIGURE E-21: **Items added to the Start menu**

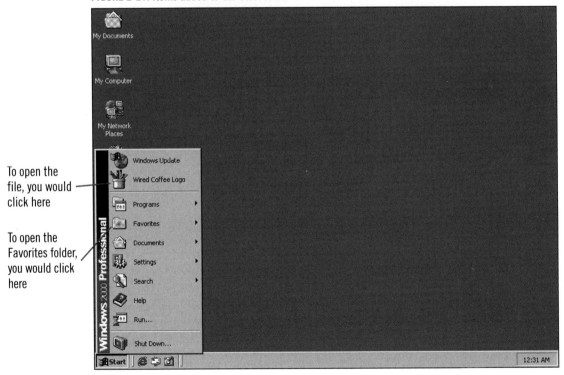

To open the file, you would click here

To open the Favorites folder, you would click here

Rearranging Start menu items

If you don't like the location of an item on the Start menu, you can move the item to a different location by dragging it to the desired location. A black line appears as you move the mouse pointer indicating the new location of the item. For example, to move the Windows Explorer menu item from the Program submenu to the Start menu, open the Start menu, then drag the Windows Explorer item to the Start menu.

Practice

► Concepts Review

Label each of the elements of the screen shown in Figure E-22.

FIGURE E-22

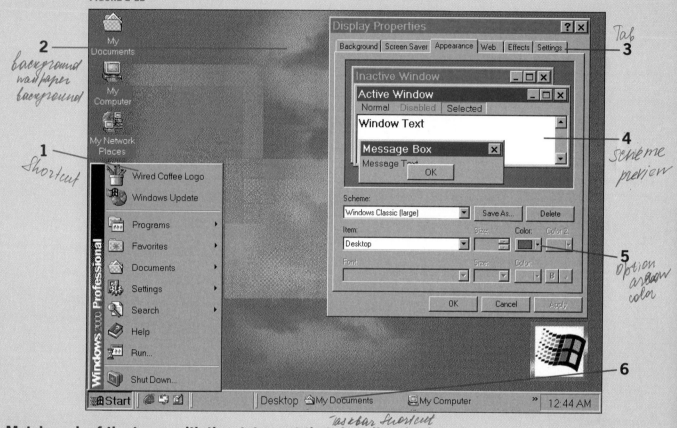

Handwritten annotations:
- 2 — background wallpaper background
- 1 — Shortcut
- 3 — Tab
- 4 — scheme preview
- 5 — Option arrow color
- 6 — Taskbar Shortcut

Match each of the terms with the statement that describes its function.

7. Patterns *d*
8. Screen saver *c*
9. Desktop schemes *b*
10. Control Panel *a*
11. Start menu *e*

a. Used to change properties of various computer elements
b. Preset combinations of desktop colors
c. Used to prevent damage to the monitor
d. Preset designs for the desktop
e. Used to start programs and open documents

Select the best answer from the list of choices.

12. To customize the Active Desktop, you need to open the
 a. Folder Options dialog box.
 b. Display Properties dialog box.
 c. Desktop Settings dialog box.
 d. Custom Desktop dialog box.

13. To change the pattern on the desktop from the Display window in the Control Panel, click the
 a. Background tab.
 b. Screen Saver tab.

c. Appearance tab.

d. Settings tab.

14. **An Internet document or Paint file used as a background is called a**

a. pattern.

b. wallpaper.

c. display.

d. shortcut.

15. **To set the date and time using the Control Panel, you double-click the**

a. Regional Settings icon.

b. Date/Time icon.

c. Scheduled Tasks icon.

d. System icon.

16. **A power failure when your computer is in this state can cause you to lose unsaved information.**

a. Sleep

b. Standby

c. Hibernation

d. Locked

▶ Skills Review

1. **Customize the Active Desktop.**

a. Right-click in an empty area on the desktop.

b. Point to Active Desktop, then click Customize My Desktop.

c. Click the Show Web content on my Active Desktop check box to select it.

d. Click Apply.

e. Click the Show Web content on my Active Desktop check box to deselect it.

f. Click Apply.

2. **Change the desktop background and screen saver settings.**

a. Click the Background tab in the Display Properties dialog box.

b. Click Greenstone in the Wallpaper section, then click Apply

c. Click the Screen Saver tab, click the Screen Saver list arrow, click 3D Pipes, then click Preview.

d. Move the mouse to end the Screen Saver preview.

e. Click the Screen Saver tab, click the Screen Saver list arrow, then click (None).

f. Click the Background tab, click (None) in the Wallpaper section, then click Apply.

3. **Change the desktop scheme.**

a. Click the Appearance tab.

b. Click the Item list arrow, then click Desktop.

c. Click any color you want for the desktop, then click Apply.

d. Click Save As, type **Fred**, then click OK.

e. Click Delete.

f. Click the Scheme list arrow, then click Windows Standard, then click OK.

4. **Set the date and time.**

a. Click the Start button, point to Settings, then click Control Panel.

b. Double-click the Date/Time icon.

c. Double-click the number of minutes.

d. Click the up arrow three times, then click Apply.

    e. Double-click the number of minutes.

    f. Click the Down Arrow button three times, then click OK.

5. Work with fonts.

    a. Double-click the Fonts icon in the Control Panel.

    b. Double-click a Times New Roman icon.

    c. Click Print, click Print again, click Done, then click the Back button on the toolbar.

6. Manage power options.

    a. Double-click the Power Options icon in the Control Panel.

    b. Click the Turn off monitor list arrow, then click After 1 min.

    c. Click Apply, then wait one minute without moving the mouse or pressing a key.

    d. Move the mouse to restore the desktop.

    e. Click the Turn off monitor list arrow, click Never, then click OK.

7. Add a scheduled task.

    a. Double-click the Scheduled Tasks icon in the Control Panel.

    b. Double-click the Add Scheduled Task icon, then click Next.

    c. Click Character Map, click Next, click the One time only option button, then click Next.

    d. Change the time to one minute ahead, select the current day, then click Next.

    e. Type your password, press [Tab], type your password again, then click Next.

    f. Click Finish, wait for the task to take place, then click the Close button on the program window.

    g. Right-click the Character Map icon, click Delete, then click Yes.

    h. Close the Scheduled Tasks window.

8. Customize the taskbar.

    a. Right-click the taskbar, point to Toolbars, then click Quick Launch to remove that toolbar from the taskbar.

    b. Click the Start button, point to Settings, then click Taskbar & Start Menu.

    c. Click the Auto hide check box to select it, then click OK.

    d. Move the mouse pointer to the bottom of the screen.

    e. Right-click the taskbar, point to Toolbars, then click Quick Launch to add the toolbar back to the taskbar.

    f. Click the Start button, point to Settings, then click Taskbar & Start Menu.

    g. Click the Auto hide check box, then click Apply.

9. Customize the Start menu.

    a. Click the Advanced tab.

    b. Click the Expand Control Panel check box to select it.

    c. Click Apply.

    d. Click the Start button, point to Settings, point to Control Panel, then press [Esc].

    e. Click the Expand Control Panel check box to deselect it, then click OK.

▶ Independent Challenges

1. You have been retained as a consultant by a large law firm that has just installed Windows 2000. The firm's employees need to be taught how to customize Windows 2000 to fit their needs. As you prepare your presentation, you decide to customize the display so it is easier for them to see. Make the following changes and be sure to change them back to the default setting or setup when you are finished.

   To complete this independent challenge:

    a. Open the Display Properties dialog box from the Control Panel.

    b. Change the background to a background of your choice.

    c. Set the screen saver for one minute so you can show them how it works without waiting too long.

    d. On the Appearance tab, set the scheme to High Contrast Black (extra large).

e. Save the scheme as *Demo*, then apply the changes.

f. Print the screen. (Press the Print Screen key to make a copy of the screen, open Paint, click Edit on the menu bar, click Paste to paste the screen into Paint, click Yes to paste the large image if necessary, click File on the menu bar, click Print, then click Print in the Print dialog box.)

g. Delete the Demo scheme, then select the Windows Standard scheme.

h. Set the screen saver for five minutes.

2. As the owner of a small optical laboratory, you want to abide by the Americans with Disabilities Act, which states that employers should make every reasonable effort to accommodate workers with disabilities. You have one worker who is visually impaired. Customize the Windows desktop for this employee so that it is easier to work in, desktop items are easier to see and read, and desktop colors are strongly contrasted with each other, but still easy on the eyes. Save this custom configuration so that this employee can use it when necessary.

To complete this independent challenge:

a. Open the Display Properties dialog box from the Control Panel.

b. Change the Desktop color to red.

c. Change the font size of menu text to 12.

d. Change the size and color of the text in the title bar for the Active Window to 24 and light blue (the second color in the fifth row).

e. Change the font style for the message box to bold.

f. Save the custom configuration as *Visible*.

g. Apply the scheme.

h. Print the screen. (See Independent Challenge 1, Step f for screen printing instructions.)

i. Delete the Visible scheme.

j. Select the Windows Standard.

3. As the system administrator of a small computer network for a chain of specialty book stores, you want to make sure all the computers run efficiently. To accomplish this goal, you want to set up a scheduled task to clean up the hard disk drives of all the computers on a weekly basis.

To complete this independent challenge:

a. Open the Scheduled Tasks window from the Control Panel.

b. Schedule the Disk Cleanup program as a task.

c. Schedule the task for a weekly time period.

d. Set the time one minute ahead of the current time.

e. When the Disk Cleanup program appears, print the screen. (See Independent Challenge 1, Step f for screen printing instructions.)

f. Delete the Disk Cleanup scheduled task.

4. As the owner of Lew's Office Supply, you need to make your business computers easier for your employees to use. One way to do this is to add programs to the Start menu. Your employees use WordPad and Paint almost exclusively, and they also use the same documents quite often.

To complete this independent challenge:

a. Add a WordPad shortcut to the Start menu. (*Hint*: Select WordPad.exe located in the Accessories folder within the Program Files folder.)

b. Add a Paint shortcut to the Start menu. (*Hint*: Select MSpaint.exe located in the same place as WordPad.)

c. Create a memo to employees about the upcoming company picnic using WordPad, then save the memo on your Project Disk as *Company Picnic Memo*.

d. Close the memo and WordPad.

e. Add the Company Picnic Memo to the Start menu.

f. Open the Company Picnic Memo from the Start menu.

g. Print the screen. (See Independent Challenge 1, Step f for screen printing instructions.)

h. Remove all the shortcuts you created.

► Visual Workshop

Re-create the screen shown in Figure E-23, which displays the Windows desktop, then print the screen. (See Independent Challenge 1, Step f for screen printing instructions.)

FIGURE E-23

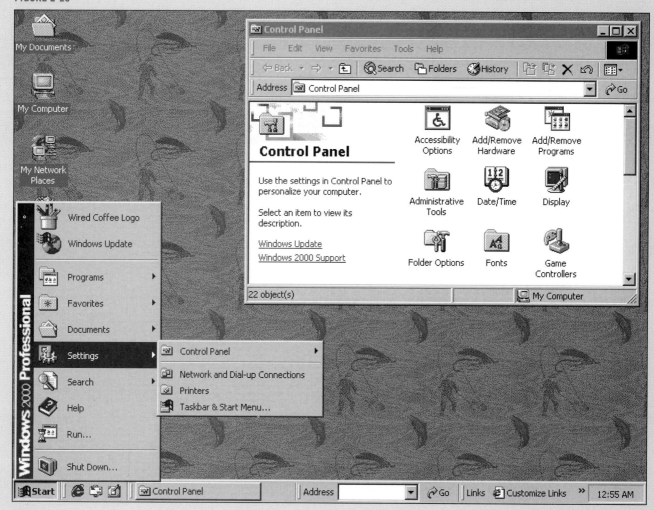

Unit F

Exploring

the Internet with Microsoft Internet Explorer

Objectives

► **Understand Web browsers**
► **Start Internet Explorer**
► **Explore the browser window**
► **Open a Web page and follow links**
► **Add a Web page to the Favorites list**
► **Make a Web page available offline**
► **Change your home page and add a link button**
► **Search the Web**
► **Print a Web page**

A valuable component included with Windows 2000 is Microsoft Internet
Explorer 5, a software program that helps you access the World Wide Web.
In this unit, you will learn about the benefits of the World Wide Web,
examine the basic features of Internet Explorer 5, and access Web pages.
This unit requires a connection to the Internet. If your computer is not
connected to the Internet, check with your instructor or technical support
person to see if it's possible for you to connect. If not, simply read the
lessons to learn about using Internet Explorer. ✎ Wired Coffee
Company is a growing business that wants to take advantage of Internet
technology. John uses Internet Explorer to open the company Web page
and find information related to the coffee business.

Understanding Web Browsers

[handwritten: soft wear programm Internet Explore, Netscape Navigator]

The Internet is a worldwide collection of more than 40 million computers from all over the world linked together to share information. The Internet's physical structure includes telephone lines, cables, satellites, and other telecommunications media, as depicted in Figure F-1. Using the Internet, computer users can share many types of information, including text, graphics, sounds, videos, and computer programs. The **World Wide Web** (also known as the Web or WWW) is a part of the Internet that consists of Web sites located on different computers around the world. A **Web site** contains Web pages that are linked together to make looking for information on the Internet easier. **Web pages** are documents that contain highlighted words, phrases, and graphics, called hyperlinks (or simply links) that open other Web pages when you click them. Some Web pages contain frames. A **frame** is a separate window within a Web page. Frames give you the ability to show more than one Web page at a time. Figure F-2 shows a sample Web page. **Web browsers** are software programs that you use to "browse the Web," or access and display Web pages. Browsers make the Web easy to navigate by providing a graphical, point-and-click environment. This unit features Internet Explorer 5, a popular browser from Microsoft that comes with Windows 2000. Netscape Communicator is another popular browser. John realizes that there are many uses for Internet Explorer in his company.

[handwritten left margin: Upload from my comp. Download to my comp. заполн. пуфа завершил]

[handwritten left margin: Home page.]

Display Web pages from all over the world
John can look at Web pages for business purposes, such as checking the pages of other coffee companies to see how they are marketing their products.

Display Web content on your desktop
John can make his desktop look and work like a Web page. John can display Web content, such as the Microsoft Investor Ticker, ESPN SportsZone, Expedia Maps Address Finder, or MSNBC Weather Map, directly on his desktop and have the content updated automatically.

Use links to move from one Web page to another
John can click text or graphical links (which appear as either underlined text or as graphics) to move from one Web page to another, investigating different sources for information. Because a Web page can contain links to any location on the Internet, you can jump to Web pages all over the World.

Play audio and video clips
John can click links that play audio and video clips, such as the sound of coffee grinding or a video of workers picking coffee beans. He can also play continuous audio and video broadcasts through radio and televisions stations over the Internet.

Search the Web for information
John can use search programs that allow him to look for information about any topic throughout the world.

Make favorite Web pages available offline
John can create a list of his favorite Web pages to make it easy for him to return to them at a later time. He can also make a Web page available offline. When he makes a Web page available offline, he can read its content when his computer is not connected to the Internet.

Print the text and graphics on Web pages
If John finds some information or images that he would like to print, he can easily print all or part of the Web page, including the graphics.

FIGURE F-1: Structure of the Internet

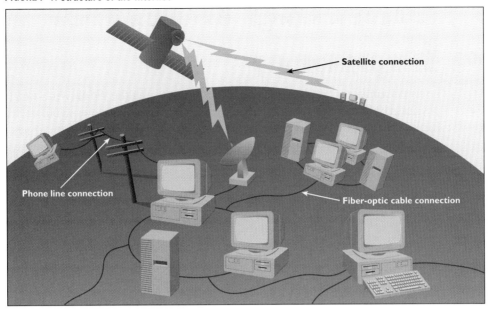

FIGURE F-2: Sample World Wide Web page

Title of Web page and name of browser

Text hyperlink

Graphic hyperlink

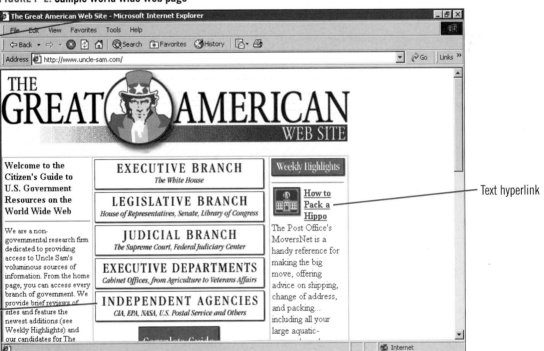

The history of the Internet and World Wide Web

The Internet has its roots in the Advanced Research Projects Agency Network (ARPANET), which the United States Department of Defense started in 1969. In 1986, the National Science Foundation formed NSFNET, which replaced ARPANET. NSFNET expanded the foundation of the U.S. portion of the Internet with high-speed, long distance data lines. In 1991, the U.S. Congress expanded the capacity and speed of the Internet further and opened it up to commercial use. The Internet is now accessible in over 300 countries. The World Wide Web was developed in Switzerland in 1991 to make finding documents on the Internet easier. Software programs designed to access the Web (Web browsers) use "point-and-click" interfaces. The first such Web browser, Mosaic, was introduced at the University of Illinois in 1993. Recently, Microsoft Internet Explorer and Netscape Communicator have become the two most popular Web browsers.

Starting Internet Explorer

Internet Explorer is a Web browser that you use to search the World Wide Web (you also need a physical connection to the Internet). When you install Windows 2000, an icon for Internet Explorer will appear on the desktop and a button for it will appear on the Quick Launch toolbar on the taskbar. You can also make your desktop look and work like a Web page. You can display a Web page or custom Web content directly on your desktop and have the content updated automatically. The specialized Web content, known as a **channel,** is designed to deliver content from the Internet to your computer. To display Web content on your desktop, simply right-click the desktop, point to Active Desktop, then click Show Web Content. ◀▬▬ Before John can take advantage of the many features of the World Wide Web, he must start Internet Explorer.

Trouble?
If your computer is not connected to the Internet, check with your instructor or technical person to see if it's possible for you to connect.

1. Establish a connection to the Internet via the network or telephone
   If you connect to the Internet through a network, follow your instructor's or technical support person's directions to establish your connection. If you connect by telephone, create a new connection using the Connection Wizard to establish your connection or use an existing Dial-Up Networking connection.

2. Locate the **Internet Explorer icon** 🖉 on your desktop
   The icon will probably appear on the left side of your screen, as shown in Figure F-3, but it doesn't matter where it is or even if it is not on your desktop. There are several different ways to start Internet Explorer, depending on your circumstances. If you have upgraded from Internet Explorer 4 or Windows 98, the desktop Channel Bar and the View Channels button on the Quick Launch toolbar are also available on the desktop.

Trouble?
If the Internet Explorer icon isn't on your desktop, click the Start button, point to programs, then click Internet Explorer.

3. Double-click 🖉 or click the **Launch Internet Explorer Browser button** 🖉 on the Quick Launch toolbar
   Internet Explorer opens. If you connect to the Internet through a network, follow your instructor's or technical support person's directions to log on. If you connect to the Internet by telephone using a Dial-Up Networking connection, you need to enter your user name and password to connect to the Internet. See your instructor or technical support person for this information.

4. If necessary, enter your **user name**, press **[Tab]**, enter your **password**, then click **Connect**
   Upon completion of the dial-up connection, you are connected to the Internet (unless an error message appears).

5. If necessary, click the **Maximize button** 🔲 to maximize the Internet Explorer window
   Internet Explorer displays a Web page, as shown in Figure F-4. It's okay if the Web page on your screen is not the same as the one shown in Figure F-4. Later in this unit, you will learn how to change the Web page that appears when you first start Internet Explorer. Continue with the next lesson to view the various elements of the browser window.

FIGURE F-3: Windows desktop

Your desktop icons might be different

Internet Explorer icon

Click to establish a connection to the Internet

Quick Launch toolbar

Launch Internet Explorer Browser button

FIGURE F-4: Web page featuring the Microsoft Corporation

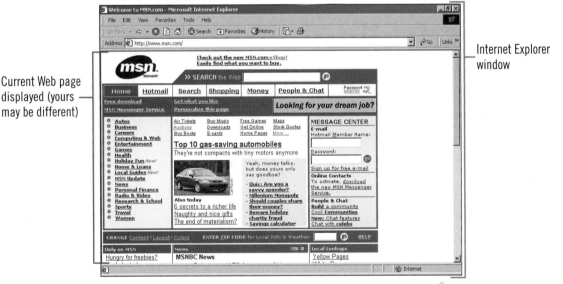

Current Web page displayed (yours may be different)

Internet Explorer window

Connecting to the Internet

Sometimes connecting your computer to the Internet can be the most difficult part of getting started. The Connection Wizard simplifies the process, whether you want to set up a new connection using an existing account or you want to select an **Internet Service provider (ISP)**—a company that provides access to the Internet for a fee—and set up a new account. You might need to obtain connection information from your ISP or your system administrator. To get connected to the Internet using the Connection Wizard, double-click the Internet Connection Wizard icon on the desktop or click the Start button, point to Programs, point to

Accessories, point to Communications, click Internet Connection Wizard, and then follow the step-by-step instructions. If you are on a network, you might need to use a **proxy server**, which provides a secure barrier between your network and the Internet and prevents other people from seeing confidential information on your network. To configure your computer to use a proxy server, click View on the menu bar, click Internet Options, click the Connections tab, and click LAN Settings. See your instructor or technical support person for setting details to connect to your network.

Windows 2000

Exploring the Browser Window

The elements of the Internet Explorer program window, shown in Figure F-5, allow you to view, print, and search for information on the Internet. ◢▬▬ Before exploring the Web, John decides to familiarize himself with the components of the browser window.

Details

He notes the following features:

 The **title bar** at the top of the page displays the name of the Web page and the name of the browser you are using.

 The **menu bar** provides access to a variety of commands, much like other Windows programs.

 The **toolbar** provides buttons for easy access to the most commonly used commands in Internet Explorer. See Table F-1 for a description of each toolbar button. These button commands are also available on the menus.

 The **Address bar** displays the address of the current Web page or the contents of a local or network computer drive. The **Web address**, like a postal address, is a unique place on the Internet where you can locate a Web page. The Web address is also referred to as the **URL**, which stands for **Uniform Resource Locator**.

 The **Links bar** displays link buttons to Web pages on the Internet or documents on a local or network drive.

 The **status indicator** (the Internet Explorer logo) spins to indicate a new Web page is loading.

 The **document window** displays the current Web page or the contents of a local or network computer drive. You may need to scroll down the page to view the entire contents.

 The **vertical scroll bar** allows you to move up or down the current Web page. The **scroll box** indicates your relative position within the Web page.

 The **status bar** displays information about your connection progress with new Web pages that you open, including notification that you have connected to another site and the percentage of information that has been transferred. This bar also displays the locations of the links in the document window as you move your mouse pointer over them.

FIGURE F-5: Elements of the Internet Explorer program window

Menu bar

Toolbar

Address bar

Document window

Status indicator

Title bar

Links bar

Scroll box

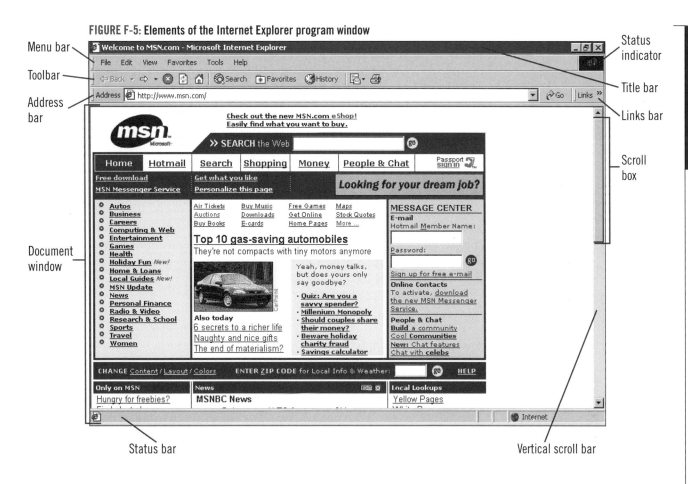

Status bar

Vertical scroll bar

TABLE F-1: Internet Explorer toolbar buttons

button	name	description	button	name	description
⟵ Back ▾	**Back**	Opens the previous page	⊛	**Favorites**	Opens the Favorites list
⇒ ▾	**Forward**	Open the next page	🕘	**History**	Opens the History list
⊗	**Stop**	Stops loading a page	📄	**Mail**	Displays options for working with Mail and News
🔃	**Refresh**	Refreshes the contents of the current page	🖨	**Print**	Prints the current Web page
🏠	**Home**	Opens the Home page	↪	**Go**	Displays the current Web address
🔍	**Search**	Opens the Search Bar			

CLUES TO USE

Getting Help with Internet Explorer

If you are new to the Internet or to Internet Explorer, you can take a tour to learn how Internet Explorer can help you efficiently browse the Web. To take the tour, click Help on the menu bar, click Tour, then follow the step-by-step instructions. If you want to get information on a general topic or a specific task, you can find the information you are looking for in Microsoft Internet Explorer Help. To access Help, click Help on the menu bar, then click Contents and Index. The Microsoft Internet Explorer Help window appears and works in the same way the Windows 2000 Help does. If you need more help, you can probably find what you need about Internet Explorer on the Web by clicking Help on the menu bar, then clicking Online Support. You can also get tips on how to use Internet Explorer more effectively. To display a tip, click Help on the menu bar, then click Tip of the Day. A Tip pane appears at the bottom of the Internet Explorer window. Read the tip, then click the *Next tip* link to display another tip. Click the Close button in the Tip pane to close the pane.

Opening a Web Page and Following Links

You can open a Web page quickly and easily using the Address bar. If you change your mind, or the Web page takes too long to **download**, or open on the screen, you can click the Stop button on the toolbar. If you stop a Web page while it is downloading and the page doesn't completely open, you can click the Refresh button on the toolbar to update the screen. Web pages can be connected to each other through links, which you can follow to obtain more information about a topic, as shown in Figure F-6. A link can move you to another location on the same Web page, or it can open a different Web page altogether. To follow a link, simply click the highlighted word, phrase, or graphic (the cursor changes to the hand pointer when it is over a link). ◀━━ John contracted a Web development company to create a Web site for Wired Coffee. He wants to access the Web site and follow some of the links in order to give feedback to the developer. John knows that the URL for the Web page is http://www.course.com/illustrated/wired/.

1. Click anywhere in the Address bar
The current address is highlighted and any text you type will replace the current address. If the current address isn't highlighted, select the entire address.

2. Type www.course.com/illustrated/wired/, then press [Enter] or click the Go button on the toolbar
Be sure to type the address exactly as it appears. When you enter a Web address, you don't have to type *http://* in the Address bar. Internet Explorer inserts it for you. The status bar displays the connection process. After downloading for a few seconds, the Web page appears in the document window.

3. Locate the <u>menu</u> link on the main page, and move the mouse pointer over the link, as shown in Figure F-7
When you move the mouse pointer over a link, the mouse pointer changes to 🖑. This indicates that the text or graphic is a link. The address of the link appears in the Status bar.

4. Click the <u>menu</u> link
The status indicator spins as the new Web page is accessed and opens. The menu Web page appears in the document window.

5. Move the mouse pointer over the **Wired Coffee logo** (the image in the upper-left corner), then click it
The Wired Coffee Company page appears in the document window.

6. Click the **Back button** ⇦ Back ▾ on the toolbar
The previous Web page appears in the document window.

7. Click the **Forward button** ⇨ ▾ on the toolbar
The Company page appears in the document window again. You could have also clicked the Wired Coffee logo link to return to the Company page again.

8. Click the **Back button list arrow** ⇦ Back ▾ on the toolbar, then click **Wired Coffee Home Page**
The Wired Coffee Home Page appears in the document window. Notice that when you have already visited a link, the color of the link changes.

Trouble?
If you receive an error message, type one of the URLs listed in Table F-2 instead to open a Web page, then follow a link.

QuickTip
You can browse folders on your hard disk drive and run programs from the Address bar. Click anywhere in the Address bar, then type the location of the folder or program. For example, typing **C:\My Documents** opens the My Documents folder.

QuickTip
To expand the document window to the full screen, click View on the menu bar, then click Full Screen. Press [F11] to return to the normal view.

FIGURE F-6: Web pages connected through links

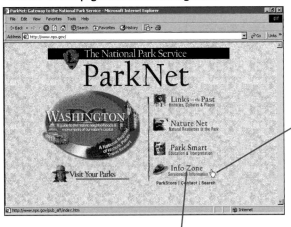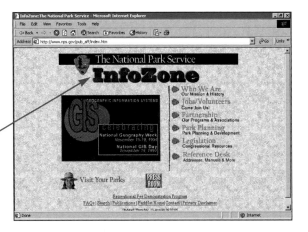

Graphic hyperlink; click to jump
to the InfoZone Web page

FIGURE F-7: Wired Coffee Company Web page

Graphic hyperlink
appears without
any distinguishing
marks

Text hyperlinks
appear in color
with an underline
(your color may be
different)

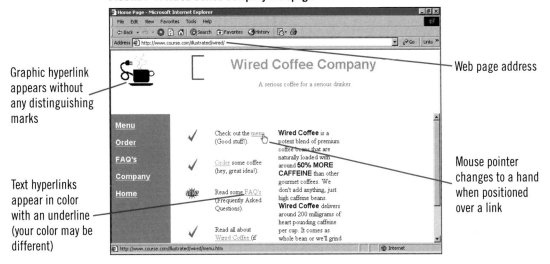

Web page address

Mouse pointer
changes to a hand
when positioned
over a link

TABLE F-2: URLs of Web sites dealing with coffee

name of company	url
Boyd Coffee Company	*http://www.boyds.com*
Peet's Coffee & Tea	*http://www.peets.com*
Seattle's Best Coffee	*http://www.seabest.com*
Starbucks Coffee	*http://www.starbucks.com*

Understanding a Web address

The address for a Web page is referred to as a URL.
Each Web page has a unique URL that begins with
"http" (HyperText Transfer Protocol) followed by a
colon, two slashes, and the name of the Web site. The
Web site is the computer where the Web pages are
located. At the end of the Web site name, another

slash may appear, followed by one or more folders
and a filename. For example, in the address,
http://www.course.com/illustrated/wired/wired_main.
htm, the name of the Web site is *www.course.com*; a
folder at that site is called */illustrated/wired*; and
within the wired folder is a file called *wired_main.htm*.

Adding a Web Page to the Favorites List

Rather than memorizing the URLs or keeping a handwritten list of Web pages you want to return to, you can use a feature called **Favorites** to store and organize the addresses. When you display a Web page in your document window that you want to display again at a later time, you can add the Web page to your Favorites list. Once you add the Web page to the Favorites list, you can return to the page by opening your Favorites list and selecting the link to the page you want. ✎ John wants to add the Wired Coffee Web page to his Favorites list.

Steps

QuickTip

To view Web pages offline, click File on the menu bar, then click Work Offline. If you want to access other Web pages, you'll need to reconnect to the Internet.

1. Click **Favorites** on the menu bar, then click **Add to Favorites**

The Add Favorites dialog box opens, as shown in Figure F-8. You have the option to make the Web page available for offline viewing. When you make a Web page available for **offline viewing**, the page is copied to your computer for later viewing when your Internet connection is disconnected. This is helpful when you want to read a Web page without having to worry about your connect time.

2. In the Name text box, select the current text, type **Wired Coffee Company**, then click **OK**

The Web page is added to your Favorites list with the name "Wired Coffee Company."

Trouble?

URLs may be case-sensitive, meaning that you must type them exactly as they appear, using uppercase and lower-case letters.

3. Click anywhere in the Address bar, type **www.course.com**, then press **[Enter]**

When you type a Web address in the Address bar, a feature called **AutoComplete** suggests possible matches from previous entries you have made for Web addresses. If a suggestion in the list matches what you want to enter, click the suggestion from the Address bar list.

4. Click the **Favorites button** 🗔 on the toolbar

The Explorer Bar opens on the left side of the document window and displays the Favorites list. The Favorites list contains several folders, including a Links folder, a Media folder, and individual favorite Web pages that come with Windows 2000.

QuickTip

You can import favorites, know as bookmarks, from Netscape Navigator by clicking File on the menu bar, then clicking Import and Export.

5. Click **Wired Coffee Company** in the Favorites list

The Wired Coffee Company Web page appears in the document window, as shown in Figure F-9. The Favorites list also includes folders to help you organize your Favorites list. You can click a folder icon in the Favorites list to display its contents.

6. Click the **Links folder** in the Favorites list

The Favorites list in the Links folder expands and appears in the Explorer Bar, as shown in Figure F-10. To open a favorite in the Links folder, position the mouse pointer over the favorite you want to open (the mouse pointer changes to a hand and the favorite appears underlined), then click the mouse button.

QuickTip

To start Internet Explorer and open a favorite, click the Start button, point to Favorites, then click a favorite Web page.

7. Click the **Links folder** in the Favorites list again

The Favorites list in the Links folder collapse to display only the Links folder icon. If you no longer use a favorite, you can delete it from the Favorites list.

FIGURE F-8: Add Favorites dialog box

Click to make Web page available offline

Displays the name of the Web page as it will appear in your Favorites list

Click to specify offline settings

Click to save the current page in another folder

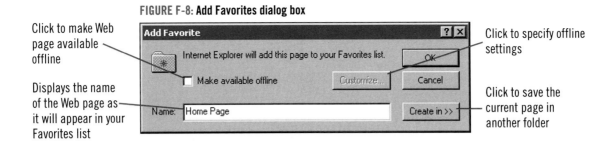

FIGURE F-9: Internet Explorer window with the Favorites list

Explorer Bar displaying the Favorites list

Individual Favorite Web pages

Click to close Explorer Bar

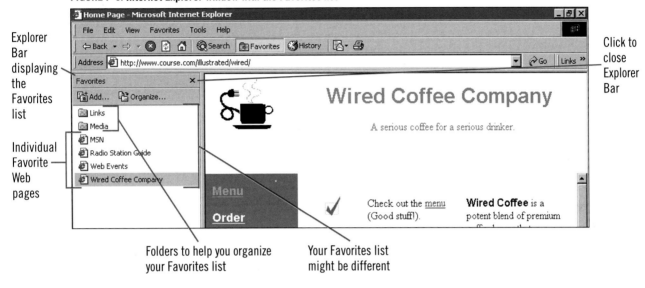

Folders to help you organize your Favorites list

Your Favorites list might be different

FIGURE F-10: Links folder with Favorites displayed

Click to display or collapse the list of Favorites in the Links folder

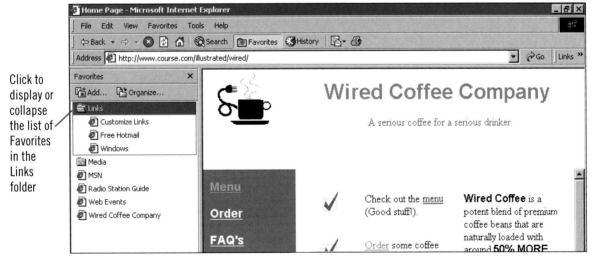

Organizing favorites

If your list of favorites gets long, you can delete favorites you don't want anymore or move favorites into folders. To delete and move your favorites, click the Favorites menu, click Organize Favorites, select one or more files from the Favorites list, then click the Delete or Move to Folder buttons. If you want to add a new folder in your Favorites list, click the Create Folder button, type the new folder name, then press Enter. If you prefer to use another name for a favorite, you can select the favorite you want to rename, click the Rename button, type the new name, then press [Enter]. When you're finished making changes, you can click Close to exit.

Making a Web Page Available Offline

When you make a Web page available offline, you can read its content when your computer is not connected to the network and Internet. For example, you can view Web pages on your laptop computer when you don't have a network or Internet connection. Or you might want to read Web pages at home but do not want to tie up a phone line. When you make a Web page available offline, the latest online version of your Web page is saved, or **synchronized**, to your hard disk drive for offline viewing. You can specify how much content you want available, such as an individual Web page or a Web page and all its links, and choose how you want to update that content on your computer. ✎ John wants to make the Wired Coffee Company Web site on the Favorites list available for offline viewing. After viewing the offline version of the Web site, John updates the offline version to make sure he has the latest data.

QuickTip

To make the current Web page available offline, click Favorites on the menu bar, click Add to Favorites, click the Make available offline check box to select it, click Custom, follow the wizard instructions, click Finish, then click OK.

QuickTip

When you choose to work offline, Internet Explorer starts in offline mode until you click File on the menu bar, then click Work Offline again to clear the check mark.

QuickTip

To specify a schedule for updating that page and how much content to download, click Properties. You can also click Setup to schedule updating when you log on to your computer and when your computer goes on idle, no activity.

1. Click **Favorites** on the menu bar, then click **Organize Favorites**
   The Organize Favorites dialog box opens.

2. In the Favorites list, click **Wired Coffee Company**
   Status information about the Wired Coffee Company favorite appears in the Organize Favorites dialog box, as shown in Figure F-11.

3. Click the **Make available offline check box** to select it, then click **Close**
   The Synchronize dialog box opens and the Wired Coffee Company Web page is synchronized; the latest version of your Web page is saved to your hard disk drive for offline viewing.

4. Click **File** on the menu bar, then click **Work Offline**
   Internet Explorer is disconnected from the network and Internet.

5. Click the **Home button** 🏠 on the toolbar, then click **Wired Coffee Company** in the Favorites list
   When you access the Wired Coffee Company Web site in offline mode, Internet Explorer displays the offline version of the Web page that is on your hard disk drive. You can view any of the offline Web pages, but if you click a link to Web page not available offline, Internet Explorer reconnects you to the network and Internet.

6. Click **File** on the menu bar, then click **Work Offline**
   When the connection to the network and Internet is re-established, you can synchronize to the latest online version of the Wired Coffee Web page to update the offline version on your hard disk drive.

7. Click **Tools** on the menu bar, then click **Synchronize**
   The Items to Synchronize dialog box opens, as shown in Figure F-12. You can select which Web pages or files you want to synchronize and specify when and how you want them to be updated.

8. Click the **Wired Coffee Company check box** to select it if necessary, deselect all other check boxes, then click **Synchronize**
   The Wired Coffee Company Web page is re-synchronized with the latest online version of the Web page to your hard disk drive and ready for offline viewing.

9. Right-click **Wired Coffee Company** in the Favorites list, click **Delete**, click **Yes**, then click the **Close button** in the Explorer Bar
   The Wired Coffee Company Web page is deleted from the Favorites list, and the Explorer Bar closes.

FIGURE F-11: Organize Favorites dialog box

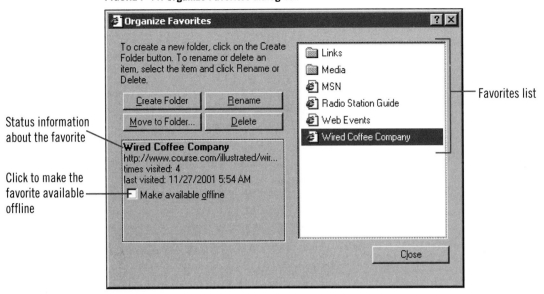

Status information about the favorite

Click to make the favorite available offline

Favorites list

FIGURE F-12: Items to Synchronize dialog box

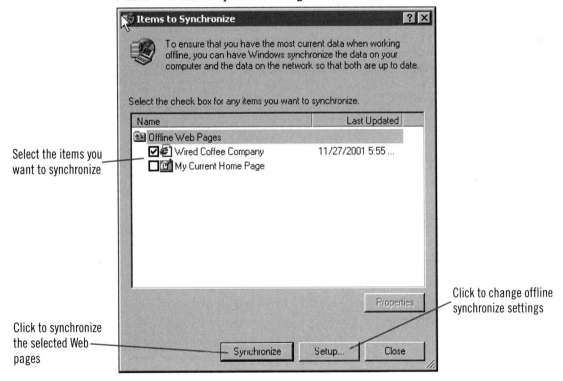

Select the items you want to synchronize

Click to change offline synchronize settings

Click to synchronize the selected Web pages

CLUES TO USE

Saving a Web page

If you want to view a Web page offline, and you don't need to update the content, you can save the page on your computer. There are several ways you can save the Web page, from just saving the text to saving all of the graphics and text needed to display that page as it appears on the Web. To save a Web page, click File on the menu bar, then click Save As. Specify the drive and folder in which you want to save the file, type the name you want for the file, click the Save As Type list arrow, select the file format type you want, then click Save. When you save a complete Web page, Internet Explorer saves all the graphic and text elements in a folder.

Changing Your Home Page and Adding a Link Button

Your **home page** in Internet Explorer is the page that opens when you start the program. When you first install Internet Explorer, the default home page is the Microsoft Network (MSN) Web site. If you want a different page to appear when you start Internet Explorer (and whenever you click the Home button), you can change your home page. You can choose one of the millions of Web pages available through the Internet or you can select a particular file on your hard drive. You can also change the Web pages associated with the buttons on the Links bar. ➤ John decides to change his home page to the Wired Coffee Web page and add a link button to the Links bar.

Steps

QuickTip

You will change your home page back to http://www.msn.com in the Skills Review exercise at the end of this unit. If you want to change it back at any other time, type *www.msn.com* in the Address bar, press [Enter], then complete Steps 1 through 3 from this lesson.

1. **Click Tools on the menu bar, click Internet Options, then click the General tab if necessary**
   The Internet Options dialog box opens, as shown in Figure F-13. The Internet Options dialog box allows you to change a variety of Internet Explorer settings and preferences. See Table F-3 for a description of each tab.

2. **In the Home page section, click Use Current**
   The address of the Wired Coffee Company Web page appears in the Address text box.

3. **Click OK**
   The Home button on the toolbar is now associated with the current Web page, Wired Coffee Company.

4. **Click the FAQ's link, then click the Home button 🏠 on the toolbar**
   The home page appears in the document window.

QuickTip

You can move the Links bar by dragging it to a new location.

5. **Double-click the word Links on the Links bar**
   The Links bar opens and may hide the Address bar. The Links bar contains buttons with links to Web pages. You can drag a link on a page or a Web site address in the Address bar to a blank area on the Links bar to create a new Links button.

6. **Drag the Order link on the main page to the left of the first button on the Links bar (the mouse pointer changes to a black bar to indicate the placement of the button), then release the mouse button**
   A new link button appears on the Links bar with the name associated with the Web site, as shown in Figure F-14. You can delete or change the properties of a links button. Simply right-click the link button you want to change, then click the Delete or Properties command on the shortcut menu.

7. **Click the Order button on the Links bar, then click the Back button ⇦ Back ▾ on the toolbar**

8. **Right-click the Order button on the Links bar, click Delete, then click Yes**
   The home page appears in the document window.

9. **Position the mouse pointer over the word Links, then drag the Links bar to the right to hide it**

FIGURE F-13: Internet Options dialog box

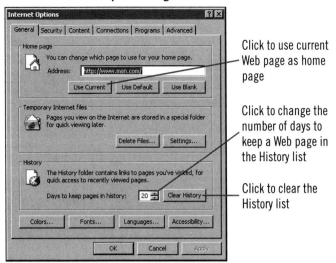

Click to use current Web page as home page

Click to change the number of days to keep a Web page in the History list

Click to clear the History list

FIGURE F-14: New button on the Links bar

Address bar (double-click to open)

New button

TABLE F-3: Internet Options dialog box tabs

tab	allows you to
General	Change your home page, temporary file settings, and history settings
Security	Select security levels for different parts of the Internet
Content	Set up a rating system for Internet content and personal information for typing Web addresses and buying items over the Internet
Connections	Change connection settings (phone and network)
Programs	Choose which programs (Mail, News, and Internet call) you want to use with Internet Explorer
Advanced	Change individual settings for browsing, multimedia, security, printing, and searching

Viewing and maintaining a History list

Sometimes you run across a great Web site and simply forget to add it to your Favorites list. With Internet Explorer there's no need to try to remember all the sites you've visited. The History feature keeps track of where you've been by date, site, most visited, or order visited today. To view the History list, click the History button 🕓 on the toolbar and click a day or week in the Explorer Bar to expand the list of Web sites visited. Because the History list can grow to occupy a large amount of space on your hard drive, it's important that you control the length of time Web sites are retained in the list. Internet Explorer deletes the History list periodically based on the settings you specify in the General tab of the Internet Options dialog box, as shown in Figure F-13.

search criteria

Searching the Web

You can find all kinds of information on the Web. The best way to find information is to use a search engine. A **search engine** is a program you access through a Web site and use to search through a collection of Internet information to find what you are looking for. There are many search engines available on the Web, such as Yahoo! and Excite. When performing a search, the search engine compares the words or phrases, known as **keywords**, you submit with words the search engine has found on various Web sites on the Internet. If it finds your keywords in the stored database, the matched sites are listed on a Web page (these matched sites are sometimes called **hits**). The company who manages the search engine determines what information is stored in their database, so search results for different search engines will vary. ➤ John wants to search for other coffee-related Web sites to check out the competition.

Steps 1 2 3 4

QuickTip

To customize the search options, click the Customize button in the Explorer Bar, click the option button to use the Search Assistant or one search engine, select the search options you want, then click OK or Update.

1. Click the **Search button** 🔍 on the toolbar

A search engine appears in the Explorer Bar, as shown in Figure F-15. In this case, the search engine is MSN Web Search; your search engine might be different. If you prefer another search engine, you can choose the search engine you want to use from the custom search options.

2. Click the **Find a web page option button** in the Explorer Bar if necessary

You can select search options to find a person's or business address, display a list of links to previous searches, and find a map for a specific address. Each search option requires different search criteria, which is information related to what you want to find. To search for a Web page with the information you are looking for, you need to enter a keyword or words (a word or phrase that best describes what you want to retrieve) in the search text box. The more specific you are with your search criteria, the better list of matches you'll receive from the search engine.

3. In the Find a Web page containing text box, type **coffee imports**

Now you're ready to start the search.

QuickTip

To search for other items using a search engine, such as a file, computer, or person, click the <u>Files or Folders</u> link, <u>Computers</u> link, or <u>People</u> link in the Explorer Bar.

4. Click **Search** in the Explorer Bar

The search engine retrieves and displays a list of Web sites that match your criteria, as shown in Figure F-16. The total number of Web sites found is listed at the top. The search results appear in decreasing order of relevance. The percentage next to each Web site indicates the degree of relevance. If the search results return too many hits, you should narrow down the search by adding more keywords. As you add more keywords, the search engine will find fewer Web pages that contain all of those words. See Table F-4 for other techniques to narrow down a search.

QuickTip

To perform a new search, click the New button in the Explorer Bar.

5. Click any **link** to a Web site in the list of matches

The Web site that you opened appears in the right pane of the document window. You can follow links to other pages on this Web site or jump to other Web sites. Once you are finished, close the Explorer Bar.

6. Click **Close button** ✖ in the Explorer Bar

The Explorer Bar closes.

QuickTip

To find text on the current Web page, click Edit on the menu bar, click Find (on This Page), type the text you want to find, then click Find Next.

7. Click the **Home button** 🏠 on the toolbar

John returns to the Wired Coffee Company home page.

FIGURE F-15: Explorer Bar with a search engine

Click to change
search engine

Click to select a
search type

Type search
criteria here

Click to search for
other items

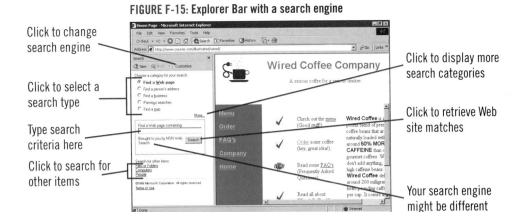

Click to display more
search categories

Click to retrieve Web
site matches

Your search engine
might be different

FIGURE F-16: Search engine results

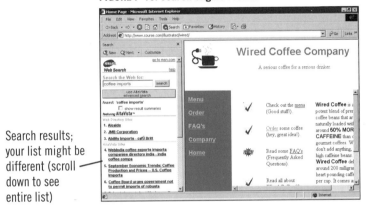

Search results;
your list might be
different (scroll
down to see
entire list)

TABLE F-4: Techniques to narrow down a search

technique	example
Use descriptive, specific words	Beaches surfing pacific
Use plain English sentences	Surfing beaches on the pacific ocean
Place exact phrases and proper names in quotes	"Sunset beach"
Use "+" sign for words your results *must* contain	Surf + beach
Use "−" sign for words your results should *not* contain	Surf + beach - Atlantic
Use AND to find results with all words	Surf AND sea AND sand
Use OR to find results with at least one word	Surf OR beach

CLUES TO USE

Searching for people on the Web

Internet Explorer includes several directory services to help
you find people you know who may have access to the
Internet (one service, Bigfoot, is shown in Figure F-17). To
find a person on the Internet, click the Start button, point to
Search, click For People, select the directory service you want
to use, type the person's name, and click Find Now. Each
directory service accesses different databases on the Internet,
so if you don't find the person you want using the first service
you use, try looking with a different directory service.

FIGURE F-17: Find People dialog box

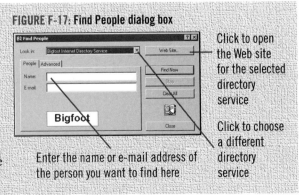

Click to open
the Web site
for the selected
directory
service

Click to choose
a different
directory
service

Enter the name or e-mail address of
the person you want to find here

Printing a Web Page

Web pages are designed for viewing on a computer screen, but you can also print all or part of one. Internet Explorer provides many options for printing Web pages. For Web pages with frames, you can print the page just as you see it, or you can elect to print a particular frame or all frames. You can even use special Page Setup options to include the date, time, or window title on the printed page. You can also choose to print the Web addresses from the links contained in a Web page. ⬛⬛⬛ John prints a Web page and then exits Internet Explorer.

Steps

1. **Click File on the menu bar, then click Print**
The Print dialog box opens, as shown in Figure F-18. See Table F-5 for a description of each tab. Make sure the printer you want to use is connected to your computer.

2. **In the Select Printer box, select the printer you want to use**

3. **Click the Current Page option button**
This option prints the currently displayed Web page.

4. **Click the Options tab**
The Options tab appears, as shown in Figure F-19. When a Web page contains one or more frames, the Print dialog box gives you several options to print the frames. You can print the Web page as laid out on the screen, only the selected frame, or all frames individually.

5. **Click the All frames individually option button**
Instead of writing down links on a Web page, you can automatically print the Web site addresses for each link.

6. **Click the Print table of links check box to select it**

7. **Click Print**
The Web page prints on the selected printer.

8. **Click the Close button ☒ in the Internet Explorer window**
The Internet Explore window closes. If you connected to the Internet by telephone, a disconnect dialog box opens. If you are connected to the Internet through a network, follow your instructor's or technical support person's directions to close your connection.

9. **If the disconnect dialog box opens, click Disconnect**

> **QuickTip**
>
> There is no need to save before you exit, because you only view documents with Internet Explorer; you do not create or change documents.

> **Trouble?**
>
> If you connected by telephone, you can right-click the Connect Icon 🖥 on the right side of the taskbar, then click Disconnect.

TABLE F-5: Print dialog box tabs

tab	allows you to
General	Select a printer and specify the page range and number of copies
Options	Print all or parts of Web site frames, all linked documents, and table of links
Layout	Specify page orientation and number of pages per sheet
Paper/Quality	Specify the paper source and quality

FIGURE F-18: Printing a Web page

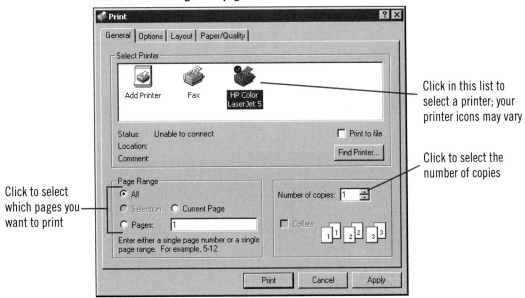

Click in this list to select a printer; your printer icons may vary

Click to select the number of copies

Click to select which pages you want to print

FIGURE F-19: Options tab in the Print dialog box

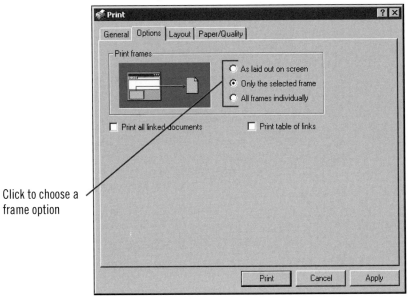

Click to choose a frame option

Setting up the page format

When you print a Web page, you can use the Page Setup dialog box to control the way text and graphics are printed on a page. The Page Setup dialog box, shown in Figure F-20, specifies the printer properties for page size, orientation, and paper source; in most cases, you won't want to change them. From the Page Setup dialog box, you can also change header and footer information. In the Headers and Footers text boxes, you can type in text that will appear as a header and footer of a Web page you print. In these text boxes, you can also use variables to substitute information about the current page, and you can combine text and codes. For example, if you type *Page &p of &P* in the Header text box, the current page number and the total number of pages will be printed at the top of each printed page. Check Internet Explorer Help for a complete list of header and footer codes.

FIGURE F-20: Page Setup dialog box

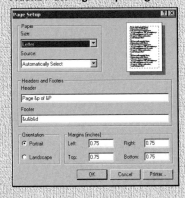

Windows 2000

Practice

▶ Concepts Review

Label each of the elements of the screen shown in Figure F-21.

FIGURE F-21

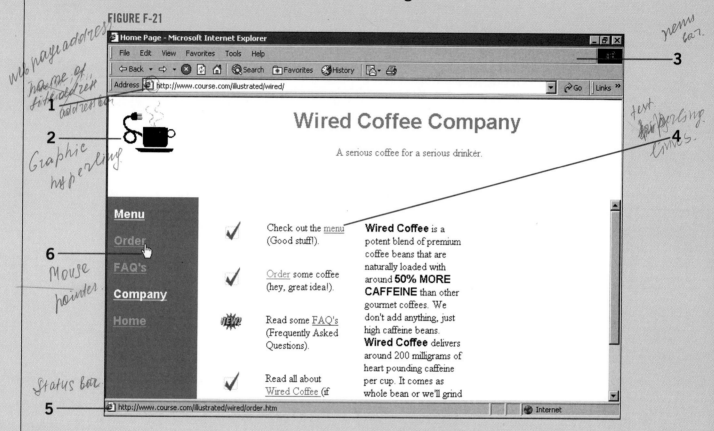

Handwritten annotations on figure:
- web page address
- name of site address
- 1
- 2 — Graphic hyperling
- 6 — Mouse pointer
- Status bar
- 5
- news bar — 3
- text hyperling lines — 4

Match each of the terms with the statement that describes its function.

b) 7. Address bar   a. Spins when Internet Explorer is loading a page

c) 8. Toolbar   b. Displays the URL for the current page

d) 9. Favorites button   c. Provides shortcuts for options on the menu bar

a) 10. Status indicator   d. Displays a list of selected Web pages and folders to organize them

e) 11. Back button   e. Displays the previously viewed page

Select the best answer from the list of choices.

12. Software programs that are used to access and display Web pages are called
    a. Web sites.
    b. search engines.
    c. Web utilities.
    d. Web browsers.

13. If you want to save the name and URL of a Web page in Internet Explorer and return to it later, you can add it to a list called
    a. Favorites.
    b. Bookmarks.
    c. Home pages.
    d. Preferences.

14. An international telecommunications network that consists of linked documents is called the
    a. NSFNET.
    b. Netscape Communicator.
    c. Internet Explorer.
    d. World Wide Web.

15. In Internet Explorer, where are the buttons located that perform common functions such as moving to a previous Web page?
    a. Address bar
    b. Toolbar
    c. Status bar
    d. Menu bar

URL
Uniform Resource Locator.

16. Which of the following is a valid URL?
    a. http:/www.usf.edu/
    b. htp://www.usf.edu/
    c. htp:/ww.usf.edu/
    d. http//www.usf.edu/

17. Underlined words that you click to jump to another Web page are called
    a. explorers.
    b. favorites.
    c. Web browsers.
    d. hyperlinks.

18. The URL of the current Web page is displayed in the
    a. title bar.
    b. document window.
    c. Address bar.
    d. status bar.

► Skills Review

1. **Start Internet Explorer.**
   a. Connect to the Internet.
   b. Start Internet Explorer.

2. **Explore the browser window.**
   a. Identify the toolbar, menu bar, Address bar, Links bar, status bar, status indicator, URL, document window, and scroll bars.
   b. In the toolbar, identify icons for searching, viewing favorites, viewing history, viewing Internet Explorer in full screen, and moving to the previous page.

3. **Open a Web page and follow links.**
   a. Click in the Address bar, type **www.cnet.com**, then press [Enter].
   b. Explore the Web site by using the scroll bars, toolbar, and hyperlinks.
   c. Click in the Address bar, type **www.sportsline.com**, then press [Enter].
   d. Follow the links to investigate the content.

4. **Add a Web page to the Favorites list.**
   a. Click in the Address bar, type **www.loc.gov**, then press [Enter].
   b. Click Favorites on the menu bar, then click Add to Favorites.
   c. Click OK.
   d. Click the Favorites button.
   e. Click the Home button.
   f. Click the link <u>Library of Congress Home Page</u> in the Favorites list.

5. **Make a Web page available offline.**
   a. Click Favorites on the menu bar, then click Organize Favorites.
   b. In the Favorites list, click Library of Congress.
   c. Click the Make available offline check box to select it, then click Close.
   d. Click File on the menu bar, then click Work Offline.
   e. Click Library of Congress Home Page in the Favorites list.
   f. Click File on the menu bar, then click Work Offline.
   g. Click Tools on the menu bar, then click Synchronize.
   h. Click the Library of Congress Home Page check to select it if necessary, then deselect all other check boxes.
   i. Click Synchronize.
   j. Right-click Library of Congress Home Page in the Favorites list, click Delete, then click Yes.
   k. Click the Close button in the Favorites list.

6. **Change your home page and add a link button.**
   a. Click in the Address bar, type *www.msn.com*, then press [Enter].
   b. Click View on the menu bar, then click Internet Options.
   c. Click the General tab.
   d. Click Use Current.
   e. Click OK.
   f. Click the Back button.
   g. Click the Home button.

7. Search the Web.

   a. Click the Search button.

   b. Click the Find a Web page option button

   c. Type **job computer training** in the search text box.

   d. Click the Search button.

   e. Click a link to a Web site from the match list.

   f. Click the Close button in the Explorer Bar.

   g. Click the Home button.

8. Print a Web page.

   a. Click File on the menu bar, then click Print.

   b. In the Select Printer box, click a printer.

   c. Click the Pages option button (use the range 1 to 1).

   d. Click Print.

   e. Click the Close button to exit Internet Explorer.

   f. Click Yes to disconnect, if necessary.

▶ Independent Challenges

1. You will soon graduate from college with a degree in business management. Before entering the workforce, you want to make sure that you are up-to-date on all of the advances in the field. You decide that checking on the Web would provide the most current information. In addition, you can look for companies with employment opportunities. Use Internet Explorer to investigate the All Business Network at http://www.all-biz.com/. When you find a promising site, print the page.

2. You are leaving tomorrow for a business trip to France. You want to make sure that you take the right clothes for the weather and decide that the best place to check France's weather might be the Web. Access one or two of the following weather sites and print at least two reports on the weather in Paris.

The Weather Channel	http://www.weather.com/
World Weather Guide	http://www.weatherlabs.com
CNN Weather	http://www.cnn.com/WEATHER/

3. Your boss wants to buy a new desktop computer (as opposed to a laptop). He assigns you the task of investigating the options. You decide that it would be more expedient to look on the Web than to visit the computer stores in the area. Visit the following Web sites and print a page from the two that you think offer the best deal.

IBM	http://www.ibm.com/
Apple	http://www.apple.com/
Dell	http://www.dell.com/

4. During the summer, you want to travel to national parks in the United States. Use one of the search engines available through your Web browser to find Web sites with maps of the national parks. Visit four or five Web sites from the match list and print a page from the three that you think offer the best maps and related information for park visitors.

▶ Visual Workshop

Re-create the screen shown in Figure F-22, which displays the document window with a search engine and a Web site. Your search results might be different. (*Hint:* Use the Custom button to change search engines.) Print the Web page and then print the screen. (Press the Print Screen key to make a copy of the screen, open Paint, click Edit on the menu bar, click Paste to paste the screen into Paint, then click Yes to paste the large image if necessary. Click File on the menu bar, click Print, then click Print in the Print dialog box.)

FIGURE F-22

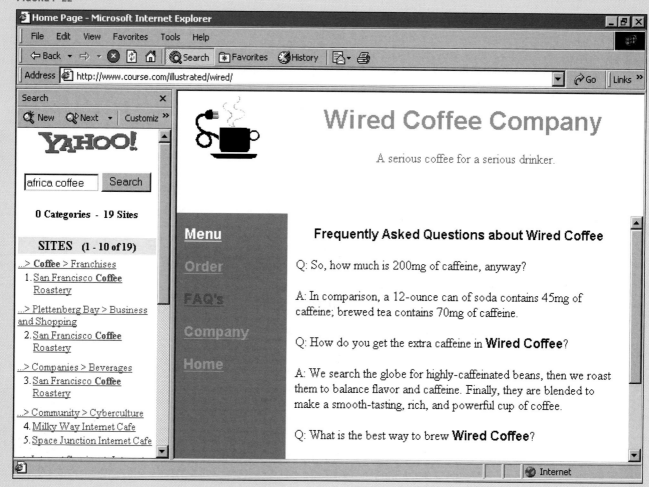

Unit **G**

Exchanging
Mail and News

Objectives

- ▶ **Start Outlook Express**
- ▶ **Explore the Outlook Express window**
- ▶ **Add a contact to the Address Book**
- ▶ **Compose and send e-mail**
- ▶ **Retrieve, read, and respond to e-mail**
- ▶ **Manage e-mail messages**
- ▶ **Select a news server**
- ▶ **View and subscribe to a newsgroup**
- ▶ **Read and post a news message**

Windows 2000 includes Microsoft Outlook Express, a powerful program for managing **electronic mail** (known as e-mail). With an Internet connection and Microsoft Outlook Express, you can exchange e-mail messages with anyone on the Internet and join any number of **newsgroups**, which are collections of e-mail messages on related topics posted by individuals to specified locations on the Internet. If you are not connected to the Internet, you will not be able to work the steps in this unit; however, you can read the lessons without completing the steps to learn what you can accomplish using Outlook Express.   In this unit John Casey, owner of the Wired Coffee Company, will use Outlook Express to send and receive e-mail messages and join a newsgroup about the coffee industry.

Starting Outlook Express

Outlook Express puts the world of online communication on your desktop. Whether you want to exchange e-mail with colleagues and friends or join newsgroups to trade ideas and information, the tools you need are here. When you install Windows 2000, a button for Outlook Express appears on the Quick Launch toolbar, which is located on the taskbar. If your computer is not connected to the Internet or you don't have an e-mail account, check with your instructor or technical support person to see if it's possible for you to connect or set up an e-mail account. ➤ John wants to use Outlook Express to exchange e-mail with his employees.

Steps

1. If necessary, establish a connection to the Internet via the network or telephone

If you connect to the Internet through a network, follow your instructor's or technical support person's directions to establish your connection. If you connect by telephone, create a new connection using the Connection Wizard to establish your connection, or use an existing Dial-Up Networking connection.

> **Trouble?**
>
> If a Browse For Folder dialog box opens, click OK to accept the default folder where Outlook Express should store your messages, then continue.

2. Click the Launch Outlook Express button 🖳 on the Quick Launch toolbar, as shown in Figure G-1

The Outlook Express window opens and displays the Outlook Express Start Page, as shown in Figure G-2. If you connect to the Internet through a network, follow your instructor's or technical support person's directions to log on. If you connect to the Internet by telephone using a dial-up networking connection, you might need to enter your user name and password to connect to the Internet. See your instructor or technical support person for this information.

3. If necessary, type your user name, press [Tab], type your password, then click Connect

Upon completion of the dial-up connection, you are connected to the Internet (unless an error message appears). When you start Outlook Express for the first time, the Internet Connection Wizard opens, asking you about your e-mail account setup information. See your instructor or technical support person for this information.

> **QuickTip**
>
> To modify or add an account, click Tools on the menu bar, click Accounts, click an account and click Properties, or click Add, click an account type, and follow the wizard instructions.

4. If necessary, enter the information required by the Internet Connection Wizard; type your name, click Next, type your e-mail address, click Next, type the name of the incoming mail server, type the name of the outgoing server, click Next, type your e-mail account name, type your password, click Next, then click Finish

Your mail account is set up.

5. If necessary, click the Maximize button 🔲 to maximize the Outlook Express window

FIGURE G-1: Windows desktop

Launch Outlook
Express button

FIGURE G-2: Outlook Express window

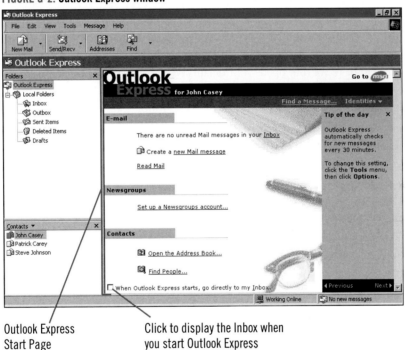

Outlook Express
Start Page

Click to display the Inbox when
you start Outlook Express

CLUES TO USE

Starting Outlook Express from your Web browser

You can set Outlook Express to be your default e-mail program, so that whenever you click an e-mail link on a Web page or choose the mail command in your Web browser, Outlook Express opens. Likewise, you can set Outlook Express to be your default news reader, so that when you click a newsgroup link on a Web page or choose the news reader command in your Web browser, Outlook Express opens. To set Outlook Express to be your default e-mail or newsgroup program, start Internet Explorer, click Tools on the menu bar, click Internet Options, click the Programs tab, click either the E-mail or Newsgroups list arrow, click Outlook Express, then click OK.

Exploring the Outlook Express Window

After you start Outlook Express, the Outlook Express window displays the Outlook Express Start Page, as shown in Figure G-3. The **Outlook Express Start Page** displays tools that you can use to read e-mail, set up a newsgroup account, read newsgroup messages, compose e-mail messages, enter and edit Address Book information, and find people on the Internet. ➤ Before reading his e-mail, John decides to familiarize himself with the components of the Outlook Express window.

Details

He notes the following features:

 The **title bar** at the top of the window displays the name of the program.

 The **menu bar** provides access to a variety of commands, much like other Windows programs.

 The **toolbar** provides icons, or buttons, for easy access to the most commonly used commands. See Table G-1 for a description of each toolbar button. These commands are also available on menus.

 The **Go to MSN link** opens your default Web browser program and displays the MSN Web page.

 The **Folders list** displays folders where Outlook Express stores e-mail messages. You can also use folders to organize your e-mail messages.

 The **Contacts list** displays the contact names in the Address Book.

 The **new Mail message link** opens the New Message dialog box where you can compose and send e-mail messages.

 The **Read Mail link** jumps to the Inbox where you can read and reply to incoming e-mail messages.

 The **Set up a Newsgroups account link** (appears instead of the Read News link if you have not set up a news group account) creates a newsgroups account.

 The **Read News link** connects to newsgroups that you can view and subscribe to.

 The **Open the Address Book link** opens the Address Book where you can enter and edit your contacts list.

 The **Find People link** opens the Find People dialog box where you can search for people on the Internet or in your Address Book.

 The **Tip of the day** on the right side of the window displays an Outlook Express tip; click Next and Previous to move between the tips.

 The **status bar** displays information about your Internet connection with a mail or newsgroup server.

FIGURE G-3: Outlook Express window with the Start Page

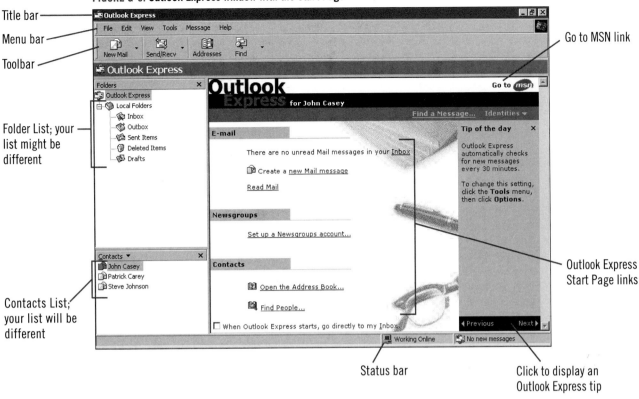

Title bar

Menu bar

Toolbar

Folder List; your list might be different

Contacts List; your list will be different

Go to MSN link

Outlook Express Start Page links

Status bar

Click to display an Outlook Express tip

TABLE G-1: Outlook Express Start Page toolbar buttons

button	description
	Opens the e-mail message composition window
	Sends e-mail messages and checks for new messages
	Opens the Address Book
	Finds e-mail messages, text in an e-mail message, or people on the Internet

Getting help in Outlook Express

If you need help connecting to the Internet to get mail or learning how to use Outlook Express features, you can get help from several different sources. To get Outlook Express Help, you can use the online Help system that comes with the program or view Outlook Express Web sites on the Internet. To open Outlook Express online Help, click Help on the menu bar, then click Contents and Index. To learn more about Outlook Express from Web sites on the Internet, click Help on the menu bar, point to Microsoft on the Web, then click Product News. Internet Explorer starts and displays the Outlook Express Web site.

Adding a Contact to the Address Book

A **contact** is a person or company that you communicate with. One contact can have several mailing addresses, phone numbers, e-mail addresses, or Web sites. You can store this information in the **Address Book**, along with other detailed information—such as the contact's title, street address, phone number, and personal Web page addresses. When you want to create a new contact or edit an existing one, you use the Properties dialog box to enter or change contact information. You can organize your contacts into **contact groups**, which are groups of related people you communicate with on a regular basis, or into folders. One contact group might be your family members or people at work. ![illustration] John wants to add a new employee to his Address Book.

Steps

1. Click the **Open the Address Book** link on the Outlook Express Start Page

The Address Book window opens, as shown in Figure G-4, displaying the current contacts in the Address Book. Your list of contacts might be different or empty. The Address Book toolbar is above the list of contacts. See Table G-2 for a description of each toolbar button. These commands are also available on the menus.

QuickTip

You can also click the Address Book button 📖 on the toolbar to open the Address Book.

2. Click the **New button** 🖼▾ on the Address Book toolbar, then click **New Contact**

The New button allows you to create new contacts, contact groups, and folders to organize contacts. The Properties dialog box opens, displaying the Name tab with empty text boxes. See Table G-3 for a description of each tab in the Properties dialog box.

QuickTip

To create a contact group, click the New button on the toolbar, click New Group, type a group name, click Select Members, double-click names from the Address Book, click OK, then click OK again.

3. Type **Shawn** in the First text box, press **[Tab]** twice to move to the Last name text box, then type **Brooks**

The complete name of the new contact appears in the Display box; this is the name that will be displayed in the list of contacts unless you click the Display list arrow and choose a different name.

4. Click the **E-Mail Addresses text box**, type **shawnbrooks@course.com**, then click **Add**

The e-mail address appears in the box below the E-Mail Addresses text box, as shown in Figure G-5. E-mail addresses are not case-sensitive (capitalization doesn't matter) and cannot contain spaces.

QuickTip

To modify an e-mail address, select it, then click Edit. To delete an e-mail address no longer in use, select it, then click Remove.

5. Click **OK**

The Properties dialog box closes and you return to the Address Book. Instead of opening the Properties dialog box every time you want to see a more complete listing of a contact's information, you can position the mouse pointer over a contact in the Address Book to display a ScreenTip summary of the contact's information.

6. Position the mouse pointer over **Shawn Brooks** in the Address Book

A ScreenTip summary appears on the screen. You can move the mouse pointer to remove the ScreenTip or wait. To edit a contact, simply double-click anywhere on the contact entry in the Address Book.

QuickTip

To print a phone list or business cards, click the Print button on the toolbar, click a print option, then click Print.

7. Double-click **Shawn Brooks**

The Shawn Brooks Properties dialog box opens and displays the selected contact's information. You can use any of the tabs in this dialog box to add to or change the contact information.

8. Click the **Business tab**, click the **Phone text box**, type **925-555-3084**, then click **OK**

Shawn's business phone number appears in the Address Book.

9. Click the **Close button** ☒ in the Address Book window

FIGURE G-4: Address Book window

Address Book toolbar

Type name here to find contact

Current contacts; your list will be different and might be blank

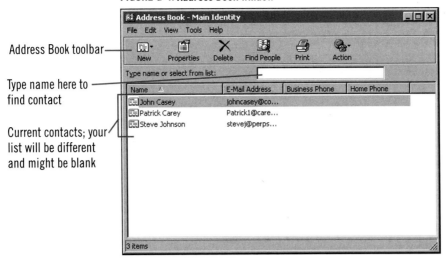

FIGURE G-5: Properties dialog box with a new contact

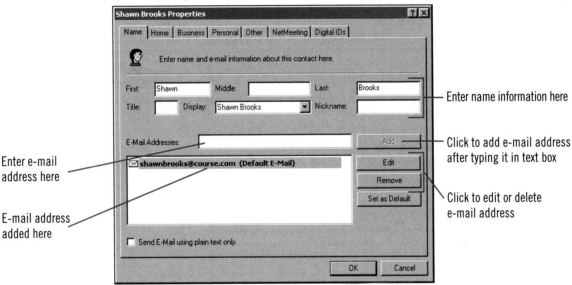

Enter name information here

Click to add e-mail address after typing it in text box

Click to edit or delete e-mail address

Enter e-mail address here

E-mail address added here

TABLE G-2: Address Book toolbar buttons

button	description	button	description
	Creates a new contact, group, or folder		Finds people on the Internet
	Opens the selected contact		Opens the Print dialog box
	Deletes the selected contact		Sends mail, dials a connection, or places an Internet call

TABLE G-3: New contact Properties dialog box tabs

tab	description	tab	description
Name	Enter name and e-mail information	Other	Enter notes about contact
Home	Enter information related to the contact's home	NetMeeting	Add and modify e-mail conferencing addresses and servers
Business	Enter business-related information	Digital Ids	Add, remove, and view security identification numbers for the contact
Personal	Enter personal information		

Windows 2000

Composing and Sending E-mail

E-mail is quickly becoming the primary form of written communication for many people. E-mail messages follow a standard memo format with fields for the sender, recipient, date, and subject of the message. To send an e-mail message, you need to enter the recipient's e-mail address, type a subject, and then type the message itself. You can send the same message to more than one individual, to a contact group, or to a combination of individuals and groups. You can personalize your e-mail messages (and newsgroup messages) with built-in stationery, or you can design your own. John wants to send an e-mail message to the new employee whose contact information he added to the Address Book in the previous lesson.

Steps

QuickTip

To create a new message without stationery, you can click the New Mail button on the toolbar, click the <u>new Mail message</u> link in the Outlook Express window, or double-click a name in the Contacts list.

QuickTip

To remove a name from the Message recipients list, click the person's name in the Message recipients list box, then press [Delete].

QuickTip

To save an incomplete message, click the Save button on the toolbar. The e-mail message is saved with the name of the subject and placed in the Drafts folder.

QuickTip

If you don't want to send the e-mail message right now, click File on the menu bar, then click Send Later. The e-mail message is placed in the Outbox but not sent.

1. **Click the New Mail button list arrow** on the toolbar, click **Clear Day**, then click the **Maximize button**
   The New Message window opens and is maximized, as shown in Figure G-6, displaying the Clear Day stationery in the message box.

2. **Click To next to the To text box**
   The Select Recipients dialog box opens, as shown in Figure G-7, displaying the contacts from the Address Book.

3. **In the list of contacts, click the down scroll arrow if necessary, click Shawn Brooks, then click To**
   The contact, Shawn Brooks, appears in the Message recipients list box. You can also add additional recipients to this list, select another recipient and click the Cc (carbon copy) button to send a copy of your e-mail message to that person, or click the Bcc (blind carbon copy) button to send a copy of your e-mail message to another person without displaying the names of the blind copy recipients in the e-mail message.

4. **Click OK**
   Shawn's name appears in the To text box. Shawn's e-mail address is associated with the name selected even though it is not displayed. John includes a subject title.

5. **Click the Subject text box, then type Welcome aboard!**
   The message title bar changes from New Message to the subject text, Welcome aboard!

6. **Click the text box at the bottom of the message window**
   The Formatting toolbar, just below the Subject text box, is activated. The Formatting toolbar works just like the Formatting toolbar in WordPad or other Windows programs. You can use it to change the format of your message text at any time.

7. Type **Dear Shawn:**, press **[Enter]** twice, type **I would like to welcome you to the Wired Coffee Company. We are excited that you have joined our team. Wired Coffee is a growing company, and I believe your contributions will make a big difference. Please come to a luncheon for new employees this Thursday at 12:30 in the company cafe.**, press **[Enter]** twice, then type **John**

8. **Click the Send button** on the toolbar, then click **OK** in the Information box, if necessary
   The New Message window closes, and the e-mail message is placed in the Outbox, a folder where outgoing messages are stored, and then automatically sent to the recipient. A copy of the outgoing message is saved in the Sent Items folder so you can reference the message later.

FIGURE G-6: New Message window with Clear Day stationery

Click to select a recipient from the Address Book

Click to enter subject text

Click here to begin typing message

Clear Day stationery

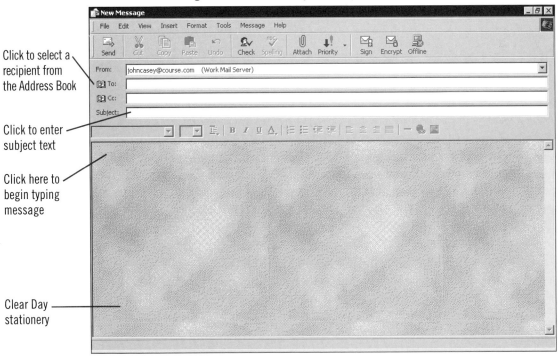

FIGURE G-7: Selecting recipients for an e-mail message

Enter name here to find a recipient, or click the Find button

Select a contact from this list, then click the To button (your list will differ)

Click to add a new contact

Click to choose the selected contact as a recipient for this message

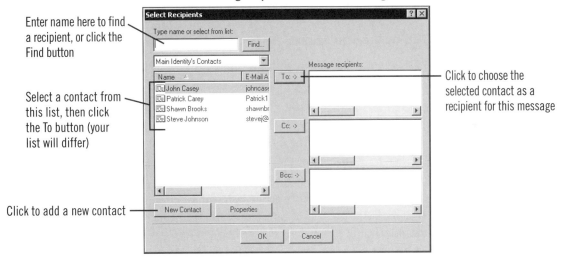

CLUES TO USE

Attaching a file to an e-mail message

You can easily share files using e-mail. You can send a file, such as a picture or a document by attaching it to an e-mail message. When the e-mail is received, the recipient can open the file in the program in which it was created or save it to disk. For example, suppose you are working on a report that you created using WordPad and that a colleague working in another part of the country needs to present it today. After you finish the report, you can attach the report file to an e-mail message and send the message to your colleague, who can then open, edit, and print the report. To attach a file to an e-mail message, create the message, click the Attach button [] on the toolbar, navigate to the drive and folder location of the file you want to attach, select the file, then click Attach.

Windows 2000

Retrieving, Reading, and Responding to E-mail

You can retrieve your e-mail manually or set Outlook Express to automatically retrieve your messages. New messages appear in the Inbox along with any messages you haven't yet stored elsewhere or deleted. One or more **message flags** may appear next to a message to indicate that the message has a certain priority, that it has a file attached to it, and whether or not it has been read. See Table G-4 for a description of the message flags. John forwards an e-mail message he received from Shawn Brooks to another person at the company.

Steps

QuickTip

To automatically check for messages every few minutes, click Tools on the menu bar, click Options, then click the check for messages option.

QuickTip

To display the Inbox when you start Outlook Express, click the When Outlook Express starts, go directly to my Inbox check box on the Outlook Express Start Page.

Trouble?

If you didn't receive a message from Shawn Brooks, click the Send/Recv button on the toolbar again. It may take a few minutes for the message to arrive.

1. Click the **Send/Recv button** 🖳 on the toolbar
   An information box displays the progress of the e-mail messages you are sending and receiving. After your e-mail messages have been sent or received, the dialog box closes. When you receive new e-mail, the Inbox folder in the Folders list is bold, indicating that it contains unread messages, and a number in parentheses indicates the number of new e-mail messages you have received.

2. In the Folders list, click **Inbox**
   The Inbox folder opens, as shown in Figure G-8. The **preview pane** displays the messages in your Inbox. The **display pane** displays the e-mail message that is selected in the preview pane. E-mail messages in the preview pane with the subject or heading text in bold are messages that have not been opened.

3. Click the **message** you received from Shawn Brooks

4. Double-click the **message** you received from Shawn Brooks in the preview pane, then click the **Maximize button** 🔲 in the message window
   When a message you receive is short, you can quickly read it by clicking the message and then reading the text in the display pane. Longer messages, like the one from Shawn Brooks, are easier to open and read in a full window. After reading a message, you can reply to the author, reply to all of the recipients, forward the message to another person, or simply close or delete the message. John forwards the message to his human resources administrator to ask her to add Shawn Brooks to the list of luncheon attendees. You will forward the message to your instructor or technical support person or to someone else whose e-mail address you know.

5. Click the **Forward button** 🔁 on the message toolbar
   The Forward Message window opens, as shown in Figure G-9, displaying the original e-mail message you sent. At the top of the message box, you can add additional text to the message.

6. Click in the upper-left corner of the message box, then type **Please add Shawn Brooks to Thursday's luncheon guest list.**

Trouble?

If you don't know an e-mail address to send the forwarded message to, click the Close button in the message window, then continue with the next lesson.

7. Click the **To text box**, type the e-mail address of your instructor, technical support person, or someone else you know, then click the **Send button** 🖳 on the toolbar
   The e-mail message is sent.

8. Click the **Address Book button** 📖 on the toolbar, click **Shawn Brooks**, click the **Delete button** ✖, click **Yes**, then click the **Close button** ✖
   Shawn is deleted from John's Address Book.

FIGURE G-8: Outlook Express window with the Inbox

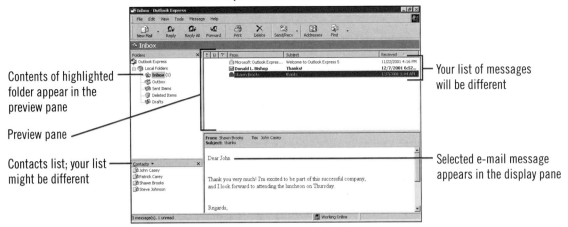

Contents of highlighted folder appear in the preview pane

Preview pane

Contacts list; your list might be different

Your list of messages will be different

Selected e-mail message appears in the display pane

FIGURE G-9: Forward Message window

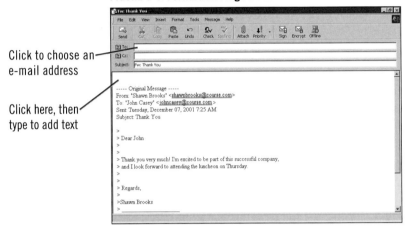

Click to choose an e-mail address

Click here, then type to add text

TABLE G-4: Mail message flag icons

icon	description
✉	Message has not been read; message heading text appears bold
✉	Message has been read
📎	Message has one or more files attached to it
!	Message has been marked as high priority by the sender
↓	Message has been marked as low priority by the sender

Printing e-mail messages and contacts

You can print your e-mail messages from any folder at any time using Outlook Express. To print an e-mail message, open the message, then click the Print button on the toolbar. You can also open the Address Book and print contact information in a variety of formats, such as Memo, Business Card, and Phone List. The Memo style prints all the information you have for a contact with descriptive titles. The Business Card style prints the contact information without descriptive titles. The Phone List style prints all the phone numbers for a contact or for all your contacts. To print contact information, open the Address Book, select a specific contact (if desired), click the Print button on the toolbar, select a print range, print style, and the number of copies you want to print, then click Print.

Managing E-mail Messages

A common problem with using e-mail is an overcrowded Inbox. To help you keep your Inbox organized, you should move messages you want to keep to other folders and subfolders, delete messages you no longer want, and create new folders as you need them. Storing incoming messages in other folders and deleting unwanted messages makes it easier to see the new messages you receive and to keep track of messages to which you have already responded. ✎ John wants to create a new folder for his important messages in the Local Folders location, move a message from the Inbox to the new folder, and then delete the messages he no longer needs.

Steps

1. Click File on the menu bar, point to New, then click Folder
The Create Folder dialog box opens, displaying the list of folders contained in the Outlook Express folder, as shown in Figure G-10.

2. Type Important, then click Local Folders in the Folders list
The new folder will be named Important and will appear in the Folders list under Local Folders. To create a subfolder (a folder in a folder), you would select one of the folders in the Folders list under Local folders. The Folders list works like the left pane of Windows Explorer. When a subfolder is created, a plus sign (+) appears next to the folder that contains the subfolder.

3. Click OK
The new folder, Important, appears in the Folders list under Local Folders.

QuickTip
To block all messages from a sender, click a message from the sender, click Message on the menu bar, then click Block Sender.

4. In the preview pane of the Inbox, right-click the message you received from Shawn Brooks
A pop-up menu appears, displaying commands, such as move, copy, delete, print, and add sender to Address Book, to help you manage your e-mail messages.

5. Click Move To Folder on the pop-up menu
The Move To dialog box opens, allowing you to specify the folder where you want to move the selected message.

QuickTip
To move a message to a folder, drag the message from the preview pane to the folder in the Folders list.

6. Click the Important folder, then click OK

7. In the Folders list, click the Important folder
The e-mail message you just moved appears in the preview and display panes, as shown in Figure G-11.

QuickTip
To sort messages by sender, subject, date, priority or flag, click a header in the preview pane.

8. In the Folders list, right-click the Important folder, click Delete, then click Yes
The Important folder is placed in the Deleted Items folder. The Delete Items folder works just like the Recycle Bin. Deleted messages are temporarily stored in the folder until they are automatically or manually deleted.

9. In the Folders list, right-click the Deleted Items folder, click Empty 'Deleted Items' Folder
The Important folder and all of its contents are permanently deleted.

FIGURE G-10: Create Folder dialog box

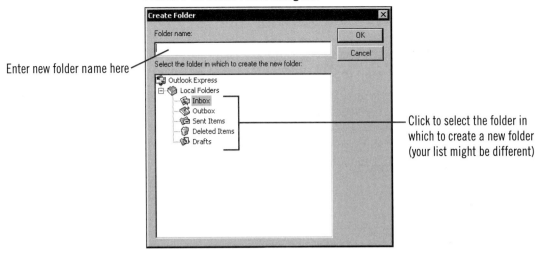

Enter new folder name here

Click to select the folder in which to create a new folder (your list might be different)

FIGURE G-11: Important folder

Click to display the contents of the folder

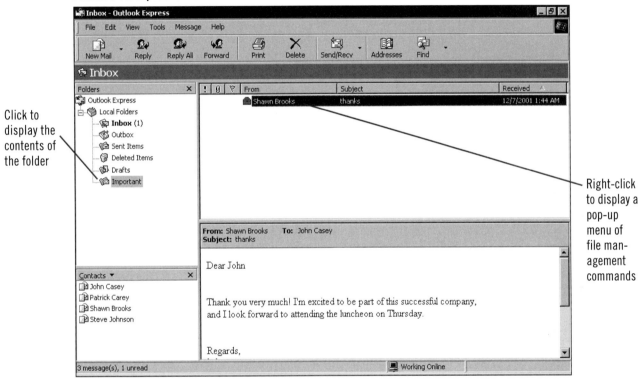

Right-click to display a pop-up menu of file management commands

Diverting incoming e-mail to folders

Outlook Express can direct incoming messages that meet criteria to other folders in the Folders list rather than to your Inbox. Let's say that you have a friend who loves sending you funny e-mail, but you often don't have time to read it right away. You can set message rules to store any messages you receive from your friend in a different folder so they won't clutter your Inbox. When you are ready to read the messages, you simply open the folder and access the messages just as you would in the Inbox. To set criteria for incoming messages, click Tools on the menu bar, point to Message Rules, then click Mail. If the New Mail Rule dialog box opens, no previous message rules exist. Otherwise, the Message Rules dialog box opens; click New to create a new message rule. The New Mail Rule dialog box opens. Select the conditions for your rule, select the actions for your rule, click any undefined value (such as the e-mail address you want to divert and the folder where you want to store the diverted messages) and provide information, type a name to identify the rule, then click OK.

Selecting a News Server

A newsgroup is an electronic forum where people from around the world with a common interest can share ideas, ask and answer questions, and comment on and discuss any subject. You can find newsgroups on almost any topic, from the serious to the lighthearted, from educational to controversial, from business to social. Before you can participate in a newsgroup, you must select a news server. A **news server** is a computer located on the Internet where newsgroup messages, also called **articles**, on different topics are stored. Each news server contains several newsgroups from which to choose. The Internet Connection Wizard walks you through the process of selecting a news server. This wizard also appears the first time you use Outlook Express News. To complete the wizard and the steps in this lesson, you'll need to get the name of the news server you want to use from your instructor, technical support person, or Internet service provider (ISP), and possibly an account name and password. John wants to add a news server account so he can access coffee-related newsgroups.

Steps

Trouble?

If you do not already have a news server selected, the Internet Connection Wizard will open, and you should skip to Step 4 to complete the wizard. If you already have a news server, continue with the next step.

QuickTip

To add a new e-mail account, click Add, click Mail, then follow the Internet Connection Wizard instructions.

QuickTip

To change a news server name, right-click the news server in the Folders list, click Properties, type a name in the News Accounts text box, then click OK.

1. In the Folders list, click Outlook Express, then click the **Read News** link or click the **Set up a Newsgroups account** link in the Outlook Express Start Page

2. Click **Tools** on the menu bar, click **Accounts**, then click the **News tab**

   The Internet Accounts dialog box opens, as shown in Figure G-12, displaying the News tab with your list of available news servers. Using the Internet Accounts dialog box, you can add, remove, and view properties for news servers, mail servers, and directory services.

3. Click **Add**, then click **News**

   The Internet Connection Wizard dialog box opens.

4. Type your **name**, if necessary, then click **Next**

   The name you enter appears in messages you post to a newsgroup.

5. Type your **e-mail address**, if necessary, then click **Next**

   Individuals participating in the newsgroup need to know your e-mail address so they can reply to your news messages either by posting another news message or by sending you an e-mail message.

6. Type the **name of the news server** provided by your instructor, technical support person, or ISP, as shown in Figure G-13, then click **Next**

7. Click **Finish**, click **Close** if the Internet Accounts dialog box opens, then click **No** to download a list of available newsgroups

   The news server name appears in the Folders list, as shown in Figure G-14. You'll view a list of available newsgroups in the next lesson.

FIGURE G-12: Internet Accounts dialog box

Click tab to select
server type

Click to add a server

Click to remove the
selected server (appears
dimmed when no servers
are listed)

Click to view properties
of selected server
(appears dimmed when
no servers are listed)

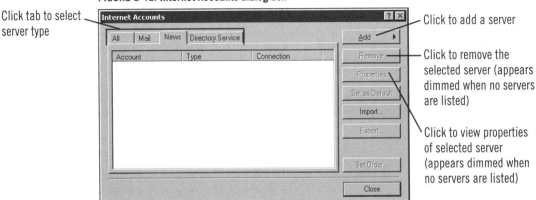

FIGURE G-13: Internet Connection Wizard dialog box

Enter news server
here; your news
server will probably
be different from
the one shown here

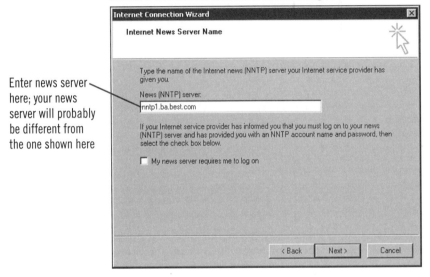

FIGURE G-14: Outlook Express window with news server

News server;
your news
server name
might be
different

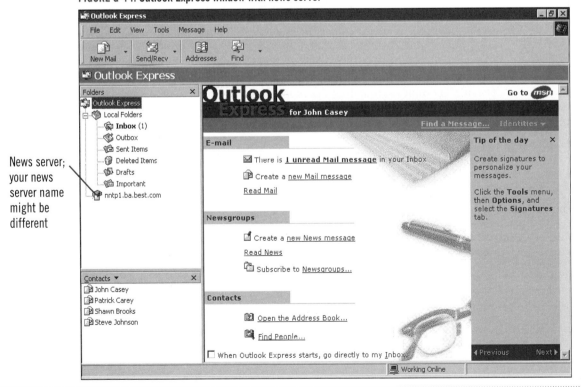

Viewing and Subscribing to a Newsgroup

When you add a news server account to Outlook Express, it retrieves a list of newsgroups available on that server. Often this list is quite lengthy. Rather than scroll through the entire list looking for a particular topic, you can have Outlook Express search the list for that topic. Similarly, you can search a newsgroup for a particular message from all the messages you retrieve from a newsgroup. Once you select a newsgroup, you can merely view its contents, or, if you expect to come back to the newsgroup often, you can subscribe to it. Subscribing to a newsgroup places a link to the group in the news server folder in your Outlook Express Folders list, providing easy access to the newsgroup. John wants to find and subscribe to a newsgroup for coffee drinkers, so he can keep track of what people want from a coffee company.

1. Click the **Read News** link in the Outlook Express Start Page, then click **Yes** if necessary, to view a list of available newsgroups
   The Newsgroups dialog box opens, as shown in Figure G-15, displaying news servers on the left (if more than one exists) and related newsgroups on the right.

2. In the News server list, click the **news server you added in the previous lesson** if necessary
   A list of the newsgroups you have subscribed to appears in the preview pane. Your list might be empty.

QuickTip

To subscribe to a newsgroup, double-click it in the Newsgroup Subscriptions dialog box.

3. Type **coffee** in the Display Newsgroups which contain text box
   Newsgroups related to coffee appear in the News groups list box, as shown in Figure G-16.

4. Scroll if necessary, click the newsgroup **rec.food.drink.coffee** (if available), or click a different newsgroup from your list, then click **Go To**
   The newsgroup name you have chosen appears selected in the Folders list and the newsgroup messages appear in the preview pane of the Outlook Express window, as shown in Figure G-17. John thinks this newsgroup looks promising, so he decides to subscribe to it.

QuickTip

To download new newsgroup messages, click the newsgroup in the Folders list, then click Synchronize Account.

5. Right-click the **newsgroup server** in the Folders list, then click **Subscribe**
   The number of newsgroup messages appears next to the newsgroup name in the Folders list. The icon next to the newsgroup changes from gray to color to indicate the subscription is complete.

Filtering unwanted newsgroup messages

After you become familiar with a newsgroup, you might decide that you don't want to retrieve messages that are from a particular person, about a specific subject, of a certain length, or older than a certain number of days. This is called **filtering** newsgroup messages. To filter unwanted messages, click Tools on the menu bar, point to Message Rules, then click News. If the New News Rule dialog box opens, no previous message rules exist. Otherwise, the Message Rules dialog box opens; click New to create a new message rule. The New News Rule dialog box opens. Select the conditions for your rule, select the actions for your rule, click any undefined value (such as the e-mail address you want to divert and the folder where you want to store the unwanted messages) and provide the information, type a name for the rule, then click OK.

FIGURE G-15: **Newsgroup dialog box**

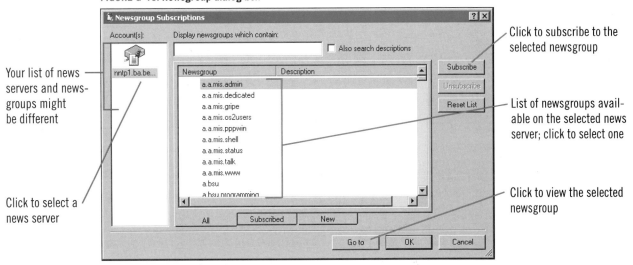

Your list of news servers and newsgroups might be different

Click to select a news server

Click to subscribe to the selected newsgroup

List of newsgroups available on the selected news server; click to select one

Click to view the selected newsgroup

FIGURE G-16: **List of newsgroups relating to coffee**

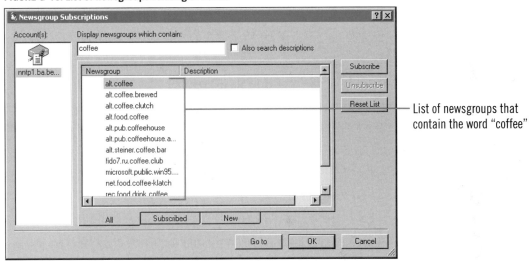

List of newsgroups that contain the word "coffee"

FIGURE G-17: **Outlook Express window with a newsgroup**

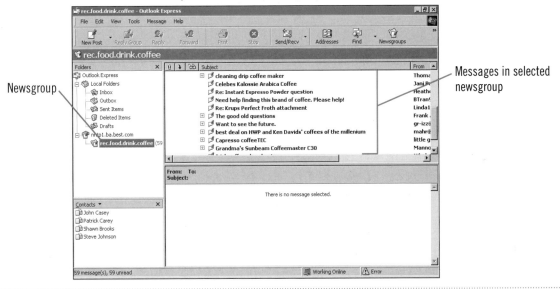

Newsgroup

Messages in selected newsgroup

Reading and Posting News Messages

Windows 2000

After retrieving new newsgroup messages, you can read them. Newsgroup messages appear in the preview pane, just as e-mail messages do. To view a newsgroup message in the display pane, click the title of the message in the preview pane. If a plus sign (+) in a box appears to the left of a newsgroup message, then the message contains a conversation thread. A **conversation thread** consists of the original message on a particular topic along with any responses that include the original message. To read the responses, click the + to display the message titles, and then click the title of the message you want to read. John decides to read some of the messages in the newsgroup. When he is finished, he will restore his news server settings by unsubscribing from this newsgroup and removing the news server from the Folders list.

Steps

Trouble?

If a newsgroup message doesn't have a +, click a message without a +, then skip to Step 3.

1. **Click a newsgroup message** in the preview pane with a + to the left of the title, then read the message in the display pane
   The newsgroup message appears in the display pane.

2. Click the **+** next to the newsgroup message
   The titles of the responses to the original message appear under the original newsgroup message, as shown in Figure G-18.

QuickTip

To view only unread messages, click View on the menu bar, point to Current View, then click Hide Read Messages.

3. Click **each reply message under the original message**, and read the reply
   As you read each message, you have the choice to compose a new message, send a reply message to everyone viewing the newsgroup (known as posting), send a reply message to the author's private e-mail address (rather than posting it on the newsgroup), or forward the message you are reading to another person.

4. After reading the last reply message, click the **Reply Group button** on the toolbar, then click the **Maximize button** if necessary

QuickTip

To watch a conversation of messages and replies, click a message in the thread, click Message on the menu bar, then click Watch Conversation.

5. Type a response to the newsgroup message, as shown in Figure G-19

6. Click the **Send button** on the toolbar, then click **OK**
   Your reply message appears in the preview pane along with the other replies to the original message. Everyone viewing the newsgroup can download and read your response.

7. Right-click the **newsgroup** in the Folders list, click **Unsubcribe**, then click **OK** (if necessary, click No to subscribe to the Newsgroup and click No to view a list of the newsgroups)

8. Right-click the **news server** in the Folders list, click **Remove Account**, then click **Yes**

9. Click **File** on the menu bar, click **Exit**, then click **Yes** if necessary to disconnect from the Internet

FIGURE G-18: Reading a newsgroup message

Click + to display
or − to hide replies
to newsgroup
messages

Click a message
to display it in the
display pane

Your list of
messages might
be different

Message selected
in preview pane
appears here

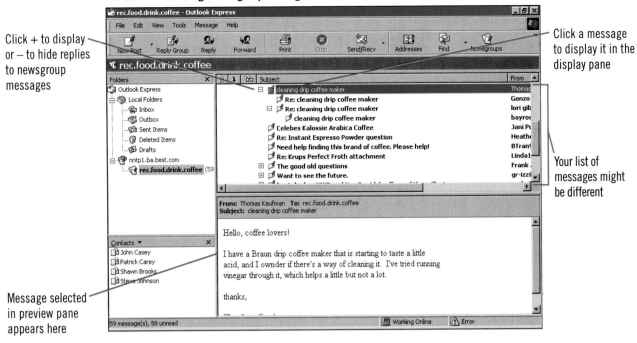

FIGURE G-19: Posting a newsgroup message

Click to post the
message to the
newsgroup

Type your reply to
the message here

Your message will
be different

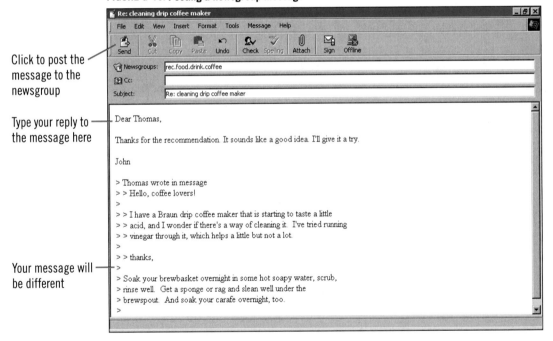

![Clues To Use]

Deleting old news messages

Newsgroup messages are stored on your hard drive, so you should delete messages you don't need to free up disk space. Outlook Express gives several cleanup options to help you optimize your hard drive space. You can delete entire messages (titles and bodies), compress messages, remove just the message bodies (leaving the title headers), or reset the information stored for selected messages, which allows you to refresh messages (download again). To clean up files on your local hard drive, select a news server in the Folders list, click Tools on the menu bar, click Options, then click the Maintenance tab. You can select any of the cleanup options to delete or compress news messages at a specified time or click Clean Up Now, then click the button for the cleanup option you want to perform now.

Practice

▶ Concepts Review

Label each of the elements of the screen shown in Figure G-20.

FIGURE G-20

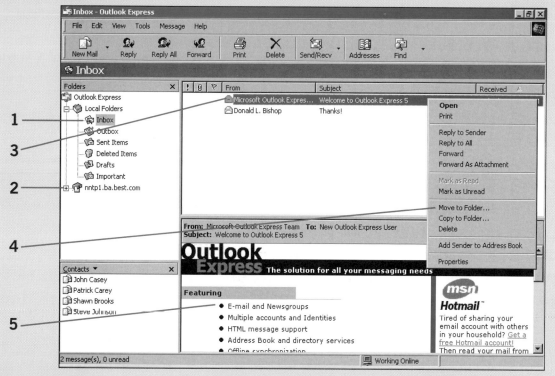

Match each of the terms with the statement that describes its function.

6. **Message flag**
7. **Outlook Express Start Page**
8. **Message Rules**
9. **Outlook Express window**
10. **News server**

a. A computer on the Internet where articles are stored
b. Displays e-mail and newsgroups
c. An icon that indicates e-mail to folders
d. Diverts selected incoming e-mail status
e. Jumps to folders and opens tools

Select the best answer from the list of choices.

11. **The location that allows you to jump to folders and open tools is called the**
    a. Outlook Express window.
    b. Outlook Express Start Page.
    c. Folders list.
    d. Outlook Express Link Page.
12. **To compose a message, you can**
    a. click the new Mail message link.
    b. click New Mail button on the toolbar.
    c. click Message on the menu bar, then click New Message.
    d. All of the above.

13. **A contact is a**
    a. person you communicate with.
    b. mailing address.
    c. newsgroup.
    d. program.

14. **When you click the Send button on the toolbar in the New Message window, an e-mail message is sent first to the**
    a. e-mail address.
    b. outbox.
    c. Internet.
    d. Cc and Bcc addresses.

15. ✉ **indicates that the message has**
    a. not been read.
    b. been read.
    c. one or more files attached to it.
    d. been marked as low priority by the sender.

▶ Skills Review

1. **Start Outlook Express and explore the Outlook Express window.**
   a. Connect to the Internet.
   b. Click the Launch Outlook Express button on the Quick Launch toolbar.
   c. Identify the title bar, menu bar, toolbar, Internet Explorer link, Folders list, Read Mail link, Read News link, new Mail message link, Open the Address Book link, Find People link, and status bar.
   d. On the toolbar, identify icons for opening the Address Book, sending and receiving e-mail messages, composing a message, and finding a message.
   e. If necessary, enter your user name and password, then click Connect.

2. **Add a contact to the Address Book.**
   a. Click the Address Book button.
   b. Click the New button, then click New Contact.
   c. Type John in the First name text box, press [Tab] twice, then type Asher
   d. Click in the E-Mail Addresses text box, then type JohnA@course.com
   e. Click Add, then click OK.
   f. Click the Close button.

3. **Compose and send e-mail.**
   a. Click the New Mail button, then click the Maximize button if necessary.
   b. Click the To button.
   c. Click the name John Asher.
   d. Click To, then click OK.
   e. Click the Subject text box, then type Financial Update Request
   f. Press [Tab] to move to the message window, then type John: Please send 2001 year-end financial report ASAP. Thanks.
   g. Click the Send button.

4. **Retrieve, read, and respond to e-mail.**
   a. Click the Send/Recv button. It may take a few minutes before you receive a message from John Asher.
   b. In the Folders list, click Inbox.
   c. Click the message you just received from John Asher.

    d. Click the Forward Message button, then click the Maximize button if necessary.

    e. Click the To text box, then enter your e-mail address.

    f. Enter a response in the message window.

    g. Click the Send button.

5. **Manage e-mail messages.**

    a. Click File on the menu bar, point to New, then click Folder.

    b. Type Archive.

    c. Click Local Folders in the Folders list, then click OK.

    d. Right-click the message received from John Asher, then click Move To Folder on the shortcut menu.

    e. Click Archive, then click OK.

    f. In the Folders list, click the Archive folder.

    g. Right-click the message received from John Asher, then click Delete on the shortcut menu.

    h. Right-click the Archive folder, click Delete, then click Yes.

    i. Click the Address Book button.

    j. Click John Asher, click the Delete button, then click Yes.

    k. Click the Close button.

6. **Select a news server.**

    a. In the Folders list, click Outlook Express.

    b. Click the Read News link or the Set up a Newsgroup account link.

    c. If the Internet Connection Wizard appears, skip to Step e. Otherwise, click Tools on the menu bar, click Accounts, then click News tab.

    d. Click Add, then click News.

    e. Type your name, then click Next.

    f. Type your e-mail address, then click Next.

    g. Type the name of a news server (see your instructor, technical support person, or ISP for a name), then click Next.

    h. Click Finish, click Close (if necessary), then click No.

7. **View and subscribe to a newsgroup.**

    a. Click the Read News link, then click Yes if necessary.

    b. In the News server list, click the news server you just added (if available).

    c. Type caffeine (If no items appear, type tea or chocolate.)

    d. Click a newsgroup.

    e. Click Go To.

    f. Right-click the newsgroup in the Folders list, then click Subscribe.

8. **Read and post a news message.**

    a. Click a newsgroup message with a +.

    b. Click the + next to the newsgroup message.

    c. Click each reply and read it.

    d. Click the Reply Group button, then type a response.

    e. Click the Send button, then click OK.

    f. Right-click the newsgroup in the Folders list, click Unsubscribe, then click OK.

    g. Right-click the news server in the Folders list, click Remove Account, then click Yes.

    h. Click File on the menu bar, click Exit, then click Yes if necessary to disconnect.

► Independent Challenges

1. You are a new lawyer at Bellig & Associates. You have a computer with Windows 2000 and Outlook Express. Because email is an important method of communication at the law firm, you want to start Outlook Express, open the Address Book, and enter colleagues' e-mail addresses.

To complete this independent challenge:

a. Start Outlook Express, then open the Address Book.
b. Enter the following names and e-mail addresses:
  Greg Bellig   gregb@bellig_law.com
  Jacob Bellig   jacobb@bellig_law.com
  Jarod Higgins   jarodh@bellig_law.com
c. Print the Address Book in both the Business Card and Memo styles.
d. Delete the names and e-mail addresses you just entered in the Address Book.

2. As president of Auto Metals, you have just negotiated a deal to export metal auto parts to an assembly plant in China. Your lawyer, Josh Higgins, has drawn up a preliminary contract. You want to send Josh an e-mail indicating the terms of the deal so he can finish the contract. When Josh responds, move the e-mail into the Legal folder. (*Note*: If you do not have a connection to the Internet, ask your instructor or technical support person for help completing this challenge.)

To complete this independent challenge:

a. Open a New Message window using the stationery called Technical.
b. Type jhiggins@course.com in the To text box in the message window and **China Deal Contract** in the Subject text box.
c. Enter the following message:
  Dear Josh,
  I have completed the negotiations with the assembly plant. Please modify the following terms in the contract:
  1. All parts shall be inspected before shipping.
  2. Ship 10,000 units a month for 3 years with an option for 2 more years.
  Sincerely yours,
  [your name here]
d. Send the e-mail.
e. Print the e-mail you receive from Josh Higgins.
f. Create a new folder called *Legal*, then move the e-mail message you received from Josh Higgins to the new folder.
g. Delete the Legal folder.

3. You are a legal assistant at a law firm specializing in international law. Your boss has asked you to research international contracts with China. You decide to start your research with newsgroups on the Internet.

To complete this independent challenge:

a. Select a news server (see your instructor, technical support person, or ISP to provide you with a news server).
b. Subscribe to a newsgroup about China, then read several newsgroup messages and replies.
c. Reply to a message, then post a new message.
d. Print the newsgroup messages including the original message and replies.
e. Unsubscribe to the newsgroup, then remove the newsgroup server.

4. You like to play sports, watch sports, read about sports, and talk about sports all the time, so you decide to join a sports newsgroup.

To complete this independent challenge:

a. Select a news server (see your instructor, technical support person, or ISP to provide you with a news server).
b. Subscribe to a newsgroup about sports, then read several newsgroup messages and replies.
c. Reply to a message, then post a new message.
d. Print the newsgroup messages including the original message and replies.
e. Unsubscribe to the newsgroup, then remove the newsgroup server.

▶ Visual Workshop

Re-create the screen shown in Figure G-21, which displays the Outlook Express window with a message that has been sent. Print the Outlook Express window. (To print the screen, press the Print Screen key, open Paint, click File on the menu bar, click Paste to paste the screen into Paint, then click Yes to paste the large image if necessary. Click File on the menu bar, click Print, then click Print in the Print dialog box.)

FIGURE G-21

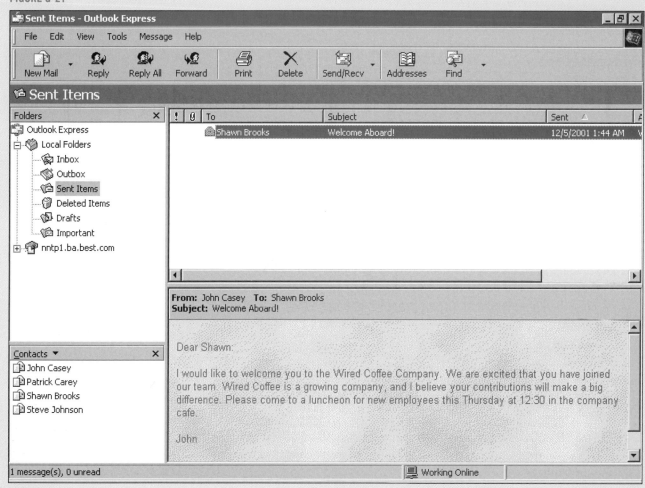

Managing

Shared Files Using
My Network Places

Objectives

- ► **Understand network services**
- ► **Examine network computer properties**
- ► **Open and view My Network Places**
- ► **Create a shared folder**
- ► **Map a network drive**
- ► **Copy and move shared files**
- ► **Open and edit a shared file**
- ► **Disconnect a network drive**

Windows 2000 includes My Network Places, a powerful tool for managing files and folders across a network. A **network** is a system of two or more computers connected together to share resources. **My Network Places** is integrated with Windows Explorer, allowing you to view the entire network and share files and folders with people from other parts of the network. If you are not connected to a network, you will not be able to actually work the steps in this unit. However, you can read the lessons without completing the steps to learn what is possible in a network environment. In this unit, John will use My Network Places to manage files and folders that will be used by multiple users on the Wired Coffee network.

Windows 2000

Understanding Network Services

Windows 2000 is a secure, reliable network operating system that allows people using many different computers to share programs, files, folders, and printers that are stored on computers other than their own. A single computer, called a **server**, can be designated to store these resources. Other computers on the network, called **clients** or **workstations**, can access the resources on the server instead of having to store them. You can share resources using two or more client computers, or you can designate one computer to serve specifically as the server. Windows 2000 provides software specifically designed for a server or a client computer. See Table H-1 for a description of the different Windows 2000 versions. If the network computers are close together, the network is called a **local area network**, or **LAN**. If the computers are spread out over a wider area, the network is called a **wide area network**, or **WAN**. **File sharing** allows many people to work on the same files without the need for creating or storing multiple copies. In this unit, you will integrate the essential Windows file management skills you have already acquired with the specific methods required to take full advantage of Windows networking capabilities. ✎ John realizes there are many benefits to using the Wired Coffee network to manage files and folders.

Share central resources through client/server networking
Windows 2000 provides the option of using a setup called **client/server networking**. Under this arrangement, a single computer is designated as a server, allowing access to resources for any qualified user. Client/server networking provides all users on a network a central location for accessing shared files. Figure H-1 shows an example of a typical network configuration.

Share resources through peer-to-peer networking
The Windows 2000 network operating system also offers a network configuration called peer-to-peer networking. **Peer-to-peer networking** enables two or more computers to link together without designating a central server. In this configuration, any computer user can access resources stored on any other computer, as long as those resources aren't restricted. Peer-to-peer networking allows individual computer users to share files and other resources, such as a printer, with other users on the network. Using peer-to-peer networking, you can transfer files from one computer directly to another without having to access a server.

Share resources through network and dial-up connections
Windows 2000 provides connectivity between your computer and a network, another computer, or the Internet using Network and Dial-up Connections. **Network and Dial-up Connections** enables you to access network resources, whether you are physically connected using a direct cable or remotely connected using a modem. You can connect securely to a network over the Internet using a **Virtual Private Network** connection. You can also connect your computer to another computer or network by having another computer call your computer. For example, you can enable your office computer to be accessed by your home computer.

Grant permission to share designated files and folders on your computer with other users
Windows 2000 provides support for security, so that even though your computer is connected to a network, you can designate which resources on your computer you want to share with others on the network. Before being able to take advantage of any resources on your computer, other users must be granted the required permission.

Map drives on your computer to automatically connect to resources of another client or server
If you have rights to share resources on another computer, Windows 2000 includes a method for connecting automatically to the other computer. You can add a drive letter to your computer that is automatically linked to the shared folder on the other computer every time you log on.

FIGURE H-1: A typical client/server network

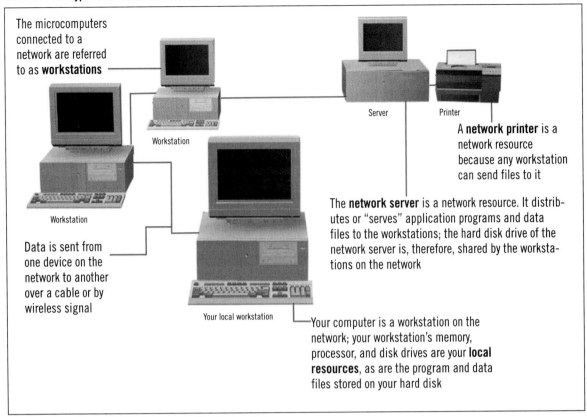

The microcomputers connected to a network are referred to as **workstations**

Workstation

Workstation

Data is sent from one device on the network to another over a cable or by wireless signal

Your local workstation

Server   Printer

A **network printer** is a network resource because any workstation can send files to it

The **network server** is a network resource. It distributes or "serves" application programs and data files to the workstations; the hard disk drive of the network server is, therefore, shared by the workstations on the network

Your computer is a workstation on the network; your workstation's memory, processor, and disk drives are your **local resources**, as are the program and data files stored on your hard disk

TABLE H-1: Windows 2000 versions

Windows 2000 version	description
Professional	A client computer for a client/server network or a peer-to-peer network; successor to Windows NT Workstation 4.0
Server	A standard server computer to perform file, print, application, Web, and communications services; successor to Windows NT Server 4.0
Advanced Server	A server computer for large networks to handle more database-intensive work as well as standard file, print, application, Web, and communication services; successor to Windows NT Server 4.0, Enterprise Edition
Datacenter Server	A server computer for large networks to handle large data storage, ISPs, online transaction processing, and large-scale science and engineering simulations

CLUES TO USE

File permission properties

Every file in the Windows 2000 file system includes **permissions** for each user, or settings that designate what each user can and cannot do to each file. Two basic types of file permissions are available for users: read and full. **Read permission** allows the user to open and view the file, but not to make changes that can be saved to the file. When you open a read-only file, the words "Read Only" appear in the title bar. You can makes changes to the file, but an error message appears when you try to save it. You can save the file with a new name in a different location (one you have full access to). **Full permission** allows the user to edit and save changes to the file (or "write") and execute programs on server or client computers. Qualified users or system administrators use file permissions and passwords to control who has access to any specific area of the network. In this way, the network remains secure against unauthorized use.

Examining Network Computer Properties

Computers are identified on networks by names and locations. The computer's name refers to the individual machine, whereas the computer's location refers to how the machine is grouped together with other computers. In a peer-to-peer network, individual computers are often organized into workgroups. A **workgroup** is a group of computers that performs common tasks or belongs to users who share common duties and interests. In a client/server network, individual computers are often grouped into domains. A **domain** is a collection of computers that the person managing the network creates to group computers that are used for the same tasks together and to simplify the set up and maintenance of the network. The difference between a domain and a workgroup is that the network administrator defines the domains that exist on the network and controls access to computers with those domains. In a workgroup, each user determines who has access to his or her computer. Computers anywhere on the network can be located easily through the naming hierarchy and can be addressed individually by name. You can find out the name and workgroup or domain of a computer on the network by examining the network computer properties. John decides to check the properties of his network computer.

QuickTip

To view the current status of the local area connection, double-click the Local Area Connection icon in the Network and Dial-up Connections window.

QuickTip

To examine network properties for your computer, you can also right-click the My Computer icon, click properties, then click the Network Identification tab.

1. Right-click the **My Network Places icon** 🖳 on the desktop, click **Properties**, then click the **Maximize button** ☐ if necessary

   The Network and Dial-up Connections window opens, as shown in Figure H-2, and displays an icon to make a new network connection and an icon to connect to for the local area connection. When you start your computer and log on to the network, Windows 2000 automatically detects your local area network and creates a connection (unless you have previously disconnected your local area connection).

2. Click the **Network Identification link**

   The System Properties dialog box for your network computer opens with the Network Identification tab in front, as shown in Figure H-3. In Figure H-3, the network computer name appears at the top of the tab. The domain or workgroup name appears below the network computer name. In this case, the network computer name is JOHNCASEY and the domain name is NETONE.

3. Click **Properties**

   The Identification Changes dialog box opens. In the Properties dialog box, you can change the computer name and domain or workgroup name.

4. Click **Cancel**

   The Identification Changes dialog box closes.

5. Click **OK** to close the System Properties dialog box

6. Click the **Close button** ☒ in the Network and Dial-up Connections window

FIGURE H-2: Network and Dial-up Connections window

Double-click to create a new connection

Click to identify your network interface card (NIC)

Click to identify your network computer

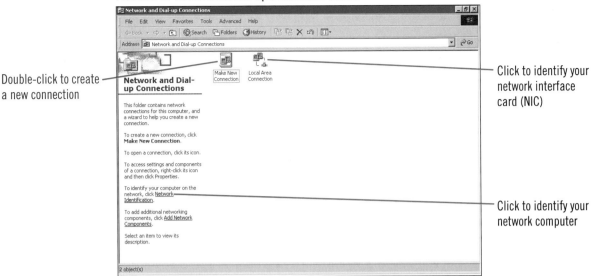

FIGURE H-3: Network Identification tab of System Properties dialog box

Click to change computer or domain name

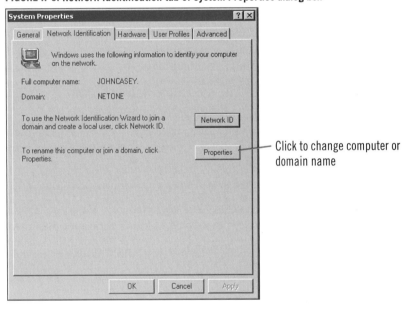

Viewing network properties

A computer that uses a Windows 2000 network must be configured so that other machines on the network recognize it. On a small network, you might be responsible for configuring your computer or that responsibility might fall to the network administrator. You can view and modify some of the network settings for your computer using the Network and Dial-up Connections dialog box. Right-click the My Network Places icon, click Properties, click Advanced on the menu bar, then click Advanced Settings. The network configuration consists of four components: adapter, protocol, service, and binding. The **adapter** is a device that connects your computer to the network. Adapters are usually cards, called **network interface** cards, or **NICs**, inserted into a slot in the back of your computer. To display the name of your NIC, click the Local Area Connection icon in the Network and Dial-up Connections window. The **protocol** is the language that the computer uses to communicate with other computers on the network. The **service** allows you to share your computer resources, such as files and printers, with other networked computers. A **binding** is a connection that enables communications among the adapters, protocols, and services installed in Windows 2000. Understanding which components have been installed on your computer helps you understand the capabilities and limitations of your computer on the network.

Windows 2000

Opening and Viewing My Network Places

The key to managing files and folders in a network environment is understanding the structure of your particular network. Most networks are comprised of multiple types of computers and operating systems. My Network Places lets you view the entire network or just your part of the network at a glance. The My Network Places window gives you access to the servers, domains, and workgroups on the network. From the My Network Places window, you can open the Entire Network window. The Entire Network window allows you to view a list of servers not in your workgroup and to view other network domains. If you want to add a server to your workgroup, you can use the Add Network Place wizard to help you through the process. ✒ John uses My Network Places to see where his computer fits in with all the others on his network.

Steps 1234

QuickTip

To search for a computer on the network, double-click the My Network Places icon, click Search on the toolbar, type the name of the computer you want to find, then click Search Now.

1. Double-click the **My Network Places icon** 🖳, then click the **Maximize button** 🔳 if necessary
   The icon is usually located right below the My Computer icon on the desktop. The My Network Places window opens, as shown in Figure H-4, and displays icons for all of the networked computers in John's immediate network, an icon for the Entire Network, and an icon to add a network to My Network Places. John's immediate network is currently running server and client computers.

2. Double-click the **Entire Network icon** 🌐, then click the **entire contents** link in the left pane to display the entire network
   My Network Places displays the various types of networks connected to John's computer. If you are on a large network, you might have other choices that will display more segments of the network.

QuickTip

To search for computers in the same workgroup, click Computers Near Me.

3. Double-click the **Microsoft Windows Network icon** 🖧
   The Microsoft Windows Network window displays the computer network domains and workgroups connected to John's computer, as shown in Figure H-5.

4. Double-click a **Network Domain icon** 🖧 in your immediate network
   The My Network Places window displays the individual computers (including one for John) associated with the selected network domain.

QuickTip

My Network Places automatically keeps track of all your favorite folders on the local network. The first time you open a file on your network, a shortcut to its folder appears in My Network Places for easy access next time.

5. Double-click a **Network Computer icon** 🖥 in your immediate network
   The computer connected to your network opens and displays the contents of the drive or folder.

6. Click the **Back button list arrow** ⬅ Back ▾ on the toolbar, then click **My Network Places**
   The My Network Places window again displays the active computers in John's immediate network.

FIGURE H-4: My Network Places window

Menu bar
Toolbar
Address bar

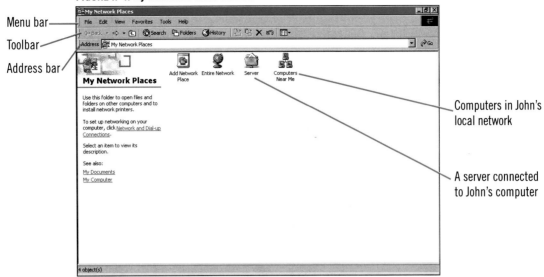

Computers in John's local network

A server connected to John's computer

FIGURE H-5: Microsoft Windows Network window

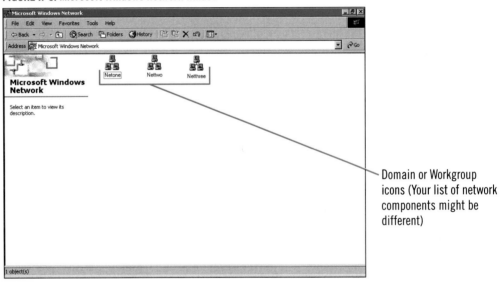

Domain or Workgroup icons (Your list of network components might be different)

CLUES TO USE

Searching for network services

Search Assistant makes it easier to search for files or folders, printers, people, and other computers on your network. Search Assistant has an indexing service that maintains an index of all the files on your computer, making searches even faster. To search for computers on your network using the Search Assistant, double-click the My Network Places icon on the desktop, click Search on the toolbar, type the computer name you want to find, then click Search Now. If you want to find files or folders, people, or information on the Internet, you can click a search option link below the Search Now button. You can also use the Search Assistant to search Active Directory for network services, such as a printer that prints in color and is located near your computer, a group of users managed by a particular individual, or a shared folder to which a unique keyword has been assigned. **Active Directory** catalogs information about all the objects on a network, including people, computers, shared folders, and printers, and distributes that information to all the computers throughout your network. Before you can use Active Directory, the feature must be installed on your network server and tailored for your organization. To perform a search using Active Directory, double-click the My Network Places icon, double-click the Entire Network icon, click the entire contents link in the left pane, double-click Directory, right-click a directory object, and then click Find.

Creating a Shared Folder

A folder on your computer can be shared with others on the network. When you share a folder, you can decide the permissions that others will be allowed or denied when they access the files in that folder over the network. To create a shared folder in My Network Places, you use many of the file management skills you learned with Windows Explorer. You must first decide where you will put the new folder. ◢◤ John has decided to create a shared folder called Sales on his computer that will allow employees from anywhere on the network to add information to Sales files. If you are working at your own computer, you might create this shared folder in a subfolder within your My Documents folder. Otherwise, you may have to ask your instructor or technical support person for permission to create a folder in another location, or you can simply read through the steps without actually creating a folder.

1. **Click the Address list arrow on the Address bar**

   My Network Places displays the desktop and drives of your own computer. You can now work with the files and folders from your computer and still have the option of connecting to various other parts of the network.

2. **Click the My Documents folder**

   My Network Places displays the contents of the My Documents folder on your hard drive.

3. **Right-click anywhere in the My Documents window (except on a file or folder), point to New, then click Folder**

   A new folder, named New Folder, appears in the window.

4. **Type Sales, then press [Enter]**

   The folder is now named Sales.

5. **Click File on the menu bar, then click Sharing**

   The Sales Properties dialog box opens. The Sales Properties dialog box is where you adjust the settings to allow other users access to the files in your shared folder. The Sharing tab allows you to designate the kind of access you want other users to have for the folder you just created.

6. **Click the Share this folder option button**

   The sharing information about the Sales folder is shown in Figure H-6. This tab includes a text box for entering the shared name of the folder. Unless you have a very good reason for naming it differently, it's best to make the shared name the same as the folder name. Keeping the names consistent will help avoid confusion. By default, Windows automatically enters the name of the folder as the shared name.

7. **Click Permissions**

   The Permissions for Sales dialog box opens. By default, Windows automatically sets the file permission to Full Control, Change, and Read.

8. **Click OK**

9. **Click OK to close the Properties window**

   The Sales folder, shown in Figure H-7, is now accessible by anyone with the right permission from anywhere on the network. A Shared Folder icon 🖐️ appears with a hand underneath the folder.

FIGURE H-6: Sharing tab of Sales Properties dialog box

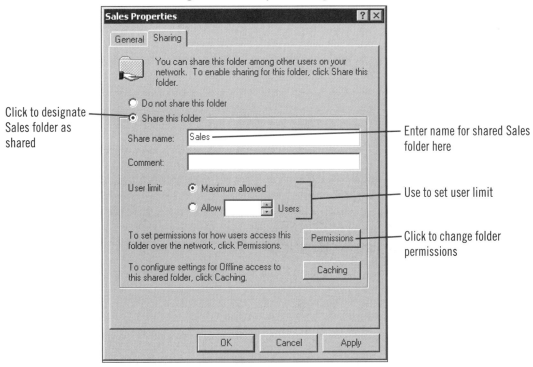

Click to designate Sales folder as shared

Enter name for shared Sales folder here

Use to set user limit

Click to change folder permissions

FIGURE H-7: Shared folder within My Documents folder

Your list of files and folders may be different

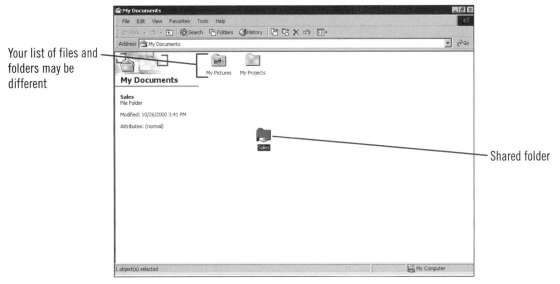

Shared folder

Password protection

With Windows 2000, you can use passwords to control access to your computer, the network, and specific files and folders. You can set different passwords and varying degrees of access for the different drives, folders, and files. You can also manage your files and printers from a remote computer and set password protection to limit access. To set or change password protection in Windows 2000 Professional, open the Control Panel and double-click the Users and Passwords icon, click the Users tab, click a user name, click Set Password, and then enter a new password. To change a user name and access privileges, click a user name, click Properties, click the General or Group Membership tab, then specify the changes you want. You can also use the Display utility to password protect files when in screen saver mode.

Mapping a Network Drive

My Network Places enables you to connect your computer to other computers on the network quite easily. If you connect to a network location frequently, you might want to designate a drive letter on your computer as a direct connection to a shared drive or folder on another computer. Instead of spending unnecessary time opening My Network Places and the shared drive or folder each time you want to access it, you can create a direct connection, called **mapping** a drive, to the network location for quick and easy access. ✐ At John's request, the network administrator created a shared folder called Wired Coffee on the computer named Server. Next John uses My Network Places to map a drive letter from his computer to that folder so that he can easily move files to this central location for others to share. To complete these steps, you need to map to a network computer and a folder specified by your instructor or technical support person. If you don't have a networked computer available, read the steps without completing them.

1. Click the **Address list arrow**, then click **My Network Places**
   My Network Places shows you all the active computers in your immediate network.

2. Click **Tools** on the menu bar, then click **Map Network Drive**
   The Map Network Drive dialog box opens, as shown in Figure H-8. By default, the Map Network Drive dialog box highlights the next available drive letter.

3. If you want to use a different drive letter, click the **Drive list arrow**, then click the **drive letter** you want to use

4. Click **Browse**
   The Browse dialog box opens and displays a tree structure of My Network Places and My Computer.

5. Click the **+** next to the drive with the networked computer you can map onto your computer (specified by your instructor or technical support person), click the **Wired Coffee folder** (or the shared folder specified by your instructor or technical support person) to select it, then click **OK**
   The Browse dialog box closes and the Map Network Drive dialog box opens.

6. If not already checked, click the **Reconnect at logon check box**, then click **Finish**
   The Map Network Drive dialog box closes, and My Network Places maps a drive connecting your computer to the Wired Coffee shared folder (or to the shared folder specified by your instructor or technical support person). When the connection is complete, a window opens for the newly mapped drive, allowing you to view the files within the mapped drive, as shown in Figure H-9. John can now easily copy folders and files from his floppy disk into the shared folder.

7. Click the **Close button** ☒ on the mapped drive window

8. Click the **Back button list arrow** ⟵ Back ▾ on the toolbar, then click **My Network Places**
   The My Network Places window displays the active computers in your immediate neighborhood.

QuickTip

If you already know the network path for the drive you want to map, right-click the My Network Places icon, click Map Network Drive, enter the network path in the Path box, then click OK.

Trouble?

If your mapped drives are not automatically reconnecting when you log on, make sure your user name and password are the same for all the networks to which you connect.

FIGURE H-8: Map Network Drive dialog box

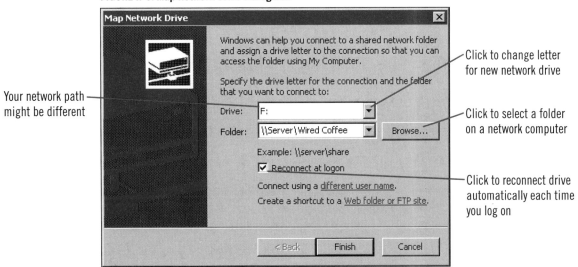

Your network path
might be different

Click to change letter
for new network drive

Click to select a folder
on a network computer

Click to reconnect drive
automatically each time
you log on

FIGURE H-9: Wired Coffee folder window

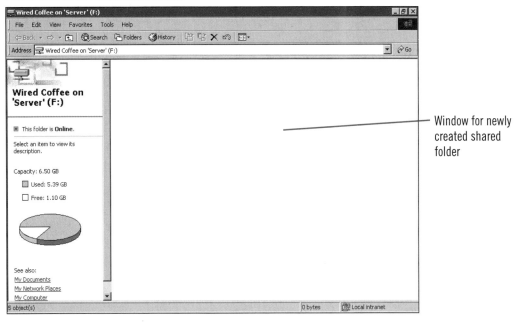

Window for newly
created shared
folder

Creating a network or dial-up connection

Network and Dial-up Connections provide connectivity between your computer and a network, another computer, or the Internet. You can create outgoing or incoming connections. **Outgoing connections** contact a remote access server by using a cable or modem to establish a connection with your computer. **Incoming connections** enable your computer to be contacted by other computers. This means your computer running Windows 2000 can operate as a remote access server. With Network and Dial-up Connections, you can establish a Virtual Private Network connection through the Internet, a direct computer connection, or a dial-up connection. To establish any one of these connection types, click the Start button on the taskbar, point to Settings, click Network and Dial-up Connections, double-click Make New Connection, click Next, click the connection option you want, and then follow the instructions in the Network Connection wizard. To grant incoming connection access rights to your computer, open Network and Dial-up Connections, right-click Incoming Connections, click Properties, click the General tab, then select the devices through which incoming connections can connect.

Copying and Moving Shared Files

Once you have created shared folders and mapped your network drives, copying and moving shared files and folders in Windows is as easy as managing files on your own computer. The only difference is data transfer can take longer over a network than it does on your local computer. You can copy and move files using any of the Windows 2000 Professional file management tools: My Network Places, My Computer, or Windows Explorer. My Network Places works just like My Computer. ▟▄▄ John wants to copy files from his floppy disk to the shared Sales folder on his hard drive to make them accessible to the other users on his network. He also needs to move a file from the shared Sales folder to the Wired Coffee folder on the network drive (F:) to make it accessible to another department. Because he's copying files to several locations, John uses Windows Explorer to drag and drop the files.

QuickTip

To prevent any changes to your Project Disk, make sure you have made a copy of it. If you need assistance, see your instructor or technical support person.

1. Make sure a copy of your Project Disk is inserted in the appropriate floppy drive

2. In the My Network Places window, click the **Address list arrow**, click **3½ Floppy (A:)** or **(B:)** (whichever drive holds your Project Disk), then double-click the **Unit H folder**
   My Network Places displays the contents of the 3½ floppy drive.

3. Right-click the **Wired Coffee folder**, click **Explore**, then click the **Sales folder** in the Explorer Bar
   Windows Explorer opens, displaying the available folders and drives in the left pane, as shown in Figure H-10. You can now copy or move files easily from your computer to anywhere on the network.

Trouble?

If you click the Sales folder by mistake, click the Sales folder on the floppy disk, then go to Step 5.

4. In the Explorer Bar, click the + next to the My Documents folder to display the shared Sales folder, as shown in Figure H-11, but *do not click the folder*

5. Click **Edit** on the menu bar, click **Select All**, then drag the files from the right pane to the shared **Sales folder** in the Explorer Bar
   The files are copied to the shared Sales folder on the hard drive. The employees who have access to John's computer can now share the files.

6. In the Explorer Bar, click the shared **Sales folder**, then click the **down scroll arrow** in the Explorer Bar if necessary until you can see the icon representing the mapped network folder
   Windows Explorer lists the contents of the Sales folder, as shown in Figure H-11.

7. Right-drag the **Suppliers file** to the mapped networked folder in the Explorer Bar, then click **Move Here**
   The Suppliers file is moved to the networked folder.

8. Click the **mapped networked folder** in the Explorer Bar to view the Suppliers file, then click the **Close button** ☒ in both the Exploring Sales and **Unit H** windows

FIGURE H-10: Exploring Sales folder

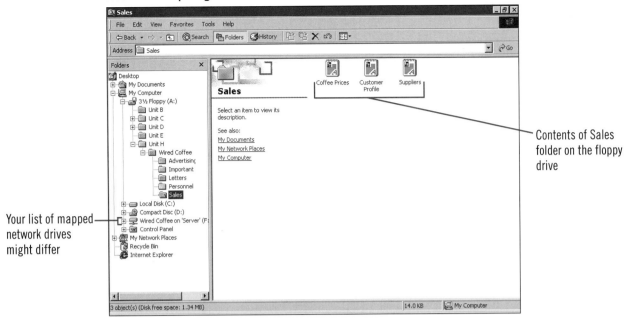

Contents of Sales folder on the floppy drive

Your list of mapped network drives might differ

FIGURE H-11: Location of Wired Coffee folder on mapped network drive (F:)

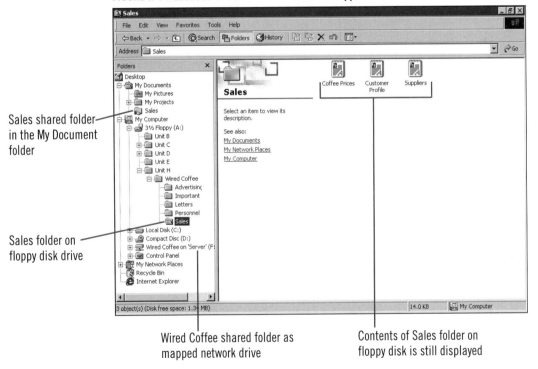

Sales shared folder in the My Document folder

Sales folder on floppy disk drive

Wired Coffee shared folder as mapped network drive

Contents of Sales folder on floppy disk is still displayed

Network traffic

Large networks may serve hundreds of users simultaneously. Like water flowing through pipes, only a certain amount of data can pass through the wires connecting the individual computers at any given time. If the amount of network traffic is of sufficient volume, then the flow of data may slow considerably, causing file operations such as opening, saving, and copying to take longer to complete.

Opening and Editing a Shared File

Working with shared files on a network is a simple task with Windows. Once you have mapped all the necessary drives to your network folders, you can use network files in any program from your computer. For example, you can use WordPad to edit text files, or Paint to create a graphic. You may also be able to use programs installed on the server specifically for the use of individual clients (ask your system administrator about available options). ✐ John uses WordPad to make corrections in the Suppliers file that he placed in the Wired Coffee folder on the server.

Steps 1 2 3 4

1. **Click the Start button** on the taskbar, point to **Programs**, point to **Accessories**, then click **WordPad**
   The WordPad window opens.

2. **Click File** on the menu bar, click **Open**, then click the **Look in list arrow**
   The Open file dialog box, shown in Figure H-12, displays the Look in list with local and networked drives. From here you can open files located on all drives and folders, including the drives mapped to the network.

3. **Click the icon for the mapped network drive to the Wired Coffee shared folder**
   The contents of the networked folder appear in the File list, as shown in Figure H-13.

4. **Click Suppliers, then click Open**
   The file named Suppliers opens.

5. **Click the bottom of the list, then type Homegrown USA Coffee**

6. **Click the Save button** 🖫 on the toolbar
   WordPad saves the changes to the file Suppliers.

7. **Click the Close button** ⊠ in the WordPad window

FIGURE H-12: **Open dialog box**

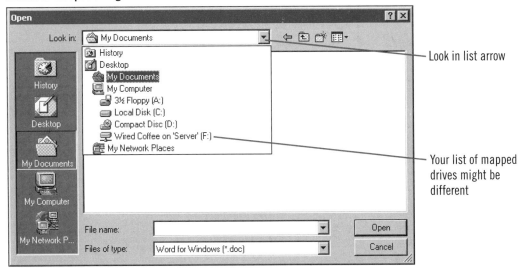

Look in list arrow

Your list of mapped drives might be different

FIGURE H-13: **Files in Wired Coffee shared folder**

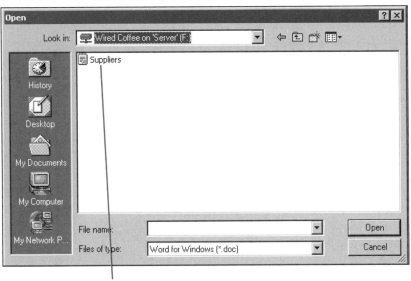

Contents of Wired Coffee on the 'Server' (F:) drive

CLUES TO USE

Working with shared network files offline

You can make shared files available offline. The Offline Files feature stores a version of them in a reserved portion of disk space on your computer called **cache**. The computer can access this cache regardless of whether it is connected to the network. You can use manual or automatic caching for documents. **Manual caching** for documents provides offline access to only those files that someone using your shared folder specifically identifies, while **automatic caching** for documents makes every file that someone opens from your shared folder available to them offline. Automatic caching does not make every file in your shared folder available offline, only those files that are opened. In Windows 2000, the Offline Files feature is enabled by default. If it's necessary to set up your computer to use Offline Files, double-click the My Computer icon, click Tools on the menu bar, click Folder Options, click the Offline Files tab, click to select the Enable Offline Files check box, then click OK.

Disconnecting a Network Drive

Windows 2000

Usually, you map a network drive to automatically reconnect every time you log on. However, sometimes you may find it necessary to manually disconnect a mapped drive. Your system administrator may have added new hard drives to the server, or he or she may have reorganized the directory structure, in which case the network path for the mapped drive may now be incorrect. Windows makes the process of disconnecting a mapped drive very easy in the case of such an event. ▶ John was informed by the system administrator of a network reorganization that will take place over the weekend. He disconnects the drive mapped to (F:) until he finds out what changes have been made. Before disconnecting the mapped drive, John cleans up his hard drive and the mapped drive.

1. Double-click the **My Computer icon** 🖳, then double-click the **mapped drive**
   The contents of the mapped drive appears.

2. Right-click the **Suppliers file**, click **Delete**, then click **Yes** to confirm the deletion

3. Click the **Back button** ⬅ Back ▾ on the toolbar

4. Click the **Address list arrow**, then click **My Documents**
   John wants to delete the Sales folder.

5. Right-click the **Sales shared folder**, then click **Delete**
   The Confirm Folder Delete dialog box opens.

6. Click **Yes**, click **Yes** again, then click the **Close button** ✕ in the My Documents window

QuickTip

To disconnect a network drive in Windows Explorer, right-click a mapped network drive in the left pane, then click Disconnect.

7. Right-click the **My Network Places icon** 📇 on the desktop
   A pop-up menu appears for My Network Places, as shown in Figure H-14. This menu provides several commands for working in a network environment. See Table H-2 for a description of the commands available through this menu.

8. Click **Disconnect Network Drive** on the pop-up menu
   The Disconnect Network Drive dialog box opens, as shown in Figure H-15. The dialog box displays a list of all the network drives that you have mapped from your computer. You should check with your system administrator or instructor before actually disconnecting a drive. To quit without actually disconnecting a drive, click Cancel.

9. Click the **mapped drive** with the Wired Coffee folder (or the one you previously mapped), click **OK**, then click **Yes** if necessary to the warning message
   Windows disconnects the drive you have selected and closes the Disconnect Network Drive dialog box.

Network paths

The path to a shared network directory is like the path to a file on a hard or floppy disk. For example, the path to the Suppliers file on your Project Disk is A:\Wired Coffee\Sales\Suppliers. Network paths replace the drive designation with the host computer name, as in \\Server\Wired Coffee. In either example, the path tells the computer where to look for the files you need.

FIGURE H-14: Shortcut menu for My Network Places

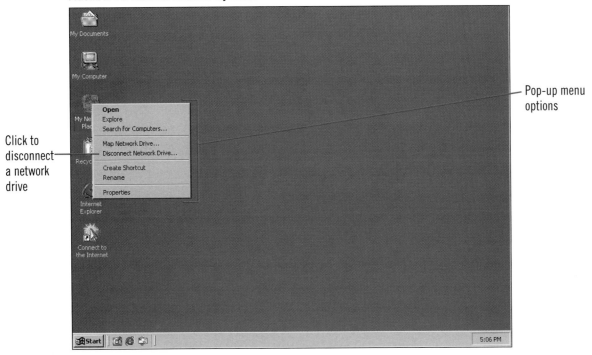

Pop-up menu options

Click to disconnect a network drive

FIGURE H-15: Disconnect Network Drive dialog box

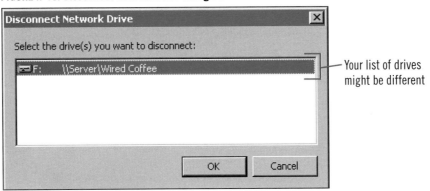

Your list of drives might be different

TABLE H-2: Pop-up menu commands for My Network Places

command	function
Open	Opens My Network Places
Explore	Opens Windows Explorer in order to copy and move files from one folder to another, whether on your local computer or the network
Search for Computers	Finds a computer whose name you know but not its location
Map Network Drive	Maps a drive from your computer to a shared directory on another computer
Disconnect Network Drive	Disconnects a drive on your computer from a shared directory on another computer
Create Shortcut	Creates a shortcut to My Network Places
Rename	Renames the My Network Places icon
Properties	Displays the properties of your network

Practice

▶ Concepts Review

Label each of the elements of the screen shown in Figure H-16.

FIGURE H-16

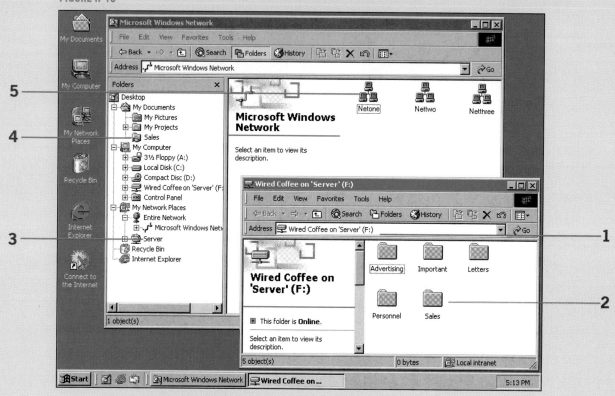

Match each of the terms with the statement that describes its function.

6. Shared folder
7. File permissions
8. Entire Network icon
9. Network path
10. Disconnect Network Drive command

a. Lists all workgroups and computers attached to a network
b. The address for an individual computer on a network
c. Determines who can read, write, or execute files
d. A location where multiple users can access the same files
e. Removes a mapped drive from the local computer

Select the best answer from the list of choices.

11. **The windows network management tool that allows you to manage the files and folders of your network is called**
    a. Windows Explorer.
    b. My Computer.
    c. My Network Places.
    d. File Manager.

12. **To disconnect a network drive,**
    a. Double-click the drive letter in My Network Places.
    b. Highlight the drive letter, click File, then click Delete.
    c. Click the drive letter, then drag it to the Recycle Bin.
    d. Right-click the My Network Places icon, then click Disconnect Network Drive.

13. **When you highlight a drive letter in My Network Places, click File on the menu bar, then click Explore,**
    a. My Computer starts, allowing you to manage files and folders.
    b. My Network Places lists the entire network.
    c. Windows Explorer starts, allowing you to manage files and folders.
    d. File Manager starts, allowing you to manage files and folders.

14. **When you map a networked drive,**
    a. My Network Places displays a graphic of the entire structure of the network.
    b. You can use the shared files and folders of another computer on the network.
    c. The computer you are using is attached to the network.
    d. My Network Places adds your computer to the network path.

15. **If the file permissions for a shared folder are set to read-only,**
    a. No one can read the files in the folder.
    b. You can edit the file and save your changes.
    c. Everyone can read the files but not write to the files.
    d. Everyone can write to the files but not read the files.

▶ Skills Review

1. **Examine network computer properties.**
   a. Right-click the My Network Places icon.
   b. Click Properties on the pop-up menu.
   c. Click the Network Identification link.
   d. View the network properties.
   e. Click OK.
   f. Click the Close button.

2. Open and view My Network Places.
  a. Double-click the My Network Places icon.
  b. Double-click the Entire Network icon.
  c. Click the entire contents link.
  d. Double-click the Microsoft Windows Network icon.
  e. Double-click a network domain icon.
  f. Double-click a network computer icon.
  g. Click the Back button list arrow, then click My Network Places.

3. Create a shared folder.
  a. Click the Address list arrow, then click the My Document folder.
  b. Right-click in the My Documents window, point to New, then click Folder.
  c. Name the new folder *Memos*, then press Enter.
  d. Click File on the menu bar, then click Sharing.
  e. Click the Share this folder option button.
  f. Click OK.

4. Map a network drive.
  a. Click the Address list arrow, then click My Network Places.
  b. Click Tools on the menu bar, then click Map Network Drive.
  c. Click Browse, then find the shared folder to which you want to map.
  d. Click the shared folder.
  e. Click OK.
  f. Click the Reconnect at logon check box to select it if necessary.
  g. Click Finish.
  h. Click the Close button on the mapped drive window.

5. Copy and move shared files.
  a. Insert a copy of your Project Disk into the appropriate floppy drive.
  b. Click the Address list arrow, click 3½ Floppy (A:) or (B:), then double-click the folder that contains your Project files.
  c. Click the Wired Coffee folder.
  d. Click File on the menu bar, then click Explore.
  e. Click the Letters folder in the Explorer Bar.
  f. Click the + next to the My Documents folder.
  g. Click Edit on the menu bar, then click Select All.
  h. Drag all the files to the shared Memos folder you created in the My Documents folder.
  i. Click the shared Memos folder in the Explorer Bar.
  j. Right-drag the IRS Letter file to the mapped networked folder in the Explorer Bar, then click Move Here.
  k. Click the mapped networked folder in the Explorer Bar to view the file.
  l. Click the Close buttons in the Explorer and Unit H windows.

6. Open and edit a shared file.
  a. Start WordPad.
  b. Open the IRS Letter file located on the mapped networked folder.
  c. In the document, change *April 25* to *May 10*.
  d. Save the file, print it, then close the file and WordPad.

7. **Disconnect a network drive.**
   a. Double-click the My Computer icon, then double-click the mapped drive.
   b. Click the IRS Letter File, press [Delete], then click Yes.
   c. Click the Address list arrow, then click My Documents.
   d. Right-click the shared Memos folder, then click Delete.
   e. Click Yes, then click Yes again to confirm the deletion.
   f. Click the Close button.
   g. Right-click the My Network Places icon.
   h. Click Disconnect Network Drive.
   i. Select the drive you mapped in Step 4.
   j. Click OK, then click Yes if necessary.

▶ Independent Challenges

1. As the new clerk at Holly's (a craft store), you have been asked to create a list of suppliers' names. Your task is to enter the supplier information into a new file and place that file in two places for others to use. You must create a shared folder on your computer that will store the file, then map a drive to a network folder that will also contain the file. (*Note*: Ask your instructor or technical support person which networked computer you can map onto your computer. If you are working in a lab environment, you may not be able to create a shared folder. If so, do not create a shared folder, and instead use the folder supplied by your instructor.)

To complete this independent challenge:

a. Open My Computer on the desktop.
b. Open your local hard drive.
c. Open the My Documents folder.
d. Create a shared folder called *Suppliers* with read only permissions.
e. Open WordPad and enter the following information in a new document:

Name	Address	City & State
Baskets & Things	101 Hopyard Road	Chicago, IL
Frames R Us	1934 Hummingbird Lane	Los Angeles, CA
Season's	125 34th Street	New York, NY

f. Save the file as *Supplier List* in the newly created Suppliers folder.
g. Print the Supplier List file.
h. Map a drive to a shared folder on another computer to which you have permission.
i. Create a *US Suppliers* folder on that drive.
j. Copy the Supplier List file from the Suppliers folder on the local computer to the US Suppliers folder on the mapped drive.
k. Print the Screen (Press the Print Screen key to make a copy of the screen, open Paint, click Edit on the menu bar, click Paste to paste the screen into Paint, then click Yes to paste the large image if necessary. Click File on the menu bar, click Print, then click Print in the Print dialog box.)
l. Delete the Suppliers folder on your hard drive and the US Suppliers folder on the mapped drive.
m. Disconnect the network drive you mapped and delete the shared folder you created.

2. As the president of your company, you have decided to increase the pay rates for two of your employees, Jessica Thielen and Debbie Cabral. You will use WordPad to write a memo that you can edit and use for both employees. After completing the memos, you will print the documents for the employees. You also want to copy the documents to the company server so they can be stored in their employee folders.

To complete this independent challenge:

a. Create a *Memos* folder on your Project Disk.

b. Open WordPad and enter the following memo in a new document:

Dear Jessica,

Your service to this company is greatly appreciated. To show my appreciation to such an outstanding employee as you, I have decided to give you a 10% raise in salary. The raise will go into effect with the next pay period.

Sincerely yours,

[your name here]

c. Use the Save As command to name the document *Thielen Raise* and save it in the Memos folder, then print the document.

d. Change *Dear Jessica* to *Dear Debbie* in the Thielen Raise memo.

e. Save the file as *Cabral Raise* in the Memos folder and print the document.

f. Close the file and WordPad.

g. Map a drive to a shared folder on another computer to which you have permission.

h. Create a shared folder on that mapped drive called *Thielen* and copy the Thielen Raise file from your Project Disk into the Thielen folder.

i. Create a shared folder on that mapped drive called *Cabral*, and copy the Cabral Raise file from your Project Disk to the Cabral folder.

j. Print the screen. (See Independent Challenge 1, Step k for screen printing instructions.)

k. Delete the Thielen and Cabral shared folders on the mapped drive.

l. Disconnect the network drive you mapped.

3. You are the system administrator for your company's computer network. During peak usage of the network, you want to monitor who is on the network. You will use the Properties command in the My Network Places to find out who is connected to the network. You also want to check the properties for a few servers to verify the connect information.

To complete this independent challenge:

a. Using My Network Places, open Computers Near Me.

b. Display the network identification for two connected computers to find out their name and domain.

c. Print the screen for the Computers Near Me window and the network identification for the connected computers (see Independent Challenge 1, Step k for screen printing instructions).

d. Map two drives to a shared folder on another computer to which you have permission.

e. Display the network identification for the mapped drives.

f. Print the screen for the network identification for the mapped drives (see Independent Challenge 1, Step k for screen printing instructions).

g. Disconnect the network drives you mapped.

4. The system administrator for your network calls and informs you that he needs to make some changes to the directory structure. He advises you to move any files you have put on the server recently and to disconnect any mapped drives.

To complete this independent challenge:

a. Map a drive to a shared folder on another computer to which you have permission, and copy two files from your Project Disk to this mapped drive.

b. Using My Network Places, create a folder on your local hard disk called *Network Files*.

c. Move the files from the folder on the network drive to the Network Files folder on the local hard disk.

d. Print the screen. (See Independent Challenge 1, Step k for screen printing instructions.)

e. Disconnect the mapped drive from the network.

f. Delete the Network Files folder on your local hard drive.

▶ Visual Workshop

Re-create the screen shown in Figure H-17, which displays the My Network Places window. Print the screen. (See Independent Challenge 1, Step k for screen printing instructions.)

FIGURE H-17

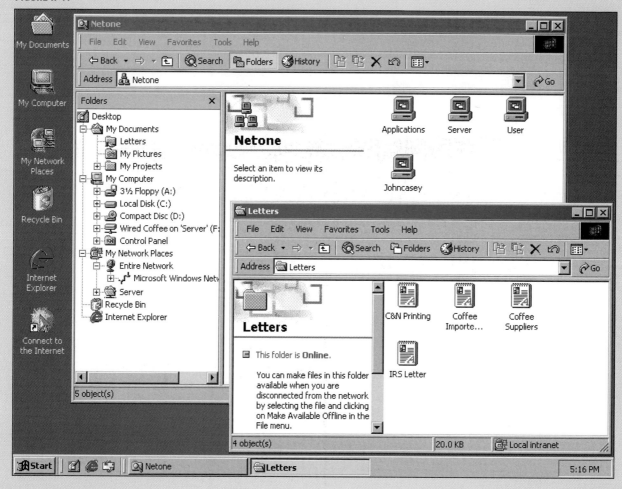

Glossary

Windows 2000

Accessibility Wizard A series of dialog boxes that guides you through steps to configure Windows 2000 for vision, hearing, and mobility needs.

Accessories Built-in programs that come with Windows 2000 that you can use for day-to-day tasks.

Active Desktop The desktop that allows you to access the Internet and view Internet content (Active Desktop items) directly from it. *See also* Desktop.

Active Desktop item An element you can place on the desktop to access or display information from the Internet.

Active Directory A catalog of information, including people, computers, shared folders, and printers, on a network.

Active program The program that is currently running.

Active window A window that you are currently using; if a window is active, its title bar changes color to differentiate it from other windows, and its program button on the taskbar appears indented.

Adapter The device that connects a computer to a network.

Address bar A bar that displays the address of the current Web page or the contents of a local or network computer drive.

Address Book An electronic database where you can store detailed information about a person or company.

Article A newsgroup message.

Auto hide A feature that automatically hides the taskbar when you are not using it.

AutoComplete A File name feature in the Open and Save dialog boxes that suggests possible matches with previous filename entries in the File name text box.

Automatic caching An offline file option that makes every file someone opens from a shared folder available for offline access.

Background The surface of your desktop on which icons and windows appear; you can customize its appearance using the Display Properties dialog box.

Backup The process you perform to save your data quickly and compress it into a small space on a set of disks or a tape cartridge.

Binding A connection that enables communications among the adapters, protocols, and services installed in Windows 2000.

Bitmapped character A character that consists of small dots organized to form it.

Bookmark A reference point in a document to which you want to create a link.

Browser A program, such as Microsoft Internet Explorer, designed to access the Internet. *See also* Web browser.

Bullet mark An indicator that shows an option is enabled.

Cache A reserved portion of disk space on a computer.

Cascading menu An additional list of commands available from a menu item with an arrow next to it. Pointing to the arrow displays the submenu.

Center A Display properties option that positions the wallpaper picture or pattern in the center of the desktop screen.

Channel A specialized Web page that delivers content from the Internet.

Check mark An indicator that shows a feature is enabled.

Click To press and release the left mouse button once.

Client A computer that accesses shared resources on a server.

Client/server network A network setup that provides all users on a network a central location for accessing shared files.

Clipboard Temporary storage space on a hard drive that contains information that has been cut or copied.

Close To exit a program or remove a window from the desktop. The Close button usually appears in the upper-right corner of a window.

Command Directive that provides access to a program's features.

Contact Information about a person or company with whom you communicate; in Outlook Express, contacts are stored in the Address Book.

Contact group A group of contacts that you can organize together; in Outlook Express, contact groups are stored in the Address Book.

Contacts list A list in Outlook Express that displays the contacts and contact groups in the Address Book.

Context-sensitive help Help that relates to the task on which you are currently working.

Control bar A bar in Windows Media Player that contains buttons to play all or part of a video or sound clip.

Control Panel A Windows utility for changing computer settings.

Copy To copy data to another location while leaving it in the original location.

Conversation thread A collection of newsgroup messages that consists of the original message on a particular topic along with any responses.

Criteria A set of information on which to make a decision.

Cut To remove data and place it on the Clipboard to be pasted in another location.

Cut and paste To move information from one place to another using the Clipboard as the temporary storage area.

Defragment A feature that allows you to rewrite the files on your disk to contiguous blocks rather than in random blocks.

Delete To remove a file or folder that is placed in the Recycle Bin, then removed from the disk.

Desktop An on-screen version of a desk that provides a workspace for different computing tasks. *See also* Active Desktop.

Dialog box A window that requests information. Many dialog boxes have options you must choose before Windows or a program can carry out a command.

Disk label Name that you assign to a disk by using the Properties dialog box.

Display pane The bottom pane of Outlook Express that displays the e-mail message selected in the preview pane. *See also* Preview pane.

Document A file that a program, such as WordPad, creates.

Document window The part of a program window that displays the current document.

Domain A collection of computers that the person managing the network creates to group computers that are used for the same tasks together and to simplify the set up and maintenance of the network.

Domain Name System (DNS) A database service that helps computers look up the names of other computers and locate their corresponding IP addresses.

Double-click To press and release the left mouse button twice quickly.

Download The process by which you access and display a Web page from the Internet.

Drag To press and hold the left mouse button while moving the mouse in order to move an item or text to a new location.

Edit To change the contents of a file without having to re-create it.

Electronic mail (e-mail) A system used to send and receive messages electronically.

Explorer Bar The pane on the left side of the screen in Windows Explorer that displays all objects available to the computer.

Favorite A shortcut to a Web address.

File An electronic collection of information that has a unique name, distinguishing it from other files.

File hierarchy A logical structure for folders and files that mimics how you would organize files and folders in a filing cabinet.

File management The process of organizing and keeping track of files and folders.

File sharing A networking option that allows many people to work on the same file without the need for creating or storing multiple copies.

Filter The process of retrieving newsgroup messages from a particular person, about a specific subject, of a certain length, or older than a number of days.

Floppy disk A disk that you insert into the disk drive of your computer and on which you can save files.

Folder A storage location for files and/or other folders that helps you organize your disks.

Folders list A list that displays folders where Outlook Express stores e-mail messages.

Font The design of a set of characters; for example, Times New Roman.

Format To change the appearance, but not the actual content, of information.

Format Bar A toolbar in WordPad that contains buttons to change the appearance, but not the actual content, of information.

Frame A separate window within a Web page.

Full permission A file setting that allows the user to edit and save changes to the file.

Graphical user interface (GUI) An environment made up of meaningful symbols, words, and windows that controls the basic operation of a computer and the programs that run on it.

Hard copy Paper output resulting from a print job. *See also* Printout.

Hard disk A disk (usually drive C) that is built into the computer and on which you store programs and files.

Hibernation A state in which a computer saves everything in memory on disk and shuts down.

Highlight To shade text or graphics with a different color by dragging the mouse or pressing a keyboard combination, in order to select the text or graphic. *See also* Select.

Hits A list of matched sites produced by search engine request. *See also* Search engine.

Home page The first Web page that appears when you open a Web browser.

Horizontal scroll bar A bar that moves your view from right to left through a window.

Hyperlink Highlighted words, phrases, and graphics that you click to open other Web pages. *See also* Link.

Icon A graphical representation of a file or another screen element.

Ingoing connection A network connection that enables a computer to be contacted by other computers.

Internet A collection of networks that connects computers all over the world using phone lines, coaxial cables, fiber-optic cables, satellites, and other telecommunications media. *See also* Network.

Internet service provider (ISP) A company that provides access to the Internet.

Insertion point The blinking vertical line in a document window, that indicates where text will appear when you type.

Keyword A word you submit to a search engine that is compared with words found on various Web sites on the Internet. *See also* Search engine.

Keyboard shortcut A keyboard alternative for executing a menu command; for example, [Ctrl][X] for Cut.

Link An element in a hypertext document that moves you to another place in the document. *See also* Hyperlink.

Links bar A bar that displays link buttons to Web pages on the Internet or documents on a local or network drive.

Local area network (LAN) A group of computers and other devices in a limited area connected by a communications link that allows one device to interact with another device on the network.

Manual caching An offline file option that enables offline access for selected documents in a shared folder.

Mapping The process by which you assign drive letters to network folders, making them appear as extra drives.

Margin The extra space around the edge of a document.

Maximize To enlarge a window so it fills the entire screen. Usually, the Maximize button is located in the upper-right corner of a window.

Media Player A Windows accessory that plays video, sound, or animation files.

Menu A list of available commands in a program.

Menu bar A bar at the top of the program window that organizes commands into groups of related operations.

Message flag An icon associated with an e-mail message that helps you determine the status or priority of the message.

Minimize To reduce the size of a window. The Minimize button is usually located in the upper-right corner of a window. Clicking the Minimize button shrinks the window to a button on the taskbar.

Most Frequently Used List A list of the most frequently used files organized by type.

Mouse A hand-held input device that you roll on your desk to position the mouse pointer on the Windows desktop. *See also* Mouse pointer.

Mouse buttons The buttons (right and left) on the mouse that you use to make selections and issue commands.

Mouse pointer The arrow-shaped cursor on the screen that follows the movement of the mouse as you roll the mouse on your desk and which you can use to select items, choose commands, and start programs. The shape of the mouse pointer changes depending on the program and the task being executed.

Multitasking The ability to run several programs at once and easily switch among them.

My Computer A window that displays the devices and folders available on your computer.

My Network Places An icon on the Windows 2000 desktop that lists the computers on the network.

Navigate To reposition the insertion point in a document.

Navigation bar A bar in Windows Media Player that contains buttons to move backward and forward between open video or sound clip files and start your Web browser and open media Web sites on the Internet.

Network Two or more computers connected together in order to exchange and share data, programs, and hardware.

Network and Dial-up Connection A network connection using a direct cable or modem.

Network folder A folder on a network that is made available to other computers on the network.

Network interface card (NIC) An adapter card inserted into a slot in the back of a computer that connects to the network.

Network operating system The software that creates, maintains, and controls the operations of the network.

Network printer A printer made available to other computers on a network.

News server A computer located on the Internet where articles on different topics are stored.

Newsgroup Online discussion groups about a particular topic, usually in an e-mail format.

Offline When the connection to the Internet is disconnected.

Offline file A version of a shared file from a network stored on a local drive.

Offline viewing When a Web page is copied to a local drive for viewing later, when the Internet connection is disconnected.

OpenType character A character that is based on a mathematical equation so the curves are smooth and the corners are sharp.

Operating system A program that controls the basic operation of your computer and the programs you run on it.

Outgoing connection A network connection that contacts a remote access server by using a cable or modem to establish a connection with a computer.

Outlook Express Start Page A page that displays tools you can use to read e-mail, compose e-mail messages, download the latest newsgroup messages, read newsgroup messages, enter and edit Address Book information, and find people on the Internet.

Pane A part of a window that divides the window into two or more sections.

Pattern A design that will display as your desktop background.

Peer-to-peer network A network setup that enables two or more computers to link together without designating a central server.

Permission A user setting, such as Read or Full, that designates what a user can and cannot do to a file.

Personalized menu A customized menu that keeps track of which programs you use and hides the programs you have not used recently.

Places bar A bar on the left side of the Open and Save dialog box that organizes navigation buttons to common locations or recently used files and folders on your computer or network.

Point To move the mouse pointer to position it over an item on the desktop.

Pop-up menu The menu that appears when you right-click an item.

Preview pane The top pane of Outlook Express that displays a list of all of the messages in your Inbox. *See also* Display pane.

Print Preview A feature that shows the layout and formatting of a document before you print it.

Printout A document that you printed on paper.

Program Task-oriented software, such as Microsoft Access, Corel WordPerfect, and Microsoft Word, that you use for a particular kind of work, such as word processing or database management.

Program button The button that appears on the taskbar that represents a program that is minimized but still running.

Properties The characteristics of a specific element (such as the mouse, keyboard, or desktop display) that you can customize.

Protocol A language that the computer uses to communicate with other computers on the network.

Proxy server An Internet connection option that provides a secure barrier between your network and the Internet.

Quick Launch toolbar A toolbar located next to the Start button on the taskbar that contains buttons to quickly start Internet-related programs and show the desktop.

Random access memory (RAM) The memory that programs use to perform necessary tasks while the computer is on, and when you turn the computer off, all information in RAM is lost.

Read permission A file setting that allows the user to view the file but not to make changes.

Recycle Bin An icon that appears on the desktop and which represents a temporary storage area on your hard drive for deleted files. Files remain in the Recycle Bin until you empty it or you restore the file(s).

Restore To reduce the window to its previous size before it was maximized. The Restore button usually is located in the upper-right corner of a maximized window.

Right-click To press and release the right mouse button once quickly.

Scheme A combination of color, fonts, or character designs for window elements.

Screen font A font that consists of bitmapped characters. *See also* Bitmapped characters.

Screen saver A moving pattern that fills your screen after your computer has not been used for a specified amount of time.

ScreenTip A description of a toolbar button that appears on your screen when you position the mouse pointer over the button.

Scroll bar A bar that appears at the bottom and/or right edge of a window whose contents are not entirely visible and which contains a scroll box and two scroll arrows.

Scroll box A box located in the vertical and horizontal scroll bars that indicates your relative position in a window. *See also* Horizontal scroll bar and Vertical scroll bar.

Search engine A program on the Web that allows you to search through a collection of information found on the Internet. *See also* Keyword.

Seek bar A bar in Windows Media Player that you drag backward or forward to play different parts of a video or sound clip.

Select To click and highlight an item in order to perform some action on it. *See also* Highlight.

Server A computer that stores and shares resources, such as programs, files, and folders, with other users on a network.

Service The network component that allows you to share resources on your computer, such as files and printers, with other networked computers.

Shortcut A link that you can place in any location that gives you instant access to a particular file, folder, or program on your hard disk or on a network.

Shut down The action you perform when you are finished working with Windows and after which it is safe to turn off your computer.

Standby A state in which a monitor and hard disks turn off after standing idle for a set time.

Start button A button on the taskbar that you use to start programs, find and open files, access Windows Help, and more.

Start menu A list of commands that allows you to start a program, open a document, change a Windows setting, find a file, or display help information.

Status bar The area along the bottom of the window that displays information about the open document or Web page.

Status indicator A graphic (the Internet Explorer logo) that spins to indicate a new Web page is loading in Internet Explorer.

Streaming media A high-quality continuous video and sound playback.

Stretch A Display properties option that displays the wallpaper picture or pattern enlarged across the desktop screen.

Submenu *See* Cascading menu.

Synchronize To save the latest version of an offline Web page to a local drive.

Tab A section at the top of the dialog box that separates options into related categories.

Task Scheduler A Windows accessory that enables you to schedule tasks to run at specific times.

Taskbar A bar at the bottom of the screen that contains the Start button and the Quick Launch toolbar, and shows which programs are running.

Title bar The area along the top of the window that contains the filename and the program used to create it.

Tile A Display Properties option that displays the wallpaper picture or pattern consecutively across the desktop screen.

Tip of the day An area on the Outlook Express Start Page that displays an Outlook Express tip.

Toggle A button that acts as an on/off switch.

Toolbar A bar that contains buttons that allow you to activate a command quickly.

Uniform Resource Locator (URL) Another name for a Web address. *See also* Web address.

Vertical scroll bar A bar that moves your view up and down through a window.

Virtual Private Network A secure network connection over the Internet.

Wallpaper An image that you display as your desktop background.

Web address A unique address on the Internet where you can locate a Web page. *See also* Uniform Resource Locator.

Web browser A program that retrieves and displays Web pages. *See also* Browser.

Web page A document that contains highlighted words, phrases, and graphics that link the document to other documents on the Internet.

Web server A computer on the Internet that hosts Web sites, making them available to the World Wide Web.

Web site A computer on the Internet that contains Web pages.

Wide area network (WAN) A group of computers and other devices spread out over a large area connected by a communications link that allows one device to interact with another device on the network.

Window A rectangular frame on a screen that might contain icons, the contents of a file, or other usable data.

Windows Explorer A Windows 2000 program that lets you manage files, folders, and shortcuts; more powerful than My Computer and allows you to work with more than one computer, folder, or file at a time.

Windows Help An online book stored on your computer, complete with an index and a table of contents, that provides information on the features and tasks associated with a Windows program.

Windows Media Player A Windows accessory that plays video, sound, and mixed-media files.

Wizard A series of dialog boxes that guides you through steps to complete a task and prompts you for information.

WordPad A word-processing accessory that comes with Windows 2000.

Wordwrap When text that will not fit on one line is automatically placed onto the next line.

Workgroup A group of computers within a network that shares resources, such as files and printers.

Workstation *See* Clients.

World Wide Web (Web, or WWW) The part of the Internet that consists of Web sites located on different computers around the world.

Index

Index

Index

Index

Properties command
   in My Network Places, WINDOWS H-17
Properties dialog box, WINDOWS C-16–17
   for new contacts, WINDOWS G-6–7
protocol, WINDOWS H-5
proxy servers, WINDOWS F-5

▶Q

Quick Format, WINDOWS C-5
Quick Launch toolbar, WINDOWS A-3, WINDOWS A-6, WINDOWS E-16–17
   defined, WINDOWS A-2

▶R

Random Access Memory (RAM), WINDOWS B-5
Read Mail link
   in Outlook Express window, WINDOWS G-4
Read News link
   in Outlook Express window, WINDOWS G-4
read permission, WINDOWS H-3
read-only files, WINDOWS H-3
Recycle Bin, WINDOWS A-3
   deleting and restoring files and folders with, WINDOWS C-12–13
   enabling, WINDOWS D-14
   properties of, WINDOWS C-13
   restoring deleted files, WINDOWS D-14–15
Regional Options dialog box, WINDOWS B-3, WINDOWS E-8–9
Rename command
   in My Network Places, WINDOWS H-17
renaming
   folders, WINDOWS C-8, WINDOWS D-8–9
resizing windows, WINDOWS A-8
resolution
   desktop size and, WINDOWS E-7
Restart option, WINDOWS A-19
Restore button, WINDOWS A-8
restoring
   files, WINDOWS C-12–13, WINDOWS D-15
   folders, WINDOWS C-12–13
   methods, WINDOWS D-15
right mouse button, WINDOWS A-4
right-clicking, WINDOWS A-4, WINDOWS A-5
Rounded Rectangle tool, WINDOWS B-10
Run submenu (Start menu), WINDOWS A-7

▶S

Save As dialog box
   in WordPad, WINDOWS B-4–5
Save button, WINDOWS B-8, WINDOWS B-12
saving
   documents, in WordPad, WINDOWS B-4–5
   files, WINDOWS B-5
   Web pages, WINDOWS F-13, WINDOWS F-18
Scheduled Task Wizard, WINDOWS E-14–15
Scheduled Tasks, WINDOWS E-14–15
schemes
   changing, WINDOWS E-6–7
   defined, WINDOWS E-6
screen fonts, WINDOWS E-10
Screen Saver tab
   in Display Properties dialog box, WINDOWS E-4–5
screen savers
   changing, WINDOWS E-4–5
   defined, WINDOWS E-4
   previewing, WINDOWS E-4
ScreenTips, WINDOWS A-4
scroll arrows, WINDOWS A-12
scroll bars
   defined, WINDOWS A-12
   in browser window, WINDOWS F-6–7
   using, WINDOWS A-12–13
scroll box, WINDOWS A-12
Search Assistant, WINDOWS H-7
Search button, WINDOWS D-10
search engines, WINDOWS F-16–17
Search for Computers command
   in My Network Places, WINDOWS H-17
Search Now button, WINDOWS H-7
Search submenu (Start menu), WINDOWS A-6, WINDOWS A-7
Search tab
   in Windows Help dialog box, WINDOWS A-16
searching
   advanced, WINDOWS D-11
   for files, WINDOWS D-10–11
   the World Wide Web, WINDOWS F-16–17
Security tab
   in Internet Options dialog box, WINDOWS F-15
Seek bar, WINDOWS B-16, WINDOWS B-18
Select Tool, WINDOWS B-12
selecting
   text, WINDOWS B-4
   with mouse, WINDOWS A-4
   words, WINDOWS B-6

Send To command, WINDOWS C-11
SerialKeys, WINDOWS A-13
servers, WINDOWS H-2
   network, WINDOWS H-3
service
   network, WINDOWS H-5
Set up a Newsgroups account link
   in Outlook Express window, WINDOWS G-4
Settings submenu (Start menu), WINDOWS A-7
Settings tab
   in Display Properties dialog box, WINDOWS E-5
shared files
   copying, WINDOWS H-12–13
   moving, WINDOWS H-12–13
   opening and editing, WINDOWS H-14–15
   working offline, WINDOWS H-15
shared folders
   creating, WINDOWS H-8–9
shortcuts
   dragging to new location, WINDOWS C-15
   placing on Start menu, WINDOWS C-15
   to files, creating, WINDOWS C-14–15
ShowSounds, WINDOWS A-13
Shut Down command, WINDOWS A-18–19
   options, WINDOWS A-19
Shut Down submenu (Start menu), WINDOWS A-7
Shut Down Windows dialog box, WINDOWS A-18–19
Similarity tool, WINDOWS E-10
sliders
   in dialog boxes, WINDOWS A-15
software. See also programs; Windows programs
   adding, WINDOWS E-15
sorting
   e-mail messages, WINDOWS G-12
sounds
   playing, WINDOWS B-18–19
SoundSentry, WINDOWS A-13
special need accessibility, WINDOWS A-13
spin boxes
   in dialog boxes, WINDOWS A-15
Standby option, WINDOWS A-19, WINDOWS E-12
Start button, WINDOWS A-3, WINDOWS A-6
   defined, WINDOWS A-2
Start menu, WINDOWS A-6–7
   adding items to, WINDOWS E-16–17
   categories on, WINDOWS A-7
   customizing, WINDOWS E-18–19
   placing shortcuts on, WINDOWS C-15
   rearranging items on, WINDOWS E-17

Index